Cooking Light
fresh food *fast*
weeknight meals

Cooking Light

fresh food *fast*

weeknight meals

Oxmoor House.

ISBN-13: 978-0-8487-3318-6
ISBN-10: 0-8487-3318-5
Library of Congress Control Number: 2009937174
Printed in the United States of America
Second Printing 2010

Be sure to check with your health-care provider
before making any changes in your diet.

Oxmoor House, Inc.

VP, Publishing Director: Jim Childs
Editorial Director: Susan Payne Dobbs
Brand Manager: Allison Long Lowery
Senior Editor: Heather Averett

Cooking Light® Fresh Food Fast
Weeknight Meals

Editor: Andrea C. Kirkland, M.S., R.D.
Project Editor: Diane Rose
Senior Designer: Emily Albright Parrish
Director, Test Kitchens: Elizabeth Tyler Austin
Assistant Director, Test Kitchens: Julie Christopher
Test Kitchens Professionals: Allison E. Cox, Julie Gunter,
Kathleen Royal Phillips, Catherine
Crowell Steele, Ashley T. Strickland
Photography Director: Jim Bathie
Senior Photo Stylist: Kay E. Clarke
Associate Photo Stylist: Katherine Eckert Coyne
Production Manager: Theresa Beste-Farley

Contributors

Copy Editor: Norma Butterworth-McKittrick
Proofreader: Adrienne S. Davis
Indexer: Mary Ann Laurens
Interns: Ina Ables, Wendy Ball, Georgia Dodge,
Perri K. Hubbard, Maggie McDaris,
Allison Sperando, Christine Taylor
Food Stylists: Margaret Dickey, Alyson Haynes,
Iris O'Brien, Laura Zapalowski
Test Kitchens Professionals: Telia Johnson, Amy Lispcomb,
Connie Nash, Angela Schmidt
Recipe Developers: Gretchen Feldtman Brown, Jaime
Harder Caldwell, Maureen Callahan,
Katherine Cobbs, Nancy Hughes,
Ana Kelly, Jean Kressy, Amelia Levin,
Caroline Wright
Photographers: Beau Gustafson, Lee Harrelson
Photo Stylists: Melanie J. Clarke, Missy Neville
Crawford, Cathy Still Johnson,
Mindi Shapiro

Cooking Light®

Editor: Scott Mowbray
Creative Director: Carla Frank
Deputy Editor: Phillip Rhodes
Food Editor: Ann Taylor Pittman
Special Publications Editor: Mary Simpson Creel, M.S., R.D.
Nutrition Editor: Kathy Kitchens Downie, R.D.
Associate Food Editors: Timothy Q. Cebula, Julianna Grimes
Associate Editors: Cindy Hatcher, Brandy Rushing
Test Kitchens Director: Vanessa T. Pruett
Assistant Test Kitchens Director: Tiffany Vickers Davis
Senior Food Stylist: Kellie Gerber Kelley
Test Kitchens Professionals: SaBrina Bone, Deb Wise
Art Director: Fernande Bondarenko
Deputy Art Director: J. Shay McNamee
Photo Director: Kristen Schaefer
Senior Photographer: Randy Mayor
Senior Photo Stylist: Cindy Barr
Photo Stylist: Leigh Ann Ross
Copy Chief: Maria Parker Hopkins
Assistant Copy Chief: Susan Roberts
Research Editor: Michelle Gibson Daniels
Editorial Production Director: Liz Rhoades
Production Editor: Hazel R. Eddins
Art/Production Assistant: Josh Rutledge
Administrative Coordinator: Carol D. Johnson

To order additional publications,
call 1–800–765–6400 or 1-800-491-0551.

For more books to enrich your life,
visit **oxmoorhouse.com**

To search, savor, and share
thousands of recipes, visit
myrecipes.com

Cover: Rotini with Chicken, Asparagus,
and Tomatoes, page 268
Front flap: Mole Chili, page 17
Back cover: Scallops with Lemon-Basil Sauce,
page 217; Raspberry–Cream Cheese Tarts,
page 337; Green Salsa Chicken, page 275

welcome

Busy weekdays call for low-key weeknights and a chance to relax and enjoy a home-cooked dinner with family and friends. That's why we've created ***Cooking Light** Fresh Food Fast Weeknight Meals*, a collection of over 280 5-ingredient, 15-minute recipes guaranteed to transform a few fresh ingredients into a tantalizing meal—fast! With this cookbook in hand, you'll be armed with strategic ways to cook smarter, make the most of your precious time, and—best of all—ensure that your efforts deliver incredibly delightful dishes night after night.

Each healthy recipe meets at least one of these two criteria: It requires five ingredients or less (excluding water, cooking spray, salt, pepper, and optional ingredients) or it can be prepared in 15 minutes or less. And many fit the bill for both!

Within these pages, we'll give you the inside track about what quick-cooking ingredients to purchase and which flavor-enhancing techniques to use so that you'll never have to sacrifice taste and nutrition to save time.

Jam-packed with 140 complete menus and 25 desserts—with a mouthwatering photo of each—we hope this cookbook will bring exciting new recipes to your weeknight repertoire and that you will discover how easy it can be to make healthy taste great!

The *Cooking Light* Editors

contents

85

41

125

164   213   348

fish & shellfish, 180
The ultimate "fast foods"—with short cook times and flavors that are hard to beat—these dishes offer a healthy option for weeknight fare.

meats, 224
Topped with robust sauces, flavorful toppings, and vibrant seasonings, you won't go wrong with this selection of beef, pork, and lamb.

poultry, 266
Whether you start with a cooked rotisserie chicken or a quick-cooking chicken breast, these dishes come together in a flash.

desserts, 306
Satisfy your sweet tooth's cravings with decadent cakes, puddings, pies, tarts, parfaits, frosty treats, and fruit desserts.

soups

Smoky Black Bean Soup with Avocado-Lime Salsa
Zesty Spinach Soup
French Onion Soup
Mole Chili
Ham and Butternut Squash Soup
Greens, Beans, and Bacon Soup
Jamaican Red Beans and Rice Soup
Sweet Pea Soup with Bacon
Sweet Potato Soup with Pancetta-Rosemary Croutons
Southern Camp Stew
Chicken-Vegetable-Barley Soup
Ginger Chicken Soup
Chicken Egg Drop Soup
Chicken Florentine Soup
Spicy Chipotle-Turkey Chili
Provençal Fish Stew
Coconut Shrimp Soup

The rich avocado topping is the secret ingredient in this recipe. It soothes the slow burn from the smoky chipotle heat and adds a burst of fresh flavor.

Smoky Black Bean Soup with Avocado-Lime Salsa

Prep: 3 minutes • Cook: 15 minutes

1 (15-ounce) can black beans, rinsed and drained
1 cup water
1 (14.5-ounce) can fire-roasted diced tomatoes, undrained
½ cup chipotle salsa
1 teaspoon ground cumin
Avocado-Lime Salsa
Reduced-fat sour cream (optional)

1. Place beans in a medium saucepan. Mash beans slightly with a potato masher. Stir in water and next 3 ingredients. Cover and bring to a boil over high heat; reduce heat, and simmer 8 minutes. Uncover, and cook 2 minutes or until soup is slightly thickened. Ladle soup evenly into each of 4 bowls; top evenly with Avocado-Lime Salsa, and, if desired, sour cream. Yield: 4 servings (serving size: 1 cup soup and ¼ cup salsa).

CALORIES 172; FAT 5.7g (sat 0.9g, mono 3.4g, poly 0.8g); PROTEIN 7.4g; CARB 29.7g; FIBER 11g; CHOL 0mg; IRON 3.1mg; SODIUM 572mg; CALC 60mg

Avocado-Lime Salsa

Prep: 5 minutes

1 cup diced peeled avocado
1 lime
2 tablespoons finely chopped fresh cilantro
⅛ teaspoon salt

1. Place avocado in a small bowl. Grate rind from lime and squeeze juice to measure ½ teaspoon and 1 tablespoon, respectively; add to avocado. Add cilantro and salt. Toss gently. Yield: 1 cup (serving size: ¼ cup).

CALORIES 55; FAT 5.2g (sat 0.8g, mono 3.2g, poly 0.7g); PROTEIN 0.7g; CARB 2.9g; FIBER 1.7g; CHOL 0mg; IRON 0.4mg; SODIUM 76mg; CALC 5mg

Grated lemon rind brightens the fresh flavor of this vegetarian soup. For an effortless meal, serve it with Crostini with Sun-Dried Tomato and White Bean Spread.

Zesty Spinach Soup

Prep: 2 minutes • Cook: 13 minutes

2 teaspoons olive oil
1½ cups chopped onion (1 small)
2 cups organic vegetable broth
1 cup (½-inch) diced Yukon Gold potato
½ teaspoon salt

¼ teaspoon freshly ground black pepper
1 (6-ounce) package fresh baby spinach
½ cup reduced-fat sour cream, divided
Reduced-fat sour cream (optional)
1 teaspoon grated lemon rind

1. Heat oil in a large saucepan over medium heat. Add onion; sauté 3 minutes. Add broth and next 3 ingredients. Cover and bring to a boil over high heat; reduce heat, and simmer 8 minutes or until potato is very tender, stirring occasionally. Add spinach; cover and cook 2 minutes or until spinach wilts.
2. Place half of soup and ¼ cup sour cream in a blender. Remove center piece of blender lid (to allow steam to escape); secure blender lid on blender. Place a clean towel over opening in blender lid (to avoid splatters). Blend until smooth. Pour into a large bowl. Repeat procedure with remaining soup and ¼ cup sour cream.
3. Pour soup evenly into 4 bowls. Top each with a dollop of additional sour cream, if desired, and ¼ teaspoon lemon rind. Yield: 4 servings (serving size: 1 cup soup and ¼ teaspoon lemon rind).

CALORIES 119; FAT 4.7g (sat 1.8g, mono 2.3g, poly 0.3g); PROTEIN 3.5g; CARB 15.5g; FIBER 2.7g; CHOL 8mg; IRON 2.5mg; SODIUM 637mg; CALC 90mg

serve with
Crostini with Sun-Dried Tomato and White Bean Spread

Prep: 2 minutes • Cook: 8 minutes

8 (½-inch-thick) diagonally-cut baguette slices
1 cup canned cannellini beans, rinsed and drained
1½ tablespoons extra-virgin olive oil
1 tablespoon fresh lemon juice

¼ teaspoon crushed red pepper
2 garlic cloves, crushed
¼ cup coarsely chopped drained oil-packed sun-dried tomato halves

1. Preheat oven to 350°.
2. Place baguette slices on a large baking sheet. Bake at 350° for 8 minutes or until lightly toasted.
3. While baguette slices toast, place beans and next 4 ingredients in a blender; process until smooth. Spread 2 tablespoons bean mixture on each baguette slice; sprinkle each with ½ tablespoon chopped tomatoes. Yield: 4 servings (serving size: 2 crostini).

CALORIES 168; FAT 6.5g (sat 0.9g, mono 4.6g, poly 0.9g); PROTEIN 4.7g; CARB 23.5g; FIBER 3.2g; CHOL 0mg; IRON 1.7mg; SODIUM 232mg; CALC 25mg

Traditionally, cheese toast tops a classic bistro-style French onion soup. However, we decided to omit it from this rich soup and add a gourmet grilled sandwich on the side instead. It's the perfect accompaniment.

French Onion Soup

Prep: 5 minutes • Cook: 25 minutes

1 tablespoon vegetable oil
3 sweet onions, cut in half vertically and thinly sliced (about 1¾ pounds)

5 sprigs fresh thyme
2 (14-ounce) cans fat-free, less-sodium beef broth

1. Heat oil in a large Dutch oven over medium-high heat. Add onion and thyme; cover and cook 20 minutes, stirring occasionally. Stir in broth; simmer 4 minutes. Remove and discard thyme. Yield: 4 servings (serving size: 1¼ cups).

CALORIES 103; FAT 3.7g (sat 0.5g, mono 1.2g, poly 1.7g); PROTEIN 3.4g; CARB 15g; FIBER 1.8g; CHOL 0mg; IRON 0.6mg; SODIUM 415mg; CALC 41mg

serve with
Gruyère-Thyme Grilled Cheese Sandwiches

Prep: 4 minutes • Cook: 6 minutes

¾ cup (3 ounces) Gruyère cheese
1 teaspoon fresh thyme leaves
2 teaspoons Dijon mustard
¼ teaspoon black pepper

8 (¼-inch-thick) slices Italian bread (about 5 ounces)
Butter-flavored cooking spray

1. Combine first 4 ingredients in a bowl. Spread filling on 4 bread slices; top with remaining bread slices.
2. Heat a large nonstick skillet over medium-high heat. Coat tops of sandwiches with cooking spray. Arrange sandwiches, top side down, in pan. Coat sandwiches with cooking spray. Cook 2 to 3 minutes on each side or until cheese melts and bread is golden brown. Yield: 4 servings (serving size: 1 sandwich).

CALORIES 185; FAT 8.1g (sat 4.3g, mono 2.4g, poly 0.9g); PROTEIN 9.5g; CARB 17.9g; FIBER 1g; CHOL 23mg; IRON 1.1mg; SODIUM 311mg; CALC 244mg

Chocolate is often added to savory Mexican dishes to cut the heat and enrich the flavor. In this recipe, chocolate adds richness and deepens the color of the chili without making it sweet.

Mole Chili

Prep: 1 minute • Cook: 14 minutes

1 pound ground round
1 cup chopped onion (about 1 small onion)
1 garlic clove, minced
1 (14.5-ounce) can diced tomatoes, undrained
1 cup water
2 tablespoons chili powder
1 ounce semisweet chocolate, coarsely chopped

1 teaspoon ground cumin
1 teaspoon salt
½ teaspoon dried oregano
Reduced-fat sour cream (optional)
Chopped fresh cilantro (optional)

1. Cook beef in a large saucepan over medium-high heat until browned, stirring to crumble. Drain, if necessary, and return beef to pan. Add onion and garlic to pan; cook 4 minutes or until tender. Add tomatoes and remaining ingredients; cover and simmer 7 minutes. Serve immediately. Top with sour cream and cilantro, if desired. Yield: 6 servings (serving size: ¾ cup).

CALORIES 127; FAT 4.7g (sat 2.2g, mono 1.4g, poly 0.2g); PROTEIN 17.3g; CARB 8.2g; FIBER 1.8g; CHOL 40mg; IRON 1.9mg; SODIUM 597mg; CALC 25mg

serve with
Jalapeño Corn Bread Mini Muffins

Prep: 9 minutes • Cook: 17 minutes

¾ cup self-rising white cornmeal mix
½ cup fat-free buttermilk
2 tablespoons minced seeded jalapeño pepper

1½ tablespoons canola oil
1 large egg
Cooking spray

1. Preheat oven to 425°. Lightly spoon self-rising white cornmeal mix into measuring cups; level with a knife, and place in a large bowl. Combine buttermilk, jalapeño pepper, oil, and egg in a small bowl. Pour buttermilk mixture into cornmeal mixture; stir just until combined. Coat 12 miniature muffin cups with cooking spray; spoon batter evenly into cups. Bake at 425° for 17 minutes or until lightly browned. Remove from pans immediately; serve warm. Yield: 6 servings (serving size: 2 mini muffins).

CALORIES 127; FAT 4.8g (sat 0.5g, mono 2.5g, poly 1.4g); PROTEIN 3.7g; CARB 17.4g; FIBER 1.3g; CHOL 30mg; IRON 1.2mg; SODIUM 312mg; CALC 93mg

Celebrate fall all year long with the help of frozen butternut squash. Complement the velvety texture of this sweet-savory soup by serving it with warm, crusty bread.

Ham and Butternut Squash Soup

Prep: 2 minutes • Cook: 8 minutes

2 (12-ounce) packages frozen butternut squash (such as McKenzie's)
1 cup fat-free, less-sodium chicken stock
2 tablespoons cinnamon sugar
½ teaspoon black pepper
2 teaspoons olive oil
1½ cups diced ham (such as Cumberland Gap)
1 tablespoon chopped fresh rosemary

1. Microwave packages of squash at HIGH 5 minutes or until thawed. Combine squash with stock, cinnamon sugar, and pepper in a large microwave-safe bowl. Microwave at HIGH 3 to 5 minutes or until thoroughly heated.
2. While squash mixture cooks, heat oil in a large nonstick skillet over medium-high heat. Pat ham dry with paper towels. Add ham to pan, and cook 2 minutes or until lightly browned. Add rosemary, and cook 1 minute, stirring occasionally.
3. Ladle soup evenly into 4 bowls, and sprinkle ham topping evenly in center of each bowl. Yield: 4 servings (serving size: about ¾ cup soup and 3 tablespoons ham topping).

CALORIES 185; FAT 7.6g (sat 1.2g, mono 1.7g, poly 3g); PROTEIN 9.9g; CARB 19.8g; FIBER 2.6g; CHOL 19mg; IRON 2.2mg; SODIUM 828mg; CALC 55mg

choice ingredient

Chicken stock, available in cartons or cans, is a staple ingredient for quick cooking. Use it as a foundation for soups and sauces, and you'll have a dish with rich, savory flavor that's ready in a snap. Be sure to read the nutrition label because the sodium and fat amounts vary among brands.

This hearty soup, which is chock-full of antioxidants and fiber from the kale and beans, pairs well with a crunchy slice of toasted ciabatta. Look for packages of prechopped kale in the produce section of your supermarket.

Greens, Beans, and Bacon Soup

Prep: 3 minutes • Cook: 36 minutes

3 slices lower-sodium bacon, cut crosswise into ¼-inch pieces
3 cups packed prechopped kale
2¼ cups water
1 (15-ounce) can no-salt-added cannellini beans, rinsed and drained
1 (14.5-ounce) can roasted garlic chicken broth
1 cup frozen chopped onion
¼ teaspoon black pepper
Hot sauce (optional)

1. Cook bacon in a large saucepan over medium-high heat 8 minutes or until crisp. Reserve 2 teaspoons drippings in pan; discard excess drippings.
2. Add kale and next 5 ingredients to bacon and drippings in pan. Stir in hot sauce, if desired. Cover and bring to a boil over high heat. Reduce heat, and simmer 25 minutes. Serve immediately. Yield: 3 servings (serving size: 1⅔ cups).

CALORIES 200; FAT 8.1g (sat 3.3g, mono 3.1g, poly 1.1g); PROTEIN 10.5g; CARB 23.2g; FIBER 5.5g; CHOL 15mg; IRON 2.9mg; SODIUM 792mg; CALC 127mg

This quick recipe is loaded with beans and rice, making this soup a filling one-dish meal. Mashing the beans slightly adds body.

Jamaican Red Beans and Rice Soup

Prep: 3 minutes • Cook: 11 minutes

2 bacon slices, cut crosswise into thin strips
½ cup chopped onion (1 small)
2 (14-ounce) cans fat-free, less-sodium chicken broth
2 teaspoons Jamaican jerk seasoning (such as McCormick)
1 (16-ounce) can red beans, rinsed and drained (such as Bush's)
1 (8.8-ounce) package microwaveable precooked whole-grain brown rice (such as Uncle Ben's Ready Rice)
¼ cup chopped fresh cilantro

1. Cook bacon and onion in a large saucepan over medium heat 2 minutes.
2. While bacon mixture cooks, place broth in a large microwave-safe bowl. Cover with plastic wrap; vent. Microwave at HIGH 2 minutes.
3. Add hot broth and jerk seasoning to bacon mixture. Stir in beans, mashing slightly. Cover; bring to a boil over high heat. Uncover, reduce heat, and simmer 5 minutes. Stir in rice; cover and simmer 3 minutes. Ladle soup evenly into 4 bowls; sprinkle with cilantro. Yield: 4 servings (serving size: 1¼ cups).

CALORIES 375; FAT 7.2g (sat 1.7g, mono 2.6g, poly 0.9g); PROTEIN 11.7g; CARB 65.5g; FIBER 7.7g; CHOL 8mg; IRON 2.1mg; SODIUM 887mg; CALC 34mg

serve now or later

Make this quick soup ahead, and divide it into small, shallow containers with lids to ensure quick cooling in the refrigerator and easy portability. Use within 3 to 4 days after cooking, or freeze for up to 6 months. For safe transporting, pack the soup in an insulated lunch bag with gel packs to help keep it cool.

Half-and-half and refrigerated potatoes add creamy, rich texture to this soup, while the bacon provides crunch and smoky flavor.

Sweet Pea Soup with Bacon
Prep: 5 minutes • Cook: 35 minutes

6   slices lower-sodium bacon
1½ cups refrigerated diced potatoes with onions (such as Simply Potatoes)
4   cups fat-free, less-sodium chicken broth
1   (16-ounce) package frozen petite green peas
½   cup fat-free half-and-half
¼   teaspoon freshly ground black pepper

1. Cook bacon in a large Dutch oven over medium-high heat 8 minutes or until crisp. Drain bacon on a paper towel; crumble. Reserve 2 tablespoons drippings in pan; discard excess drippings.
2. Add potatoes to drippings in pan, and sauté 5 minutes or until slightly brown. Add broth and peas to pan; bring to a boil. Cover, reduce heat to medium-low, and simmer 15 minutes. Place 4½ cups soup in a blender. Remove center piece of blender lid (to allow steam to escape); secure blender lid on blender. Place a clean towel over opening in blender lid (to avoid splatters). Blend until smooth. Return pureed soup to pan; add half-and-half and pepper. Heat 4 minutes or until thoroughly heated. Ladle soup evenly into 6 bowls, and top evenly with crumbled bacon. Yield: 6 servings (serving size: 1 cup soup and 1 tablespoon bacon).

CALORIES 194; FAT 7.9g (sat 2.8g, mono 3.4g, poly 1g); PROTEIN 9.7g; CARB 20g; FIBER 4g; CHOL 13mg; IRON 1.4mg; SODIUM 673mg; CALC 31mg

Sweet Potato Soup with Pancetta-Rosemary Croutons

Prep: 12 minutes • Cook: 28 minutes

¼ cup finely chopped pancetta (about
    1½ ounce)
2 cups chopped sweet onion
4 cups cubed peeled sweet potato (2 medium)
1 (12-ounce) can low-fat evaporated milk

2 cups water
¼ teaspoon salt
½ teaspoon freshly ground black pepper
Pancetta-Rosemary Croutons

1. Cook pancetta in a large Dutch oven over medium-low heat 4 minutes until golden brown and crisp. Add onion; cook 5 minutes, stirring occasionally. Add sweet potato and next 4 ingredients. Cover and bring to a boil. Cover, reduce heat, and simmer 15 minutes. Place 3 cups soup in a blender. Remove center piece of blender lid (to allow steam to escape); secure blender lid on blender. Place a clean towel over opening in blender lid (to avoid splatters). Blend until smooth. Pour blended soup into a large bowl. Repeat procedure with remaining soup. Stir soup to blend. Ladle soup evenly into 6 bowls; sprinkle with Pancetta-Rosemary Croutons. Yield: 6 servings (serving size: 1 cup).

CALORIES 251; FAT 7.5g (sat 3.6g, mono 1.5g, poly 1.2g);; PROTEIN 9.8g; CARB 36.2g; FIBER 3.7g; CHOL 22mg; IRON 1.5mg; SODIUM 630mg; CALC 198mg

Pancetta-Rosemary Croutons

Prep: 3 minutes • Cook: 13 minutes

⅓ cup finely chopped pancetta (about
    2 ounces)

2 cups (1-inch) cubed sourdough bread
1 teaspoon chopped fresh rosemary

1. Cook pancetta in a nonstick skillet over medium-low heat 4 minutes or until golden brown and crisp. Remove pancetta from skillet; drain. Cook bread cubes in drippings in pan, stirring frequently, 7 minutes or until golden and crisp. Stir in rosemary; cook 1 minute. Stir pancetta into bread cubes. Yield: 6 servings (serving size: about ⅓ cup).

CALORIES 80; FAT 3.5g (sat 1.4g, mono 1g, poly 1g); PROTEIN 3.1g; CARB 9.3g; FIBER 0.6g; CHOL 7mg; IRON 0.8mg; SODIUM 263mg; CALC 18mg

To save time, use cubed peeled sweet potato from the produce department of your supermarket.

This hearty dish is reminiscent of Brunswick stew, a Southern comfort-food favorite made with pork, beef, and chicken. In this version, we opted to only use chicken to keep the ingredient list short and the preparation quick.

Southern Camp Stew

Prep: 2 minutes • Cook: 13 minutes

1½ cups frozen whole-kernel corn
1 cup chicken stock (such as Swanson)
2 tablespoons white vinegar
1 tablespoon light brown sugar
¼ cup no-salt-added tomato paste
1 (14.5-ounce) can no-salt-added diced tomatoes

1 (15.25) can medium-size green lima beans, rinsed and drained
2 teaspoons hot sauce (optional)
1 small rotisserie chicken

1. Combine first 7 ingredients and hot sauce, if desired, in a large Dutch oven. Cover and bring to a boil; reduce heat, and simmer 6 minutes.
2. While soup simmers, skin and bone chicken. Shred chicken to measure 3½ cups; add chicken to soup. Cook 3 minutes. Yield: 6 servings (serving size: 1 cup).

CALORIES 225; FAT 2.9g (sat 0.8g, mono 1g, poly 0.7g); PROTEIN 27g; CARB 23.8g; FIBER 5g; CHOL 60mg; IRON 2.4mg; SODIUM 257mg; CALC 38mg

choice ingredient

Tomato paste is a richly flavored tomato concentrate made from ripened tomatoes that have been cooked for several hours, strained, and reduced. The final product is a thick red paste that's perfect for adding depth of flavor to soups and sauces. This recipe calls for a small amount, so you'll have some paste leftover. To freeze the remaining paste, spoon it by the tablespoon onto a baking sheet, and freeze. Remove the frozen paste from the baking sheet, and store in a heavy-duty plastic freezer bag. It will already be measured and ready for your next recipe.

Warm up on a cold winter day with a bowl of this simple and healthful soup. It's rich in fiber, potassium, and magnesium—all of which protect against heart disease. Serve this soup with toasted slices of cheese-topped *bâtarde,* a small French bread loaf.

Chicken-Vegetable-Barley Soup

Prep: 5 minutes • Cook: 21 minutes • Other: 5 minutes

5 cups fat-free, less-sodium chicken broth
2 cups shredded rotisserie chicken breast
½ teaspoon kosher salt
½ teaspoon freshly ground black pepper

1 (16-ounce) package frozen vegetable soup mix with tomatoes
¾ cup quick-cooking barley
2 cups chopped bagged baby spinach leaves

1. Combine first 5 ingredients in a large Dutch oven. Cover and bring to a boil. Stir in barley; cover, reduce heat, and simmer 10 minutes, stirring occasionally. Remove from heat; stir in spinach, and let stand 5 minutes. Yield: 8 servings (serving size: about 1 cup).

CALORIES 156; FAT 2.9g (sat 0.8g, mono 1.1g, poly 0.6g); PROTEIN 15.9g; CARB 17.6g; FIBER 3g; CHOL 29mg; IRON 0.8mg; SODIUM 494mg; CALC 11mg

serve with
Garlic Cheddar Toast

Prep: 2 minutes • Cook: 8 minutes

1 cup (4 ounces) shredded reduced-fat sharp cheddar cheese
1 tablespoon light mayonnaise
½ teaspoon chopped fresh oregano

2 garlic cloves, minced
1 (8-ounce) multigrain bâtarde, cut diagonally into 16 slices

1. Preheat oven to 400°.
2. Combine first 4 ingredients. Top bread slices with cheese mixture. Place on a baking sheet. Bake at 400° for 8 minutes or until cheese browns and bread is lightly toasted. Yield: 8 servings (serving size: 2 slices).

CALORIES 252; FAT 5.6g (sat 2.1g, mono 0.5g, poly 1.3g); PROTEIN 11.6g; CARB 38.4g; FIBER 4g; CHOL 11mg; IRON 2.2mg; SODIUM 495mg; CALC 182mg

Ponzu sauce adds subtle saltiness to this Asian-inspired soup. Ponzu, a traditional Japanese sauce, is made with lemon juice or rice vinegar, soy sauce, and mirin.

Ginger Chicken Soup

Prep: 1 minute • Cook: 14 minutes

1 tablespoon dark sesame oil
2 tablespoons finely chopped fresh peeled ginger
6 garlic cloves, sliced
2 cups diced cooked chicken breast

4 cups chicken stock (such as Swanson)
2 tablespoons ponzu sauce (such as Kikkoman)
4 cups thinly sliced bok choy
1 cup diagonally sliced green onions

1. Heat oil in a Dutch oven over medium-low heat. Add ginger and garlic; sauté 1 minute. Add chicken and next 3 ingredients. Bring to a boil over high heat. Reduce heat and simmer, uncovered, 5 minutes. Stir in green onions. Ladle soup evenly into 6 bowls. Yield: 6 servings (serving size: about 1 cup soup).

CALORIES 128; FAT 4.2g (sat 0.8g, mono 1.5g, poly 1.4g); PROTEIN 18.4g; CARB 4.3g; FIBER 1g; CHOL 40mg; IRON 1.2mg; SODIUM 708mg; CALC 74mg

serve with
Crispy Sesame Wontons

Prep: 6 minutes • Cook: 7 minutes

1 teaspoon sugar
2 teaspoons ponzu sauce (such as Kikkoman)
1 teaspoon rice vinegar
1 teaspoon dark sesame oil

12 wonton wrappers, stacked and cut diagonally into triangles
Cooking spray
1 tablespoon sesame seeds

1. Preheat oven to 400°.
2. Combine first 4 ingredients. Arrange wonton wrappers on a large baking sheet coated with cooking spray. Brush wontons evenly with oil mixture; sprinkle with sesame seeds.
3. Bake at 400° for 5 to 7 minutes or until lightly browned and crisp. Yield: 6 servings (serving size: 4 crisps).

CALORIES 98; FAT 2.6g (sat 0.4g, mono 0.9g, poly 1.1g); PROTEIN 2.9g; CARB 15.6g; FIBER 0.7g; CHOL 2mg; IRON 1.1mg; SODIUM 238mg; CALC 33mg

Egg drop soup is noted for its strands of shredded egg. To achieve this characteristic look and texture, make sure you blend the egg mixture well, and stir it slowly into the broth.

Chicken Egg Drop Soup

Prep: 4 minutes • Cook: 9 minutes

3½ cups fat-free, less-sodium chicken broth
1½ tablespoons reduced-sodium soy sauce
2 tablespoons cornstarch
¼ teaspoon freshly ground black pepper
1 tablespoon water
1 large egg

1 large egg white
2 cups chopped cooked chicken breast (about 8 ounces)
¼ cup chopped green onions (about 2)
1 tablespoon dark sesame oil
¼ cup chopped cilantro (optional)

1. Combine broth and soy sauce in a medium saucepan. Bring to a boil over high heat. While broth mixture comes to a boil, combine cornstarch, pepper, and water in small bowl, stirring with a whisk until smooth. Gradually whisk cornstarch mixture into broth mixture. Reduce heat, and simmer, stirring frequently, 1 minute or until soup is slightly thickened.
2. Combine egg and egg white, stirring with a whisk until blended. Slowly add egg mixture to soup, stirring gently. Add chicken, green onions, and sesame oil; cook 1 minute or until thoroughly heated.
3. Ladle soup evenly into 4 bowls; garnish with cilantro, if desired. Yield: 4 servings (serving size: 1¼ cups).

CALORIES 203; FAT 7g (sat 1.5g, mono 2.7g, poly 2.1g); PROTEIN 27.3g; CARB 5.9g; FIBER 0.2g; CHOL 105mg; IRON 1.1mg; SODIUM 810mg; CALC 23mg

serve with
Asian Slaw

Prep: 6 minutes

¼ cup reduced-fat mayonnaise
1 tablespoon reduced-sodium soy sauce
1 teaspoon dark sesame oil

4 cups packaged 3-color coleslaw (such as Fresh Express)
½ cup chopped fresh cilantro

1. Combine first 3 ingredients in a medium bowl, stirring with a whisk. Add coleslaw and cilantro; toss well. Yield: 4 servings (serving size: ¾ cup).

CALORIES 46; FAT 3.2g (sat 0.2g, mono 0.5g, poly 1.5g); PROTEIN 0.8g; CARB 4.8g; FIBER 1.1g; CHOL 0mg; IRON 0.2mg; SODIUM 290mg; CALC 21mg

Round out this rustic one-dish meal with warm crusty bread, and use it to soak up the richly flavored broth. Orzo makes a fine substitute for the ditalini.

Chicken Florentine Soup

Prep: 2 minutes • Cook: 13 minutes

½ cup uncooked ditalini (very short tube-shaped macaroni)
1¼ pounds skinless, boneless chicken thighs, chopped
3 cups fat-free, less-sodium chicken broth
1 cup water
1 (14.5-ounce) can diced tomatoes with basil, garlic, and oregano
1 (6-ounce) package fresh baby spinach
2 tablespoons commercial pesto
¼ teaspoon freshly ground black pepper
Grated fresh Parmesan cheese (optional)

1. Cook pasta according to package directions, omitting salt and fat. Set aside.
2. While pasta cooks, combine chicken, broth, and water in a large Dutch oven. Cover and bring to a boil. Reduce heat, and simmer 3 minutes or until chicken is cooked. Remove chicken with a slotted spoon; keep warm. Stir in tomatoes; cook 1 minute or until thoroughly heated. Stir in spinach; cook 2 minutes or until spinach wilts. Add cooked chicken and pasta to pan; cook 1 minute or until thoroughly heated. Stir in pesto and pepper. Ladle soup evenly into 6 bowls, and sprinkle with Parmesan cheese, if desired. Yield: 6 servings (serving size: 1½ cups).

CALORIES 219; FAT 6.2g (sat 1.4g, mono 2.4g, poly 2g); PROTEIN 23.7g; CARB 17.1g; FIBER 2.4g; CHOL 80mg; IRON 3.3mg; SODIUM 810mg; CALC 88mg

choice ingredient

Packaged fresh baby spinach, found in your grocer's produce section, can be a real time-saver when preparing weeknight meals. There's no need to trim the stems from the tender leaves, and their small size eliminates the need to chop them.

Add heat and smokiness to this robust chili with a hint of chipotle chili powder. This Southwestern seasoning is made by grinding smoke-dried jalapeños into a powder. Look for it in the spice aisle along with regular chili powder.

Spicy Chipotle-Turkey Chili

Prep: 5 minutes • Cook: 10 minutes

1 tablespoon vegetable oil
1 pound ground turkey
1 large poblano pepper, seeded and finely chopped
2 cups water
1 teaspoon chipotle chili powder (such as Spice Islands)

2 (16-ounce) cans pinto beans, rinsed and drained
1 (16-ounce) jar mild salsa
Shredded cheddar cheese (optional)

1. Heat oil in a medium saucepan over medium-high heat. Add turkey and poblano pepper; cook 5 minutes or until turkey is browned; stir to crumble. Stir in water and next 3 ingredients. Cover and bring to a boil. Mash beans lightly with a potato masher until soup is slightly thickened; ladle evenly into 6 bowls. Garnish with cheddar cheese, if desired. Yield: 6 servings (serving size: 1⅓ cups).

CALORIES 234; FAT 10.5g (sat 2.5g, mono 4.3g, poly 3.5g); PROTEIN 17.4g; CARB 14.6g; FIBER 3.2g; CHOL 65mg; IRON 3.7mg; SODIUM 812mg; CALC 33mg

serve with
Corn Muffins

Prep: 5 minutes • Cook: 15 minutes

1 cup self-rising white cornmeal mix (such as White Lily)
½ cup plain nonfat yogurt
1 large egg

1 tablespoon canola oil
½ cup frozen whole-kernel corn
Cooking spray

1. Preheat oven to 425°.
2. Place 6 muffin cups in oven while it preheats. Place cornmeal mix in a medium bowl, and make a well in center. Combine yogurt, egg, and oil in a bowl, stirring well with a whisk; stir in corn. Add yogurt mixture to cornmeal mix, stirring just until moist.
3. Remove muffin cups from oven; coat with cooking spray. Spoon batter evenly into cups. Coat batter with cooking spray. Bake at 425° for 15 minutes or until lightly browned. Yield: 6 muffins (serving size: 1 muffin).

CALORIES 122; FAT 3.8g (sat 0.4g, mono 2g, poly 1.3g); PROTEIN 3.7g; CARB 19.8g; FIBER 1.7g; CHOL 30mg; IRON 0.9mg; SODIUM 310mg; CALC 57mg

If you're concerned about the grouper overpowering the light, fresh taste of this stew, you can rest easy. Grouper is a mild fish, and it quickly absorbs the flavors with which it is seasoned. Wait until the last 3 minutes to add the shrimp and fish; they don't need to cook long.

Provençal Fish Stew

Prep: 4 minutes • Cook: 11 minutes

1 teaspoon olive oil
1¼ cups chopped leek
½ cup chopped fennel bulb
1 garlic clove, minced
1 (14.5-ounce) can diced tomatoes
1¼ cups organic vegetable broth

¼ cup dry white wine
3 tablespoons chopped fresh parsley, divided
6 ounces grouper or other firm white fish, cut into 1½-inch pieces
¼ pound peeled and deveined medium shrimp
Parsley sprigs (optional)

1. Heat oil in a large Dutch oven over medium-high heat. Add leek, fennel, and garlic to pan; sauté 4 minutes or until tender. Stir in tomatoes, broth, wine, and 1 tablespoon parsley; bring to a boil. Add fish and shrimp; cook 3 minutes or until done. Sprinkle with remaining 2 tablespoons parsley, and garnish with parsley sprigs, if desired. Yield: 4 servings (serving size: 1¼ cups).

CALORIES 127; FAT 2g (sat 0.3g, mono 1.2g, poly 0.5g); PROTEIN 14.2g; CARB 10.5g; FIBER 2.5g; CHOL 58mg; IRON 2.1mg; SODIUM 391mg; CALC 60mg

choice ingredient

Fennel, an aromatic plant native to the Mediterranean region, has licorice-like flavor and is delicious raw or cooked. Chopped and sautéed, the fennel bulb adds body and rich flavor to soups. Look for small, heavy, white bulbs that are firm and free of cracks, browning, or moist areas. Store fennel bulbs in a perforated plastic bag in the refrigerator for up to 5 days.

Light coconut milk adds subtle flavor to this spicy soup for two. Use a vegetable peeler to remove the strip of rind from the lime, but be careful to avoid the bitter white pith.

Coconut Shrimp Soup

Prep: 3 minutes • Cook: 6 minutes

1   cup light coconut milk
1   cup water
½   teaspoon red curry paste
¼   teaspoon salt

1   (2 x ½-inch) strip lime rind
¾   pound peeled and deveined large shrimp
¼   cup julienne-cut fresh basil

1. Combine first 5 ingredients in a large saucepan, stirring with a whisk. Bring to a boil over medium-high heat. Add shrimp; cover, reduce heat to medium, and cook 3 minutes or until shrimp turn pink. Remove and discard lime rind; stir in basil. Yield: 2 servings (serving size: 1⅔ cups).

CALORIES 199; FAT 7.5g (sat 6.1g, mono 0.7g, poly 0.7g); PROTEIN 28.7g; CARB 5.2g; FIBER 0.4g; CHOL 252mg; IRON 4.7mg; SODIUM 633mg; CALC 61mg

serve with
Edamame Salad

Prep: 5 minutes

1   cup frozen shelled edamame
¾   cup frozen petite corn kernels
¼   cup chopped red onion

1   tablespoon chopped fresh parsley or cilantro
1½ tablespoons light olive oil vinaigrette

1. Place edamame and corn in a colander, and rinse under cool running water to thaw; drain well. Combine edamame, corn, red onion, parsley or cilantro, and vinaigrette in a medium bowl; toss well to coat. Serve immediately, or cover and chill until ready to serve. Yield: 2 servings (serving size: 1 cup).

CALORIES 152; FAT 5.6g (sat 0.2g, mono 1.5g, poly 3.9g); PROTEIN 8g; CARB 19.9g; FIBER 1.4g; CHOL 0mg; IRON 1.4mg; SODIUM 95mg; CALC 43mg

sandwiches

Tuna Florentine Sandwiches with Lemon-Caper Vinaigrette
Open-Faced Avocado-Bacon Tuna Melt
Tilapia Sandwich with Greek Tapenade
Open-Faced Salmon BLTs
Shrimp Rolls
Portobello Melts with Smoky Red Pepper Mayo
Roasted Tomato and Goat Cheese Baguette with Parsley Aïoli
Blue Cheese and Pear Sandwiches
Margherita Piadine
Mediterranean Flatbread Sandwiches
Black Pepper Sirloin Wrap with Kickin' Chipotle Spread
Sweet-Spiked Pork Sandwiches
Pressed Italian Sandwich with Pesto
Pulled Chicken Sandwiches with White Barbecue Sauce
Southwestern Chicken Lettuce Wraps with Spicy Chipotle Dipping Sauce
Greek Chicken Salad Pitas
Avocado Chicken Salad Sandwiches
Grilled Chicken, Pear, and Arugula Wrap with Cranberry Vinaigrette
Grilled Chicken and Tomato Pesto Baguettes
Turkey Cobb Salad Roll-Ups
Sun-Dried Turkey Burgers with Basil Aïoli

Fresh basil leaves and a homemade lemon-caper vinaigrette lend a vibrant Italian flair to this easy sandwich. For a simple, sweet-yet-healthful accompaniment, serve with juicy red grapes.

Tuna Florentine Sandwiches with Lemon-Caper Vinaigrette

Prep: 4 minutes • Cook: 3 minutes

1 (12-ounce) can albacore tuna in water, drained and flaked
1½ cups bagged baby spinach leaves
1 cup fresh basil leaves

Lemon-Caper Vinaigrette
8 (1.5-ounce) multigrain bread slices (such as Arnold Healthy Multigrain), toasted

1. Combine first 4 ingredients; toss well. Spoon tuna mixture evenly over each of 4 toasted bread slices. Top with remaining bread slices. Yield: 4 servings (serving size: 1 sandwich).

CALORIES 326; FAT 7.2g (sat 0.5g, mono 2.9g, poly 2.9g); PROTEIN 25.3g; CARB 43.1g; FIBER 6g; CHOL 26mg; IRON 3.3mg; SODIUM 572mg; CALC 291mg

Lemon-Caper Vinaigrette

Prep: 4 minutes

3 tablespoons fresh lemon juice
2½ tablespoons minced shallots (1 small)
1 tablespoon drained capers

1 tablespoon olive oil
½ teaspoon freshly ground black pepper
½ teaspoon Dijon mustard

1. Combine all ingredients in a small bowl, stirring with a whisk. Yield: ½ cup (serving size: 2 tablespoons).

CALORIES 39; FAT 3.5g (sat 0.5g, mono 2.5g, poly 0.5g); PROTEIN 0.4g; CARB 2.4g; FIBER 0.2g; CHOL 0mg; IRON 0.1mg; SODIUM 63mg; CALC 6mg

Shorten the prep time by baking the sweet potato fries while you make the sandwiches. Then add the assembled sandwiches to the baking sheet used for the potatoes during the last 2 minutes of cooking so that everything is ready at the same time.

Open-Faced Avocado-Bacon Tuna Melt

Prep: 13 minutes • Cook: 2 minutes

1 (12-ounce) can albacore tuna in water, drained and flaked
3 tablespoons light mayonnaise
$\frac{1}{8}$ teaspoon black pepper
4 (1-ounce) slices whole wheat bread, toasted

4 center-cut bacon slices, cooked and halved
$\frac{1}{4}$ avocado, thinly sliced
4 (0.74-ounce) slices reduced-fat Swiss cheese (such as Sargento)

1. Preheat oven to 425°.
2. Combine first 3 ingredients in a bowl. Spoon tuna mixture evenly over toasted bread slices. Top tuna mixture evenly with bacon, avocado, and cheese. Place sandwiches on a baking sheet.
3. Bake at 425° for 2 minutes or until cheese melts. Yield: 4 servings (serving size: 1 sandwich).

CALORIES 264; FAT 11.7g (sat 3.1g, mono 3.5g, poly 3.4g); PROTEIN 29.4g; CARB 11.1g; FIBER 3.6g; CHOL 47mg; IRON 1.2mg; SODIUM 514mg; CALC 269mg

serve with
Spicy Sweet Potato Fries

Prep: 2 minutes • Cook: 16 minutes

2½ cups frozen sweet potato fries
Butter-flavored cooking spray

¼ kosher salt
⅛ teaspoon ground red pepper

1. Preheat oven to 425°.
2. Place potatoes in a single layer on a large baking sheet coated with cooking spray. Coat potatoes with cooking spray.
3. Bake at 425° for 16 minutes or until crisp and golden.
4. Combine salt and ground pepper in a small bowl. Remove fries from oven, and sprinkle with salt mixture. Yield: 4 servings (serving size: ½ cup).

CALORIES 202; FAT 8.2g (sat 1.7g, mono 3.7g, poly 2.3g); PROTEIN 2.7g; CARB 32.1g; FIBER 4.1g; CHOL 0mg; IRON 1mg; SODIUM 304mg; CALC 54mg

Mâche, also known as lamb's lettuce or corn salad, is a tender green with a tangy, nutty flavor. Look for it in the produce section at your supermarket. Use a minichopper—or take your time using a large chef's knife—to finely chop the olives, roasted peppers, and oregano for the Greek Tapenade before you spread the mixture over the toasted bread.

Tilapia Sandwich with Greek Tapenade

Prep: 8 minutes • Cook: 6 minutes

Greek Tapenade
2 (6-ounce) tilapia fillets
⅛ teaspoon salt
⅛ teaspoon coarsely ground black pepper
Cooking spray

4 (0.8-ounce) slices crusty Chicago-style Italian bread (about ½ inch thick), toasted
⅔ cup mâche
4 tomato slices

1. Prepare Greek Tapenade; set aside.
2. Sprinkle fillets evenly with salt and pepper. Heat a large nonstick over medium-high heat; coat pan with cooking spray. Add fish; cook 2 to 3 minutes on each side or until fish flakes easily when tested with a fork.
3. Spread about 1 tablespoon Greek Tapenade on each bread slice. Top each of 2 slices with 1 fillet, 2 tomato slices, ⅓ cup mâche, and remaining bread slices. Yield: 2 servings (serving size: 1 sandwich).

CALORIES 347; FAT 8.9g (sat 3g, mono 3.4g, poly 1.7g); PROTEIN 39.9g; CARB 26g; FIBER 1.6g; CHOL 93mg; IRON 3mg; SODIUM 768mg; CALC 113mg

Greek Tapenade

Prep: 5 minutes

2 tablespoons chopped pitted kalamata olives
2 tablespoons crumbled feta cheese
1 tablespoon chopped bottled roasted red bell peppers

½ teaspoon grated lemon rind
1 teaspoon fresh lemon juice
½ teaspoon chopped fresh oregano

1. Place all ingredients in a mini food processor; pulse 2 or 3 times or until minced. Yield: 2 servings (serving size: 2½ tablespoons).

CALORIES 52; FAT 4.3g (sat 1.7g, mono 2.2g, poly 0.3g); PROTEIN 1.5g; CARB 1.7g; FIBER 0.1g; CHOL 8mg; IRON 0mg; SODIUM 262mg; CALC 52mg

Fresh salmon and a tangy dill spread dress up
the conventional BLT. You'll need a knife and fork to
handle this hearty sandwich. To save time, toast the bread
slices while the fish cooks.

Open-Faced Salmon BLTs

Prep: 5 minutes • Cook: 10 minutes

8 slices precooked hickory-smoked bacon (such as Jimmy Dean)
2 (6-ounce) salmon fillets (about 1 inch thick)
¼ teaspoon freshly ground black pepper, divided
Cooking spray
¼ cup light mayonnaise

1½ tablespoons fresh lemon juice
1½ teaspoons minced fresh dill
4 (1-ounce) slices diagonally cut French bread, toasted
4 green leaf lettuce leaves
4 slices tomato, cut in half

1. Preheat broiler.
2. Microwave bacon slices according to package directions; set aside.
3. While bacon cooks, sprinkle fish with ⅛ teaspoon pepper. Place fish, skin sides down, on a broiler pan coated with cooking spray. Broil 10 to 13 minutes or until fish flakes easily when tested with a fork. Remove skin from fish, and cut fish into chunks.
4. While fish cooks, combine mayonnaise, lemon juice, dill, and remaining ⅛ teaspoon pepper. Spread 1 tablespoon dill mayonnaise on each French bread slice; top with 1 lettuce leaf, 2 tomato halves, 2 slices bacon, and one-fourth of salmon chunks. Drizzle remaining dill mayonnaise evenly over each sandwich. Yield: 4 servings (serving size: 1 sandwich).

CALORIES 331; FAT 15.6g (sat 3, mono 4.8g, poly 5.7g); PROTEIN 24.9g; CARB 21.4g; FIBER 1.3g; CHOL 55mg; IRON 1.7mg; SODIUM 505mg; CALC 31mg

serve with
Tomato and Cucumber Salad

Prep: 5 minutes

1 cup cherry tomatoes, halved
2 small salad cucumbers, sliced
½ cup coarsely chopped yellow or green bell pepper

½ cup light red wine vinaigrette
½ teaspoon freshly ground black pepper

1. Combine all ingredients in a medium bowl; toss well. Cover and chill until ready to serve. Yield: 4 servings (serving size: ¾ cup).

CALORIES 66; FAT 5.2g (sat 0.5g, mono 2g, poly 2g); PROTEIN 0.8g; CARB 5.6g; FIBER 1.1g; CHOL 0mg; IRON 0.3mg; SODIUM 283mg; CALC 12mg

We've chosen a traditional hot dog bun for this sandwich. However, for variety, you can also use a flour tortilla. Place a lettuce leaf on an 8-inch tortilla, spoon the shrimp mixture onto the lettuce, and then roll up the tortilla. Secure the roll with a round wooden pick, and cut it in half.

Shrimp Rolls
Prep: 10 minutes

1 small lemon	½ cup finely chopped celery
¼ cup light mayonnaise	4 (1.5-ounce) white-wheat hot dog buns
2 tablespoons chopped green onion tops	4 Boston lettuce leaves
¾ pound chopped cooked shrimp	

1. Grate ½ teaspoon lemon rind from lemon. Squeeze lemon to measure 1½ tablespoons juice. Combine lemon rind, juice, mayonnaise, and green onions in a large bowl. Add shrimp and celery; toss gently.

2. Top each bun with 1 lettuce leaf. Spoon shrimp mixture evenly onto lettuce leaves. Serve immediately. Yield: 4 servings (serving size: 1 sandwich).

CALORIES 220; FAT 7.4g (sat 1g, mono 1.2g, poly 3.4g); PROTEIN 23.1g; CARB 20.7; FIBER 4.5g; CHOL 171mg; IRON 5.5mg; SODIUM 514mg; CALC 296mg

serve with
Pear-Kiwi Salad
Prep: 6 minutes

2 tablespoons lime juice	2 cups sliced pear (about 2 pears)
1 tablespoon finely chopped fresh mint	1¾ cups peeled, sliced kiwi
1 tablespoon honey	

1. Combine lime juice, mint, and honey in a medium bowl, stirring with a whisk. Add pear and kiwi; toss gently. Yield: 4 servings (serving size: ¾ cup).

CALORIES 113; FAT 0.5g (sat 0g, mono 0.1g, poly 0.2g); PROTEIN 1.3g; CARB 29.2g; FIBER 5g; CHOL 0mg; IRON 0.4mg; SODIUM 4mg; CALC 36mg

Smoky Red Pepper Mayo and melted cheese
transform this grilled mushroom sandwich into the perfect
weeknight dinner. Make some extra mayo to dress up other
sandwiches; store it in the refrigerator for up to 1 week.

Portobello Melts with Smoky Red Pepper Mayo

Prep: 7 minutes • Cook: 10 minutes

4 large portobello mushroom caps
Olive oil-cooking spray
4 (0.7-ounce) part-skim mozzarella slices
2 tablespoons shredded Parmigiano-Reggiano cheese

Smoky Red Pepper Mayo
4 (1.5-ounce) whole-grain white sandwich thins (such as Arnold)

1. Prepare grill.
2. Coat both sides of mushroom caps with cooking spray. Place mushroom caps, gill side down, on grill rack coated with cooking spray. Grill 5 minutes; turn mushrooms over, and top evenly with cheeses. Grill 5 minutes or until cheeses melt.
3. Spread 2½ tablespoons Smoky Red Pepper Mayo evenly on cut sides of each sandwich thin. Place a mushroom cap, cheese side up, on bottom of each sandwich thin. Top with sandwich thin tops. Yield: 4 servings (serving size: 1 sandwich).

CALORIES 329; FAT 17.6g (sat 5.5g, mono 4.3g, poly 5.4g); PROTEIN 15.6g; CARB 29.6g; FIBER 7.4g; CHOL 28mg; IRON 1.8mg; SODIUM 680mg; CALC 288mg

Smoky Red Pepper Mayo

Prep: 4 minutes

½ cup light mayonnaise
2 tablespoons chopped bottled roasted red bell pepper

1 teaspoon fresh lemon juice
½ teaspoon smoked paprika
½ teaspoon minced garlic

1. Combine all ingredients in a small bowl. Yield: 10 tablespoons (serving size: 2½ tablespoons).

CALORIES 104; FAT 10g (sat 1.5g, mono 2.3g, poly 5.2g); PROTEIN 0.2g; CARB 3.1g; FIBER 0.1g; CHOL 11mg; IRON 0.1mg; SODIUM 253mg; CALC 2mg

choice ingredient

Round sandwich thins are a tasty alternative to regular sliced bread. Each serving contains 100 calories and 5 grams of fiber, which is comparable to a single slice of bread.

Roasting the tomatoes and peppers intensifies their natural sweetness, which is the key to this simple sandwich's robust flavor. Round out your meal by adding crispy sweet potato chips.

Roasted Tomato and Goat Cheese Baguette with Parsley Aïoli

Prep: 7 minutes • Cook: 12 minutes

8 (½-inch thick) slices large beefsteak tomatoes
1 large yellow bell pepper, quartered lengthwise
1 (10-ounce) whole-grain baguette, halved lengthwise
4 ounces goat cheese, crumbled
Parsley Aïoli

1. Preheat broiler.
2. Place tomato slices and bell pepper on a baking sheet lined with foil. Broil 10 minutes or until bell pepper is charred. Cut bell pepper crosswise into thin strips.
3. Place baguette halves cut sides up on a baking sheet. Broil 2 minutes or until lightly toasted.
4. Arrange tomato slices in a single layer on top of cut side of bottom half of toasted baguette. Top tomato slices evenly with goat cheese and pepper strips.
5. Spread Parsley Aïoli on cut side of top half of toasted baguette. Top pepper strips with top half of baguette. Cut crosswise into 4 equal portions. Yield: 4 servings (serving size: 1 sandwich).

CALORIES 294; FAT 10.8g (sat 6.1g, mono 3.2g, poly 0.9g); PROTEIN 12.3g; CARB 36.1g; FIBER 2.6g; CHOL 24mg; IRON 3.2mg; SODIUM 624mg; CALC 114mg

Parsley Aïoli

Prep: 4 minutes

1 cup fresh parsley leaves
1 garlic clove, crushed
1 teaspoon extra-virgin olive oil
1 teaspoon Dijon mustard
¼ cup fat-free mayonnaise
⅛ teaspoon freshly ground black pepper

1. Place all ingredients in a food processor; process until blended. Yield: ⅓ cup (serving size: about 1 tablespoon).

CALORIES 32; FAT 1.7g (sat 0.3g, mono 1.2g, poly 0.1g); PROTEIN 0.4g; CARB 4.1g; FIBER 0.5g; CHOL 1mg; IRON 1mg; SODIUM 162mg; CALC 22mg

This "salad and sandwich in one" features a hearty slice of peasant bread topped with sweet pears, pungent blue cheese, and peppery watercress. Look for artisan peasant bread in the bakery at your supermarket.

Blue Cheese and Pear Sandwiches

Prep: 4 minutes • Cook: 6 minutes

 4 (1½-ounce) slices peasant bread
Cooking spray
1⅓ cups coarsely chopped watercress
 2 teaspoons olive oil

⅛ teaspoon salt
⅛ teaspoon freshly ground black pepper
 2 medium pears, thinly sliced
½ cup (2 ounces) crumbled blue cheese

1. Preheat broiler.
2. Place bread slices on a baking sheet. Coat each slice with cooking spray; broil 2 minutes on each side or until lightly toasted.
3. While bread cooks, combine watercress, olive oil, salt, and pepper in a small bowl; toss gently.
4. Place pear slices evenly on bread slices; top with blue cheese. Broil 2 to 3 minutes or until cheese melts. Remove from oven; top with watercress mixture. Serve immediately. Yield: 4 servings (serving size: 1 sandwich).

CALORIES 211; FAT 6.9g (sat 3g, mono 2.8g, poly 0.4g); PROTEIN 7.5g; CARB 31.7g; FIBER 2.5g; CHOL 11mg; IRON 1.2mg; SODIUM 506mg; CALC 139mg

serve with
White Balsamic–Dill Pasta Salad

Prep: 2 minutes • Cook: 14 minutes

 2 cups uncooked farfalle (bow tie pasta)
 2 tablespoons white balsamic vinegar
 1 tablespoon olive oil
⅛ teaspoon salt

⅛ teaspoon freshly ground black pepper
½ cup prechopped tricolor bell pepper mix
 1 tablespoon chopped fresh dill

1. Cook pasta according to package directions, omitting salt and fat. Rinse under cold water until cool; drain well.
2. While pasta cooks, combine vinegar and next 3 ingredients in a medium bowl, stirring with a whisk. Add pasta, bell pepper mix, and dill, and toss well. Yield: 4 servings (serving size: ¾ cup).

CALORIES 196; FAT 4.1g (sat 0.7g, mono 2.5g, poly 0.6g); PROTEIN 6g; CARB 34g; FIBER 1.7g; CHOL 0mg; IRON 1.5mg; SODIUM 77mg; CALC 12mg

A *piadine* is an Italian flatbread sandwich made by cooking dough over coals and then folding the thin bread over dressed greens or vegetables. Our version is baked in the oven and uses refrigerated pizza crust for speed and ease.

Margherita Piadine

Prep: 5 minutes • Cook: 10 minutes

Cooking spray
1 (11-ounce) package refrigerated thin-crust pizza crust dough
2 teaspoons extra-virgin olive oil, divided
1 small garlic clove, minced
3 large basil leaves, cut into thin strips
¼ teaspoon freshly ground black pepper, divided

1 tablespoon balsamic vinegar
⅛ teaspoon salt
4 cups loosely packed arugula
1½ cups diced seeded plum tomato (about 2)
4 (0.67-ounce) slices reduced-fat provolone cheese (such as Sargento)

1. Preheat oven to 425°.
2. Coat a large baking sheet with cooking spray. Roll out dough onto prepared baking sheet; cut dough crosswise in half, creating 2 smaller rectangles. Brush surface of dough with 1 teaspoon oil; sprinkle with garlic, basil, and ⅛ teaspoon pepper. Bake at 425° for 8 minutes or until crust is golden but still pliable.
3. While crust bakes, combine remaining oil, remaining ⅛ teaspoon pepper, vinegar, and salt in a large bowl, stirring with a whisk. Add arugula and tomatoes; toss well.
4. Arrange cheese slices lengthwise down long side of crusts; top with arugula mixture. Fold dough over filling, creating 2 long rectangle sandwiches. Bake an additional 1 to 2 minutes or until cheese melts. Cut each rectangle crosswise in half. Serve immediately. Yield: 4 servings (serving size: 1 sandwich).

CALORIES 314; FAT 12.3g (sat 3.6g, mono 5g, poly 1.6g); PROTEIN 12.2g; CARB 39.8g; FIBER 2g; CHOL 10mg; IRON 2.2mg; SODIUM 730mg; CALC 188mg

serve with
Lemony Chickpea Salad

Prep: 2 minutes • Cook: 2 minutes

1 tablespoon chopped fresh parsley
1 tablespoon fresh lemon juice
1 tablespoon extra-virgin olive oil
⅛ teaspoon crushed red pepper

1 small garlic clove, minced
1 (15-ounce) can chickpeas (garbanzo beans), rinsed and drained

1. Combine first 5 ingredients in a medium bowl. Stir in chickpeas. Serve at room temperature. Yield: 4 servings (serving size: about ½ cup).

CALORIES 117; FAT 4.2g (sat 0.6g, mono 2.7g, poly 0.7g); PROTEIN 3.6g; CARB 16.7g; FIBER 3.2g; CHOL 0mg; IRON 1.1mg; SODIUM 128mg; CALC 26mg

Soft, tender Mediterranean flatbread offers a delightful contrast to the crisp vegetables and crunchy pilaf in this hearty meatless recipe. Round out your meal with a sweet-tart Pomegranate Refresher.

Mediterranean Flatbread Sandwiches
Prep: 10 minutes

1 (8.5-ounce) package 7-grain pilaf (such as Seeds of Change)
1 cup diced English cucumber
1 cup chopped seeded tomato (1 medium)
½ cup (2 ounces) crumbled feta cheese
2 tablespoons fresh lemon juice
1 tablespoon olive oil
¼ teaspoon salt
¼ teaspoon freshly ground black pepper
1 (7-ounce) container hummus (such as Athenos Original)
3 (2.8-ounce) Mediterranean-style white flatbreads (such as Toufayan)

1. Combine first 8 ingredients in a bowl. Spread hummus evenly over each flatbread. Spoon pilaf mixture evenly over half of each flatbread; fold flatbread over filling. Cut each sandwich in half, and serve immediately. Yield: 6 servings (serving size: ½ sandwich).

CALORIES 310; FAT 12.2g (sat 3.4g, mono 6.6g, poly 1.8g); PROTEIN 11.1g; CARB 39.2g; FIBER 6g; CHOL 11mg; IRON 1mg; SODIUM 549mg; CALC 80mg

serve with
Pomegranate Refreshers
Prep: 4 minutes

2 cups pomegranate juice, chilled
¼ cup fresh lemon juice
3 tablespoons sugar
2 cups club soda, chilled
Ice cubes
Lemon slices (optional)

1. Combine first 3 ingredients in a small pitcher, stirring until sugar dissolves. Gently stir in club soda. Serve over ice, and garnish with lemon slices, if desired. Yield: 6 servings (serving size: about ¾ cup).

CALORIES 73; FAT 0g (sat 0g, mono 0g, poly 0g); PROTEIN 0.4g; CARB 18.8g; FIBER 0g; CHOL 0mg; IRON 0.1mg; SODIUM 27mg; CALC 18mg

Mayonnaise, garlic, and adobo sauce create a spicy, smoky spread well suited for these satisfying steak wraps. To warm the tortillas, stack them together, and cover with a few layers of damp paper towels; then microwave at HIGH 1 minute or until the tortillas are soft and pliable.

Black Pepper Sirloin Wrap with Kickin' Chipotle Spread

Prep: 6 minutes • Cook: 10 minutes

1 pound lean boneless sirloin steak (¾ inch thick)
2 teaspoons coarsely ground black pepper
Cooking spray
6 (7-inch) flour tortillas (such as Mission Carb Balance)

4 cups torn mixed salad greens
1 cup (3 x ¼-inch) julienne-cut red bell pepper (about 1 medium)
Kickin' Chipotle Spread

1. Prepare grill.
2. Sprinkle both sides of steak with black pepper. Place steak on a grill rack coated with cooking spray; grill 5 to 6 minutes on each side or until desired degree of doneness. Let stand 3 minutes before slicing.
3. While steak cooks, top tortillas evenly with salad greens and bell pepper. Top with steak slices; drizzle Kickin' Chipotle Spread evenly over steak. Roll up. Yield: 6 servings (serving size: 1 wrap).

CALORIES 235; FAT 9.8g (sat 2.4g, mono 3.8g, poly 1.7g); PROTEIN 18.9g; CARB 17.7g; FIBER 2.1g; CHOL 51mg; IRON 3.3mg; SODIUM 759mg; CALC 22mg

Kickin' Chipotle Spread

Prep: 2 minutes

⅓ cup light mayonnaise
2 teaspoons adobo sauce
1 garlic clove, minced

2 tablespoons water
¼ teaspoon salt

1. Combine all ingredients in a small bowl, stirring with a whisk. Yield: about ½ cup (serving size: about 1 tablespoon).

CALORIES 35; FAT 3.4g (sat 0.7g, mono 0.8g, poly 1.7g); PROTEIN 0g; CARB 0.9g; FIBER 0.1g; CHOL 3mg; IRON 0mg; SODIUM 166mg; CALC 1mg

Although the slaw can be served as a side dish with this open-faced sandwich, we enjoyed piling it high on top of the sweet glazed pork as a condiment.

Sweet-Spiked Pork Sandwiches

Prep: 2 minutes • Cook: 25 minutes

1 (1-pound) pork tenderloin, trimmed
¼ teaspoon salt
¾ teaspoon coarsely ground black pepper
Cooking spray
1 cup cola
¼ cup bourbon
2½ tablespoons country-style Dijon mustard
4 (0.8-ounce) Chicago Italian bread slices, lightly toasted

1. Sprinkle pork evenly with salt and pepper; coat with cooking spray. Heat a large nonstick skillet over medium-high heat. Coat pan with cooking spray. Add pork; cook 3 minutes or until browned on 1 side.
2. Reduce heat to medium-low; turn pork over. Cover and cook 17 minutes or until a thermometer registers 160° (slightly pink). Remove pork from pan. Cover and let stand 5 minutes.
3. While pork is standing, increase heat to medium-high, and add cola and bourbon to pan. Bring to a boil; cook 7 minutes or until mixture is reduced to ¼ cup.
4. Spread mustard evenly on one side of bread slices. Cut pork into thin slices. Add pork slices to sauce, tossing to coat. Arrange pork slices over mustard. Spoon sauce evenly over pork. Yield: 4 servings (serving size: 1 open-faced sandwich).

CALORIES 275; FAT 4.7g (sat 1.5g, mono 1.9g, poly 0.7g); PROTEIN 25.9g; CARB 20.1g; FIBER 0.7g; CHOL 74mg; IRON 2.1mg; SODIUM 562mg; CALC 27mg

serve with
Spicy Celery Seed Coleslaw

Prep: 5 minutes

3 tablespoons light mayonnaise
1 tablespoon sugar
1 tablespoon water
1 teaspoon cider vinegar
½ teaspoon celery seed
⅛ teaspoon crushed red pepper
⅛ teaspoon salt
¼ freshly ground black pepper
3 cups cabbage-and-carrot coleslaw

1. Combine all ingredients, except coleslaw, in a medium bowl; stir with a whisk. Add coleslaw; toss well. Yield: 4 servings (serving size: about ⅔ cup).

CALORIES 61; FAT 3.8g (sat 0.8g, mono 1g, poly 2g); PROTEIN 0.4g; CARB 6g; FIBER 0.8g; CHOL 4mg; IRON 0.3mg; SODIUM 169mg; CALC 20mg

This pressed sandwich can be made a day ahead and stored in the refrigerator until ready to serve—just be sure to layer the red bell pepper strips between the prosciutto and cheese to prevent the bread from becoming soggy.

Pressed Italian Sandwich with Pesto

Prep: 14 minutes • Other: 2 hours to 24 hours

1 (16-ounce) ciabatta
Pesto
6 ounces very thinly sliced prosciutto
1 cup drained bottled roasted red bell pepper, cut into strips

8 (0.75-ounce) slices mozzarella cheese
¼ teaspoon freshly ground black pepper

1. Slice ciabatta in half horizontally. Hollow out top and bottom halves of bread; reserve torn bread for another use. Spread Pesto over bottom half of bread. Layer prosciutto, bell pepper strips, and cheese over pesto; sprinkle with pepper. Replace top half of bread. Wrap loaf in plastic wrap and foil, and place on a plate; top with a heavy skillet filled with heavy cans. Refrigerate 2 hours or overnight.
2. Remove foil and plastic wrap; cut sandwich into 8 pieces. Yield: 8 servings (serving size: 1 piece).

CALORIES 313; FAT 13g (sat 4.6g, mono 6.1g, poly 1.4g); PROTEIN 17.2g; CARB 33.2g; FIBER 1.5g; CHOL 27mg; IRON 2.5mg; SODIUM 987mg; CALC 224mg

Pesto

Prep: 9 minutes

1 garlic clove
1 tablespoon pine nuts
2 cups fresh basil leaves

¼ cup (1 ounce) grated fresh Parmesan cheese
1½ tablespoons olive oil
⅛ teaspoon salt

1. With food processor on, drop garlic and pine nuts through food chute; process until minced. Add basil and remaining ingredients; process until smooth. Yield: about ½ cup (serving size: about 1 tablespoon).

CALORIES 48; FAT 4.3g (sat 0.9g, mono 2.1g, poly 0.7g); PROTEIN 1.9g; CARB 0.7g; FIBER 0.4g; CHOL 3mg; IRON 0.4mg; SODIUM 100mg; CALC 67mg

White Barbecue Sauce, widely used in Alabama-style barbecue, is known for its vinegary taste and its use of mayonnaise as its base, rather than the usual tomato sauce. To make the sauce ahead of time, combine all the ingredients, store it in the refrigerator, and bring it to room temperature before serving.

Pulled Chicken Sandwiches with White Barbecue Sauce

Prep: 5 minutes

2 cups packaged angel hair slaw
6 (1.8-ounce) white-wheat hamburger buns
3 cups shredded rotisserie chicken

¾ cup White Barbecue Sauce
2 hamburger dill pickle slices

1. Place ⅓ cup slaw on bottom half of each bun; top each with ½ cup chicken, 2 tablespoons White Barbecue Sauce, 2 pickle slices, and a bun top. Yield: 6 servings (serving size: 1 sandwich).

CALORIES 379; FAT 8.6g (sat 2g, mono 1.9g, poly 2.8g); PROTEIN 52.3g; CARB 25.5g; FIBER 5.7g; CHOL 129mg; IRON 1.6mg; SODIUM 503mg; CALC 332mg

White Barbecue Sauce

Prep: 5 minutes

1 cup low-fat mayonnaise
¾ cup cider vinegar
2 tablespoons fresh lemon juice

1 tablespoon freshly ground black pepper
¼ teaspoon ground red pepper

1. Combine all ingredients in a small bowl, stirring with a whisk. Cover and store in refrigerator up to a week. Yield: 1¾ cup (serving size: 2 tablespoons).

CALORIES 22; FAT 1.2g (sat 0g, mono 0g, poly 0.6g); PROTEIN 0.1g; CARB 2.9g; FIBER 0.1g; CHOL 0mg; IRON 0.1mg; SODIUM 149mg; CALC 3mg

choice ingredient

Prepared produce, such as angel hair coleslaw, can shave minutes off your prep time. Look for bags of angel hair coleslaw near the bagged lettuce in the produce section of your supermarket. Always check the freshness date, and look closely at the cut edges for signs of deterioration.

Crisp iceberg lettuce cradles a Southwest-inspired mix of rice, beans, chicken, and salsa. Find fresh salsa in the produce section of your supermarket. It generally has 50 percent less sodium than bottled salsa, and it tastes like it's homemade.

Southwestern Chicken Lettuce Wraps with Spicy Chipotle Dipping Sauce

Prep: 7 minutes • Cook: 90 seconds

1 (8.8-ounce) package microwaveable precooked whole-grain brown rice (such as Uncle Ben's Ready Rice)
2 cups shredded rotisserie chicken
¾ cup fresh salsa

⅓ cup chopped green onion (about 3)
1 (15-ounce) can reduced-sodium black beans (such as Bush's), rinsed and drained
12 iceberg lettuce leaves
Spicy Chipotle Dipping Sauce

1. Prepare rice according to package directions. Place rice in a large bowl. Stir in chicken and next 3 ingredients. Spoon chicken mixture evenly in center of lettuce leaves. Fold in edges of leaves; roll up, and secure with wooden picks. Serve with Spicy Chipotle Dipping Sauce. Yield: 6 servings (serving size: 2 wraps and 2 tablespoons sauce).

CALORIES 211; FAT 5.3g (sat 2.1g, mono 1.3g, poly 0.5g); PROTEIN 18.6g; CARB 21.4g; FIBER 3.3g; CHOL 48mg; IRON 1.6mg; SODIUM 183mg; CALC 52mg

Spicy Chipotle Dipping Sauce

Prep: 2 minutes

½ cup reduced-fat sour cream
1 tablespoon chopped fresh cilantro
1 tablespoon fresh lime juice

½ teaspoon ground cumin
¼ teaspoon chili powder

1. Combine all ingredients in a small bowl. Yield: ¾ cup (serving size: 2 tablespoons).

CALORIES 28; FAT 2.4g (sat 1.5g, mono 0.7g, poly 0.1g); PROTEIN 0.6g; CARB 1.1g; FIBER 0.1g; CHOL 8mg; IRON 0.1mg; SODIUM 12mg; CALC 23mg

You'll find prepared hummus in a variety of flavors. We used roasted red bell pepper hummus for this sandwich, but either spicy three-pepper or artichoke-and-garlic hummus would make a good choice, too. Round out your meal with a refreshing side of mixed melon.

Greek Chicken Salad Pitas

Prep: 11 minutes

2 cups sliced romaine lettuce
1 cup chopped roasted chicken breast
⅔ cup diced seeded cucumber
¼ cup thinly sliced red onion
¼ cup (1 ounce) crumbled feta cheese
2 tablespoons fresh lemon juice

2 tablespoons olive oil
¼ teaspoon salt
¼ teaspoon freshly ground black pepper
6 tablespoons roasted red bell pepper hummus
2 (6-inch) whole wheat pitas, cut in half

1. Combine lettuce and next 4 ingredients in a large bowl. Add lemon juice, olive oil, salt, and pepper; toss gently.
2. Spread 1½ tablespoons hummus inside each pita half; spoon salad mixture evenly into halves. Serve immediately. Yield: 4 servings (serving size: 1 pita half).

CALORIES 278; FAT 13.5g (sat 2.9g, mono 7.3g, poly 1.8g); PROTEIN 16.7g; CARB 24.6g; FIBER 4.1g; CHOL 38mg; IRON 2mg; SODIUM 669mg; CALC 71mg

make it faster

To make this meal even faster, forgo rinsing, slicing, and chopping the fresh vegetables and fruit yourself. Look in the produce section for packaged torn romaine lettuce and containers of presliced red onion, prechopped cucumber, and prechopped mixed melon. Sometimes these items may be more expensive, but the trade-off is time saved from prepping and cleaning.

Avocado gives this chicken salad a rich, creamy texture as well as a healthy dose of monounsaturated fat, which protects against heart disease.

Avocado Chicken Salad Sandwiches

Prep: 7 minutes • Cook: 4 minutes

3 cups (½-inch) cubed cooked chicken breast
¼ cup light mayonnaise
2 tablespoons chopped fresh cilantro
¼ teaspoon salt

⅛ teaspoon black pepper
1 cup (½-inch) cubed avocado (about 1)
4 green leaf lettuce leaves
8 whole wheat bread slices, toasted

1. Combine first 5 ingredients in a large bowl. Gently stir avocado into chicken mixture until combined.
2. Place 1 lettuce leaf onto each of 4 bread slices. Spoon chicken mixture evenly onto each lettuce leaf. Top with remaining bread slices. Yield: 4 servings (serving size: 1 sandwich).

CALORIES 364; FAT 16.4g (sat 2.7g, mono 7.9g, poly 3g); PROTEIN 41.4g; CARB 24.1g; FIBER 11.9g; CHOL 95mg; IRON 4.4mg; SODIUM 647mg; CALC 322mg

serve with
Herbed Tomato-Cucumber Salad

Prep: 6 minutes

1 tablespoon olive oil
2 teaspoons champagne vinegar
¼ teaspoons salt
¼ teaspoon Italian seasoning
⅛ teaspoon black pepper

½ teaspoon minced garlic
2 medium tomatoes, cut into wedges
1 cup cucumber slices
¼ cup diced sweet onion

1. Combine first 6 ingredients in a medium bowl, stirring with a whisk. Stir in remaining ingredients. Serve immediately. Yield: 4 servings (serving size: ¾ cup).

CALORIES 51; FAT 3.6g (sat 0.5g, mono 2.5g, poly 0.4g); PROTEIN 0.9g; CARB 4.6g; FIBER 1.1g; CHOL 0mg; IRON 0.3mg; SODIUM 150mg; CALC 14mg

shortcut kitchen tip

To peel, seed, and dice an avocado, cut into the avocado vertically using a sharp knife; you'll hit the large seed in the center, so don't expect to be able to cut all the way through the fruit. Cut around the seed; twist both sides. Pull the halves apart. Whack the seed with the knife blade; then gently twist the knife, and pull to remove the seed, which will be stuck on the blade. Gently slice several horizontal and vertical lines through the flesh, but not through the skin. Use a spoon to gently scoop the diced flesh from the shell.

These sandwiches are generously stuffed, so we've wrapped them in parchment and cut them in half—right through the paper—to make them easier and less messy to eat. You can use wax paper if you don't have parchment.

Grilled Chicken, Pear, and Arugula Wrap with Cranberry Vinaigrette

Prep: 10 minutes • Cook: 12 minutes

1 pound chicken breast tenders (about 8)
¼ teaspoon salt
¼ teaspoon black pepper
2 pears, quartered lengthwise and cored
Cooking spray

6 cups arugula
Cranberry Vinaigrette
4 (8-inch) 96% fat-free whole wheat flour tortillas (such as Mission)

1. Prepare grill.
2. Sprinkle chicken with salt and pepper. Place chicken and pear on a grill rack coated with cooking spray. Grill chicken 3 to 4 minutes on each side or until done. Grill pear 2 minutes on each side or until browned. Remove chicken and pear from grill; cut pear into ¼-inch slices.
3. Combine arugula and Cranberry Vinaigrette in a large bowl; toss well. Place about 1 cup arugula mixture on each tortilla; top evenly with chicken and pear slices. Roll up tortillas, and wrap in parchment paper. Cut each wrap in half. Yield: 4 servings (serving size: 1 wrap).

CALORIES 349; FAT 7.5g (sat 0.3g, mono 3.4g, poly 3.4g); PROTEIN 29g; CARB 42.7g; FIBER 6g; CHOL 61mg; IRON 1.9mg; SODIUM 1039mg; CALC 85mg

Cranberry Vinaigrette

Prep: 2 minutes

2½ tablespoons frozen cranberry juice cocktail concentrate
1 tablespoon rice vinegar
1½ teaspoons Dijon mustard
1 tablespoon finely chopped dried sweetened cranberries

⅛ teaspoon salt
⅛ teaspoon black pepper
1 tablespoon canola oil

1. Combine first 6 ingredients in a bowl, stirring with a whisk until cranberry concentrate thaws. Gradually add oil, stirring with a whisk until blended. Yield: ⅓ cup (serving size: about 1 tablespoon).

CALORIES 46; FAT 3.5g (sat 0.3g, mono 2.1g, poly 1.1g); PROTEIN 0g; CARB 3.8g; FIBER 0.1g; CHOL 0mg; IRON 0.1mg; SODIUM 119mg; CALC 0.5mg

Work quickly when you assemble this sandwich so the chicken and bell pepper retain enough heat from the grilling to melt the cheese. Serve with raw cucumber and carrot sticks for a crunchy side.

Grilled Chicken and Tomato Pesto Baguettes

Prep: 7 minutes • Cook: 8 minutes

1 (8.5-ounce) thin whole wheat baguette
2 (8-ounce) skinless, boneless chicken breast halves
¼ teaspoon salt
⅛ teaspoon black pepper
1 red bell pepper, seeded and quartered
Cooking spray
¼ cup sun-dried tomato pesto (such as Classico)
4 curly leaf lettuce leaves
4 (0.7-ounce) slices low-fat Swiss cheese, cut in half lengthwise

1. Prepare grill.
2. Cut baguette in half lengthwise. Hollow out top half of baguette, leaving a ½-inch border; reserve torn bread for another use. Set aside.
3. Place chicken breast halves between 2 large sheets of heavy-duty plastic wrap; pound to ½-inch thickness using a meat mallet or small heavy skillet. Sprinkle chicken with salt and pepper.
4. Flatten bell pepper quarters with hands. Coat chicken breasts and bell pepper quarters with cooking spray; place on grill rack. Cover and grill 8 minutes or until chicken is done and bell peppers are tender, turning once. Place cut sides of baguette halves on grill during last 2 minutes of grilling to lightly toast. Cut each chicken breast in half crosswise.
5. Spread both cut halves of baguette evenly with pesto. Top bottom half with lettuce leaves, chicken breast halves, bell pepper quarters, and cheese slices. Place top half of baguette on top of cheese. Cut crosswise into 4 equal portions. Yield: 4 servings (serving size: ¼ of baguette).

CALORIES 345; FAT 7.2g (sat 3.2g, mono 1.8g, poly 1.9g); PROTEIN 39.3g; CARB 24.7g; FIBER 1.7g; CHOL 66mg; IRON 2.4mg; SODIUM 748mg; CALC 271mg

The original Cobb Salad made its debut at the Brown Derby Restaurant in Hollywood. It was created as a way to use a variety of leftovers—turkey, tomatoes, onions, avocado, blue cheese, and Roquefort dressing.

Turkey Cobb Salad Roll-Ups

Prep: 14 minutes

2 cups shredded romaine lettuce
1 cup chopped seeded tomato (1 medium)
¼ cup chopped green onions (2 medium)
3 tablespoons blue cheese-flavored yogurt dressing (such as Bolthouse Farms)

½ teaspoon freshly ground black pepper
8 ounces thinly sliced roast turkey
1 avocado, diced
4 (1.9-ounce) multigrain flatbreads with flax (such as Flatout)

1. Combine first 7 ingredients in a medium bowl. Spoon turkey mixture evenly onto flatbreads; roll up. Yield: 4 servings (serving size: 1 wrap).

CALORIES 301; FAT 13.3g (sat 2.3g, mono 6.4g, poly 3.4g); PROTEIN 28.8g; CARB 25.1g; FIBER 12g; CHOL 53mg; IRON 1.9mg; SODIUM 381mg; CALC 83mg

serve with
Carrot Slaw

Prep: 5 minutes

2½ tablespoons fresh lemon juice
1 tablespoon olive oil
1 tablespoon honey
⅛ teaspoon salt

¼ teaspoon freshly ground black pepper
3½ cups grated carrot (about pound)
1½ cups diced Granny Smith apple (1 small)

1. Combine first 5 ingredients in a medium bowl, stirring with a whisk. Add carrot and apple; toss well. Yield: 4 servings (serving size: about 1 cup).

CALORIES 115; FAT 3.6g (sat 0.5g, mono 2.5g, poly 0.5g); PROTEIN 1.1g; CARB 22g; FIBER 3.9g; CHOL 0mg; IRON 0.5mg; SODIUM 140mg; CALC 36mg

Take
big f
and B
Fries

salads

Chicken, Spinach, and Blueberry Salad with Pomegranate Vinaigrette
Grilled Chicken and Peach Spinach Salad with Sherry Vinaigrette
Grilled Chicken and Vegetable Arugula Salad
Grilled Romaine Chicken Caesar Salad
Chicken Salad with Red Grapes and Citrus-Honey Dressing
Chicken Salad with Asparagus and Creamy Dill Dressing
Tuna, Artichoke, and Roasted Red Pepper Salad
Grilled Southwestern Shrimp Salad with Lime-Cumin Dressing
Sweet and Spicy Shrimp and Avocado Salad with Mango Vinaigrette
Pea, Carrot, and Tofu Salad
Grilled Pork Salad with Sweet Soy and Orange Dressing
Warm Pork Salad with Apples
Heirloom Tomato and Goat Cheese Salad with Bacon Dressing
Arugula Salad with Prosciutto and Pears
Mediterranean Pasta Salad
Lemony Fusilli with Chickpeas, Raisins, and Spinach
Spinach, Tomato, and Fresh Mozzarella Pasta Salad with Italian Dressing
Grilled Pesto Salmon–Orzo Salad
Shrimp and Noodle Salad with Asian Vinaigrette Dressing
Whole Wheat Mediterranean Panzanella
Beet, Bulgur, and Orange Salad with Parsley Vinaigrette
Multigrain Tuna Tabbouleh with Creamy Black Olive Vinaigrette
Couscous Salad with Roasted Chicken
Yucatecan Rice Salad
Chicken and Wild Rice Salad with Orange-Mango Vinaigrette

Chicken, Spinach, and Blueberry Salad with Pomegranate Vinaigrette

Prep: 6 minutes • Cook: 7 minutes

Cooking spray
- 8 chicken breast tenders (about ¾ pound)
- 1½ teaspoons coarsely ground black pepper
- ¼ teaspoon salt
- 8 cups bagged baby spinach

Pomegranate Vinaigrette
- ½ cup thinly sliced red onion
- 1 cup fresh blueberries
- ¼ (1 ounce) cup crumbled blue cheese

1. Heat a grill pan or large nonstick skillet over medium-high heat. Coat pan with cooking spray. Sprinkle chicken with pepper and salt. Coat chicken with cooking spray, and add to pan. Cook 3 to 4 minutes on each side or until done.

2. Divide spinach evenly on each of 4 serving plates; drizzle evenly with Pomegranate Vinaigrette. Arrange chicken, onion, and blueberries evenly over spinach. Sprinkle evenly with cheese. Yield: 4 servings (serving size: 2 cups spinach, 2 chicken tenders, 3 tablespoons vinaigrette, 2 tablespoons onion, ¼ cup blueberries, and 1 tablespoon cheese).

CALORIES 203; FAT 4.4g (sat 1.7g, mono 1.6g, poly 0.7g); PROTEIN 23g; CARB 18.5g; FIBER 3.7g; CHOL 56mg; IRON 2.4mg; SODIUM 377mg; CALC 95mg

Pomegranate Vinaigrette

Prep: 2 minutes

- ½ cup pomegranate juice
- 3 tablespoons sugar
- 3 tablespoons balsamic vinegar
- 1 tablespoon canola oil
- 1 teaspoon grated orange rind

1. Combine all ingredients in a small bowl. Stir with a whisk until blended. Yield: ¾ cup (serving size: 3 tablespoons).

CALORIES 96; FAT 3.5g (sat 0.3g, mono 2.1g, poly 1g); PROTEIN 0.2g; CARB 15.9g; FIBER 0.1g; CHOL 0mg; IRON 0.1mg; SODIUM 7mg; CALC 9mg

choice ingredient

Antioxidant-rich pomegranate juice has found a place in a healthful diet that stretches beyond a quick cup of juice with breakfast. Pomegranate juice has a rich and tangy flavor, which makes it an ideal ingredient to use in simple salad dressings and pan sauces with short ingredient lists.

Sweet blueberries pair well with distinctive blue cheese in this chicken salad, while a bold-flavored vinaigrette lightly coats the tender baby spinach leaves.

Pairing peaches with chicken is the ultimate summer addition to a spinach salad. The Sherry Vinaigrette brings out the sweetness of the peaches, while grilling the fruit caramelizes the natural sugars.

Grilled Chicken and Peach Spinach Salad with Sherry Vinaigrette

Prep: 6 minutes • Cook: 8 minutes

Sherry Vinaigrette, divided
 2 peaches, halved and pitted
 4 (4-ounce) chicken breast cutlets
Cooking spray

4 cups fresh baby spinach
⅓ cup pine nuts, toasted
1 (3-ounce) package goat cheese, crumbled

1. Prepare grill.
2. Prepare Sherry Vinaigrette; set aside ¼ cup vinaigrette.
3. Coat peach halves and chicken with cooking spray; brush chicken with remaining 1½ tablespoons vinaigrette. Place peach halves and chicken on a grill rack coated with cooking spray. Grill chicken 3 to 4 minutes on each side. Grill peach halves 1 to 2 minutes on each side; cut each half into 4 wedges.
4. Cut chicken crosswise into thin strips. Place peach wedges, chicken strips, spinach, and pine nuts in a large bowl; drizzle with reserved ¼ cup vinaigrette, and toss well. Place 2 cups salad mixture on each of 4 plates; sprinkle evenly with cheese. Yield: 4 servings (serving size: 2 cups salad and 1½ tablespoons cheese).

CALORIES 320; FAT 17.2g (sat 4.5g, mono 6g, poly 4.7g); PROTEIN 32.9g; CARB 8.6g; FIBER 1.9g; CHOL 76mg; IRON 2.9mg; SODIUM 327mg; CALC 74mg

Sherry Vinaigrette

Prep: 4 minutes

2½ tablespoons minced shallot (about 1 large)
 1 tablespoon sherry vinegar
 1 tablespoon olive oil

½ teaspoon ground mustard
½ teaspoon freshly ground black pepper
¼ teaspoon salt

1. Combine all ingredients, stirring with a whisk. Yield: 4 servings (serving size: about 1 tablespoon and 1 teaspoon).

CALORIES 38; FAT 3.4g (sat 0.5g, mono 2.5g, poly 0.4g); PROTEIN 0.2g; CARB 1.4g; FIBER 0.2g; CHOL 0mg; IRON 0.1mg; SODIUM 156mg; CALC 4mg

Grilled Chicken and Vegetable Arugula Salad

Prep: 4 minutes • Cook: 6 minutes

4 (4-ounce) chicken cutlets
7 tablespoons light balsamic vinaigrette (such as Newman's Own), divided
1 medium (8 ounces) zucchini, cut in half lengthwise
6 (¼-inch-thick) red onion slices (1 medium)
Cooking spray
4 plum tomatoes, halved
6 cups baby arugula
½ cup (2 ounces) crumbled feta cheese

1. Prepare grill.
2. Brush chicken with 1 tablespoon vinaigrette. Place chicken, zucchini, and onion on a grill rack coated with cooking spray. Grill 3 to 4 minutes on each side or until chicken is done and vegetables are tender, adding tomato halves to grill rack after 2 minutes. Cook tomato 2 minutes on each side. Remove chicken and vegetables from grill. Cut chicken crosswise into thin slices; coarsely chop vegetables.
3. Combine chicken, vegetables, and remaining 6 tablespoons vinaigrette in a large bowl, tossing to coat. Add arugula and cheese; toss gently. Yield: 4 servings (serving size: 2¾ cups).

CALORIES 243; FAT 8.4g (sat 3g, mono 2g, poly 2.6g); PROTEIN 30.6g; CARB 11.1g; FIBER 2.5g; CHOL 78mg; IRON 1.8mg; SODIUM 661mg; CALC 153mg

serve with
Grilled Garlic Bread

Prep: 2 minutes • Cook: 4 minutes

4 (0.07-ounce) Italian bread slices
1 garlic clove, halved
2 teaspoon extra-virgin olive oil
Cooking spray

1. Prepare grill.
2. Rub bread slices with cut sides of garlic halves; brush evenly with oil. Place bread slices on a grill rack coated with cooking spray. Grill 2 minutes on each side or until lightly toasted. Yield: 4 servings (serving size: 1 slice).

CALORIES 75; FAT 3g (sat 0.5g, mono 1.8g, poly 0.6g); PROTEIN 1.8g; CARB 10.2g; FIBER 0.6g; CHOL 0mg; IRON 0.6mg; SODIUM 116mg; CALC 17mg

serve now or later

This salad is delicious served immediately, but leftovers make an equally tasty chilled lunch-to-go. Just be sure to pack the vegetable and chicken mixture, salad greens, and salad dressing in separate containers, and toss them together right before serving.

This colorful salad is packed with garden-fresh zucchini and tomatoes. Grill the bread slices along with the tomatoes so everything is ready at the same time.

Grilling sturdy hearts of romaine imparts smoky flavor to this popular salad green. You'll love the contrasting textures of the lightly wilted outer leaves and the crisp center. Be sure to keep the core intact to hold the leaves together on the grill.

Grilled Romaine Chicken Caesar Salad

Prep: 11 minutes • Cook: 14 minutes

3 (6-ounce) skinless, boneless chicken breasts
2 teaspoons olive oil
½ teaspoon salt, divided
¾ teaspoon freshly ground black pepper, divided

2 romaine hearts, cut in half lengthwise
Olive oil-flavored cooking spray
4 (1-ounce) slices French bread baguette (1 inch thick)
Caesar Dressing

1. Prepare grill.
2. Brush chicken with olive oil; sprinkle with ¼ teaspoon salt and ½ teaspoon pepper. Coat romaine hearts with cooking spray, and sprinkle with remaining salt and pepper. Coat both sides of bread slices generously with cooking spray.
3. Place chicken, romaine, and bread on a grill rack coated with cooking spray. Grill chicken 7 to 8 minutes on each side or until done. Grill romaine halves 4 to 5 minutes. Grill bread slices 3 minutes on each side or until toasted.
4. Cut chicken diagonally into thin slices; cut grilled bread into large cubes. Arrange chicken strips and grilled croutons evenly over romaine halves; drizzle evenly with Caesar Dressing. Yield: 4 servings (serving size: 1 romaine heart half, about 4 ounces chicken, ¼ cup croutons, and 3 tablespoons dressing).

CALORIES 320; FAT 9.1g (sat 3.6g, mono 3g, poly 2.2g); PROTEIN 37.6g; CARB 21.1g; FIBER 1.8g; CHOL 84mg; IRON 2.9mg; SODIUM 731mg; CALC 203mg

Caesar Dressing

Prep: 4 minutes

½ cup nonfat buttermilk
¼ cup shredded fresh Parmigiano-Reggiano cheese
2 tablespoons light mayonnaise

½ teaspoon freshly ground black pepper
½ teaspoon Dijon mustard
2 garlic cloves, pressed

1. Combine all ingredients, stirring with a whisk until smooth. Yield: ¾ cup (serving size: 3 tablespoons).

CALORIES 69; FAT 4.7g (sat 1.9g, mono 1g, poly 1.4g); PROTEIN 4.3g; CARB 3.1g; FIBER 0.1g; CHOL 10mg; IRON 0.1mg; SODIUM 188mg; CALC 102mg

In this unique sweet-savory tossed salad, juicy red grapes offer a surprising contrast to the tangy citrus dressing. You'll need to squeeze about 2 medium lemons to yield ¼ cup lemon juice for the dressing.

Chicken Salad with Red Grapes and Citrus-Honey Dressing

Prep: 10 minutes

8 cups mixed baby salad greens
2 cups shredded cooked chicken breast (about 8 ounces)

1 cup red seedless grapes, halved
⅔ cup thin diagonally cut slices celery
Citrus-Honey Dressing

1. Combine all ingredients in a large bowl; toss gently. Place 2 cups salad on each of 4 plates. Yield: 4 servings (serving size: 1 salad).

CALORIES 230; FAT 9.4g (sat 1.6g, mono 6.1g, poly 1.2g); PROTEIN 19.9g; CARB 17.8g; FIBER 3.2g; CHOL 48mg; IRON 2.3mg; SODIUM 323mg; CALC 85mg

Citrus-Honey Dressing

Prep: 5 minutes

¼ cup fresh lemon juice
2 tablespoons fresh orange juice
2 tablespoons extra-virgin olive oil
1 tablespoon honey

2 teaspoons grated lemon rind
½ teaspoon kosher salt
⅛ teaspoon coarsely ground black pepper

1. Combine all ingredients in a small bowl, stirring with a whisk. Yield: ½ cup (serving size: 2 tablespoons).

CALORIES 87; FAT 7g (sat 1g, mono 5.4g, poly 0.6g); PROTEIN 0.2g; CARB 6.7g; FIBER 0.2g; CHOL 0mg; IRON 0.1mg; SODIUM 236mg; CALC 4mg

shortcut kitchen tip

To quickly juice lemons to get the most juice, bring them to room temperature, and then roll them across the countertop while applying pressure with the palm of your hand.

This tasty salad is perfect for evenings when you're looking for a quick, no-fuss meal. We hand-pulled large pieces of chicken from a cooked chicken breast to achieve a chunky texture. Serve with crackers to complete the meal.

Chicken Salad with Asparagus and Creamy Dill Dressing

Prep: 3 minutes • Cook: 5 minutes

2½ cups (2-inch) diagonally cut asparagus
2 cups coarsely shredded cooked chicken breast (about 8 ounces)
½ cup thinly sliced radishes

Creamy Dill Dressing
8 tomato slices (about 1 large)
Freshly ground black pepper (optional)

1. Steam asparagus, covered, 3 minutes or until crisp-tender. Drain and plunge asparagus into ice water; drain.
2. Combine asparagus, chicken, radishes, and dressing in a large bowl; toss well. Arrange 2 tomato slices on each of 4 plates; top each serving with 1 cup chicken mixture. Sprinkle with pepper, if desired. Yield: 4 servings (serving size: 1 salad).

CALORIES 170; FAT 4.3g (sat 0.6g, mono 1.7g, poly 1.5g); PROTEIN 21.2g; CARB 12.2g; FIBER 2.8g; CHOL 49mg; IRON 2.6mg; SODIUM 467mg; CALC 79mg

Creamy Dill Dressing

Prep: 4 minutes

½ cup low-fat mayonnaise
½ cup nonfat buttermilk
1 tablespoon chopped fresh dill

1 tablespoon fresh lemon juice
¼ teaspoon kosher salt
¼ teaspoon freshly ground black pepper

1. Combine all ingredients in a medium bowl, stirring well with a whisk. Yield: 8 servings (serving size: 2 tablespoons).

CALORIES 21; FAT 1g (sat 0g, mono 0g, poly 0.5g); PROTEIN 0.6g; CARB 3.1g; FIBER 0g; CHOL 0.2mg; IRON 0mg; SODIUM 205mg; CALC 19mg

flavorful combinations

Low-fat mayonnaise, nonfat buttermilk, fresh dill, and fresh lemon juice form the base for superfast homemade Creamy Dill Dressing. Make extra to keep on hand to drizzle over side salads or serve as a vegetable dip. We recommend using fresh dill, but in a pinch, you can substitute 1 teaspoon of dried dill.

A medley of Mediterranean flavors perks up humble albacore tuna in this no-cook dish. It can be made ahead for a lunch-to-go or prepared for dinner. Just add the spinach and toss before serving. For sandwich variations, stuff the tuna mixture into whole wheat pita halves, or spread it between two baguette halves.

Tuna, Artichoke, and Roasted Red Pepper Salad

Prep: 9 minutes

1   (12-ounce) jar marinated quartered artichoke hearts (such as Reese)
¼   cup chopped fresh dill
1   tablespoon extra-virgin olive oil
1   tablespoon fresh lemon juice
½   teaspoon freshly ground black pepper

2   garlic cloves, minced
2   cups chopped bagged fresh baby spinach
2   (5-ounce) cans albacore tuna in water, drained and flaked
1   (12-ounce) jar roasted red bell peppers, drained and chopped

1. Drain artichokes, reserving 2 tablespoons marinade. Coarsely chop artichokes. Combine artichokes, reserved marinade, dill, and next 4 ingredients in a large bowl. Add spinach, tuna, and roasted peppers, tossing well. Yield: 4 servings (serving size: 1¼ cups).

CALORIES 153; FAT 6.8g (sat 0.5g, mono 3g, poly 2.7g); PROTEIN 15.1g; CARB 9.3g; FIBER 2.2g; CHOL 23mg; IRON 0.7mg; SODIUM 468mg; CALC 17mg

serve with
Feta Pita Crisps

Prep: 4 minutes • Cook: 10 minutes

3   (6-inch) pitas
1   (3.5-ounce) package crumbled reduced-fat feta cheese, finely chopped

Olive oil-flavored cooking spray

1. Preheat oven to 425°.
2. Split pitas; cut each into 6 wedges. Arrange pita wedges in a single layer on a large baking sheet; sprinkle with cheese, and lightly coat with cooking spray.
3. Bake at 425° for 10 minutes or until crisp and golden. Yield: 4 servings (serving size: 9 pita crisps).

CALORIES 173; FAT 3.5g (sat 2.2g, mono 0.9g, poly 0.1g); PROTEIN 10.4g; CARB 25.5g; FIBER 1.1g; CHOL 7mg; IRON 2mg; SODIUM 463mg; CALC 103mg

We tested this recipe with peeled and deveined shrimp. Whether you have your fishmonger peel and devein them or if you do it yourself, you'll need to start with 1 pound of unpeeled shrimp.

Grilled Southwestern Shrimp Salad with Lime-Cumin Dressing

Prep: 2 minutes • Cook: 12 minutes

¾ pound peeled and deveined large shrimp
1 teaspoon chili powder
2 ears corn
Cooking spray

6 cups chopped romaine lettuce
2 large tomatoes, cut into 8 wedges
Lime-Cumin Dressing
1 cup diced peeled avocado (1 small)

1. Prepare grill.
2. Sprinkle shrimp evenly with chili powder. Remove husks from corn; scrub silks from corn. Place corn on a grill rack coated with cooking spray. Grill 12 minutes, turning occasionally. Add shrimp to grill rack after 6 minutes; grill 3 minutes on each side. Cut kernels from ears of corn. Discard cobs.
3. Combine shrimp, corn, lettuce, and tomato in a large bowl; drizzle with Lime-Cumin Dressing, and toss well. Add avocado; toss gently. Serve immediately. Yield: 4 servings (serving size: 3¼ cups).

CALORIES 266; FAT 11.2g (sat 1.5g, mono 5.7g, poly 2.7g); PROTEIN 21.4g; CARB 24g; FIBER 5.9g; CHOL 129mg; IRON 3.8mg; SODIUM 404mg; CALC 90mg

Lime-Cumin Dressing

Prep: 4 minutes

¼ cup fresh lime juice
1 tablespoon canola oil
1 tablespoon honey

½ teaspoon kosher salt
½ teaspoon ground cumin
⅛ teaspoon coarsely ground black pepper

1. Combine all ingredients in a small bowl, stirring with a whisk. Yield: 4 servings (serving size: 1½ tablespoons).

CALORIES 52; FAT 3.6g (sat 0.3g, mono 2.1g, poly 1g); PROTEIN 0.1g; CARB 5.8g; FIBER 0.2g; CHOL 0mg; IRON 0.1mg; SODIUM 236mg; CALC 5mg

For casual weeknight entertaining, try serving this salad in clear glasses instead of on traditional dining plates.

Sweet and Spicy Shrimp and Avocado Salad with Mango Vinaigrette
Prep: 8 minutes

Mango Vinaigrette
- 6 cups shredded romaine lettuce (2 hearts)
- 1 cup chopped red bell pepper (1 medium)
- 6 tablespoons thinly sliced green onions (optional)

- 1 pound peeled cooked shrimp
- 1 avocado, diced

1. Place Mango Vinaigrette in a large bowl. Add lettuce, bell pepper, and green onions, if desired; toss well. Add shrimp and avocado; toss gently. Yield: 4 servings (serving size: 2¾ cups).

CALORIES 249; FAT 10.3g (sat 1.7g, mono 6g, poly 1.8g); PROTEIN 26.1g; CARB 15.1g; FIBER 5g; CHOL 221mg; IRON 5mg; SODIUM 412mg; CALC 86mg

Mango Vinaigrette
Prep: 9 minutes

- ¼ cup fresh lime juice
- 2 tablespoons chopped fresh cilantro
- 1 tablespoon olive oil
- ½ teaspoon crushed red pepper
- ½ teaspoon sugar

- ¼ teaspoon salt
- ¼ teaspoon freshly ground black pepper
- 1 garlic clove, minced
- ¾ cup diced mango (about 1 medium)

1. Combine first 8 ingredients in a large bowl, stirring with a whisk. Stir in mango. Yield: 4 servings (serving size: about ¼ cup).

CALORIES 58; FAT 3.5g (sat 0.5g, mono 2.5g, poly 0.4g); PROTEIN 0.3g; CARB 7.6g; FIBER 0.7g; CHOL 0mg; IRON 0.1mg; SODIUM 147mg; CALC 8mg

To get a beautiful brown sear on the tofu, drain the tofu slices between several layers of paper towels to absorb the extra moisture before cooking. Sear the slices in a hot skillet, and while they cook, move them only to turn them over.

Pea, Carrot, and Tofu Salad

Prep: 5 minutes • Cook: 10 minutes

1 (14-ounce) package water-packed firm tofu, drained
2 tablespoons sesame oil
½ cup light sesame ginger dressing
1 (16-ounce) package frozen petite green peas, thawed
1 cup matchstick-cut carrots
1 (8-ounce) can water chestnuts, drained
½ cup thinly sliced red onion
¼ teaspoon freshly ground black pepper
1 medium head Bibb lettuce, torn
4 teaspoons roasted, unsalted sunflower seed kernels

1. Place tofu on several layers of heavy-duty paper towels. Cover tofu with additional paper towels; gently press out moisture. Cut tofu into 1-inch cubes.
2. Heat oil in a large nonstick skillet over medium-high heat. Add tofu; cook 5 to 6 minutes on each side or until golden on all sides, stirring occasionally.
3. Combine tofu, dressing, and next 5 ingredients in a large bowl; toss gently to coat. Divide lettuce evenly among 4 plates. Top lettuce with 1¾ cups tofu mixture. Sprinkle evenly with sunflower seed kernels. Yield: 4 servings (serving size: about 1½ cups lettuce, 1¾ cups tofu mixture, and 1 teaspoon sunflower seed kernels).

CALORIES 312; FAT 14.6g (sat 2.1g, mono 4.5g, poly 7g); PROTEIN 15.9g; CARB 33.2g; FIBER 8.5g; CHOL 0mg; IRON 4.4mg; SODIUM 554mg; CALC 256mg

Be sure to grate the rind from the oranges before you peel and section them for the salad. You'll use the rind in the dressing and the sections in the salad.

Grilled Pork Salad with Sweet Soy and Orange Dressing

Prep: 5 minutes • Cook: 8 minutes • Other: 3 minutes

Sweet Soy and Orange Dressing, divided
3 (4-ounce) boneless center-cut loin pork chops (about ½ inch thick)
½ teaspoon coarsely ground black pepper

Cooking spray
6 cups thinly sliced napa (Chinese) cabbage
½ cup chopped green onions
¼ cup sliced almonds, toasted

1. Prepare grill.
2. Prepare Sweet Soy and Orange Dressing. Reserve ¼ cup dressing; set remaining dressing aside.
3. Sprinkle both sides of pork with pepper. Place pork on a grill rack coated with cooking spray. Cook 4 minutes on each side, basting with reserved ¼ cup dressing. Cover and let pork stand 3 minutes; cut into thin slices.
4. Divide cabbage evenly among 4 plates. Top evenly with pork slices, orange sections (reserved from Sweet Soy and Orange Dressing), and green onions. Drizzle salads evenly with remaining dressing, and sprinkle evenly with almonds. Yield: 4 servings (serving size: 1½ cups cabbage, 3 ounces pork, ½ orange, 2 tablespoons green onions, about 1½ tablespoons dressing, and 1 tablespoon almonds).

CALORIES 299; FAT 16.5g (sat 3.7g, mono 8.8g, poly 3g); PROTEIN 19.6g; CARB 18.7g; FIBER 3g; CHOL 44mg; IRON 1.3mg; SODIUM 876mg; CALC 133mg

Sweet Soy and Orange Dressing

Prep: 3 minutes

2 navel oranges
¼ cup low-sodium soy sauce
3 tablespoons honey

3 tablespoons rice vinegar
1½ tablespoons canola oil

1. Grate 2 teaspoons rind from oranges. Peel and section oranges; reserve orange sections for salad.
2. Combine orange rind, soy sauce, and remaining 3 ingredients in a small bowl, stirring with a whisk. Yield: 6 servings (serving size: about 1 tablespoon).

CALORIES 73; FAT 3.5g (sat 0.3g, mono 2.1g, poly 1g); PROTEIN 0.6g; CARB 10.7g; FIBER 0.2g; CHOL 0mg; IRON 0.3mg; SODIUM 356mg; CALC 3mg

Pork and apples are simply meant for each other. The pungent dressing marries well with tart Granny Smith apples.

Warm Pork Salad with Apples

Prep: 6 minutes • Cook: 7 minutes

6 teaspoons olive oil, divided
1 (1-pound) pork tenderloin, cut into 12 slices
1¼ teaspoons ground cumin, divided
½ teaspoon salt, divided
¼ teaspoon black pepper, divided
2 tablespoons cider vinegar

2 teaspoons light brown sugar
1 (7-ounce) package torn radicchio and butter lettuce (such as Fresh Express Riviera)
1 large Granny Smith apple, cored and thinly sliced

1. Heat 2 teaspoons oil in a large nonstick skillet over medium-high heat. Sprinkle pork evenly with 1 teaspoon cumin, ¼ teaspoon salt, and ⅛ teaspoon pepper. Add pork to pan; cook 3 minutes on each side or until done.
2. Combine vinegar, brown sugar, remaining 4 teaspoons oil, remaining ¼ teaspoon cumin, remaining ¼ teaspoon salt, and remaining ⅛ teaspoon pepper in a small bowl, stirring with a whisk.
3. Place lettuce, apple, and 2 tablespoons dressing in a large bowl; toss gently to coat. Divide salad evenly among 4 plates; top each with 3 slices of pork, and drizzle remaining dressing evenly over pork. Yield: 4 servings (serving size: 3 slices pork, 2 cups salad, and 1 teaspoon dressing).

CALORIES 237; FAT 11g (sat 2.3g, mono 4.1g, poly 4.3g); PROTEIN 23.4g; CARB 12g; FIBER 2.1g; CHOL 63mg; IRON 1.6mg; SODIUM 344mg; CALC 16mg

serve with
Pomegranate-Orange Sparkler

Prep: 2 minutes

1 cup pomegranate juice, chilled
1 cup orange juice, chilled
¼ cup sugar

2 cups sparkling water, chilled
4 lemon wedges

1. Combine pomegranate juice, orange juice, and sugar in a large pitcher; stir until sugar dissolves. Stir in sparkling water, and serve immediately over ice with lemon wedges. Yield: 4 servings (serving size: 1 cup sparkler and 1 lemon wedge).

CALORIES 154; FAT 0.2g (sat 0g, mono 0g, poly 0g); PROTEIN 0.8g; CARB 38.7g; FIBER 0.1g; CHOL 0mg; IRON 0.2mg; SODIUM 13mg; CALC 18mg

Three harmonious flavors converge in this simple salad: smoky bacon, earthy goat cheese, and acidic tomatoes. Serve with a warm baguette slice and a glass of dry white wine to complete the meal.

Heirloom Tomato and Goat Cheese Salad with Bacon Dressing
Prep: 7 minutes

2 heirloom tomatoes, sliced
1 (4-ounce) package goat cheese, sliced
½ cup vertically sliced onion

2 cups bagged baby spinach leaves
½ cup Bacon Dressing

1. Arrange layers of tomato slices and next 3 ingredients evenly on each of 4 serving plates. Drizzle salads evenly with Bacon Dressing. Yield: 4 servings (serving size: 1 salad and 2 tablespoons dressing).

CALORIES 173; FAT 8.5g (sat 4.9g, mono 2.4g, poly 1.2g); PROTEIN 10.2g; CARB 14.4g; FIBER 1.5g; CHOL 21mg; IRON 1.7mg; SODIUM 457mg; CALC 65mg

Bacon Dressing
Prep: 4 minutes • Cook: 7 minutes

6 center-cut 30%-less fat bacon slices
¼ cup cider vinegar
2 tablespoons honey

¼ teaspoon kosher salt
½ teaspoon freshly ground black pepper
¼ cup minced green onions (1 large)

1. Cook bacon in a skillet over medium heat until crisp. Remove bacon from pan, reserving 1 tablespoon drippings in pan; drain bacon.
2. Add vinegar and next 4 ingredients to drippings in pan, stirring with a whisk. Remove pan from heat. Crumble bacon, and add to pan, stirring with a whisk. Yield: ⅔ cup (serving size: about 2½ tablespoons).

CALORIES 76; FAT 2.3g (sat 0.8g, mono 1g, poly 0.5g); PROTEIN 3.9g; CARB 9.5g; FIBER 0.3g; CHOL 8mg; IRON 0.5mg; SODIUM 337mg; CALC 7mg

choice ingredient

We recommend using heirloom tomatoes, which are grown from the seeds of old-fashioned varieties, because of their full-bodied flavor and dazzling palette of colors. They vary from red to yellow and from green to purplish black. Look for them at farmers' markets during the summer months.

You can toast the walnut halves quickly in a dry skillet over medium-high heat. Stir frequently, and remove them from the heat as soon as you begin to smell that wonderful nutty aroma.

Arugula Salad with Prosciutto and Pears

Prep: 7 minutes • Cook: 2 minutes

2 (5-ounce) bags arugula
2 red pears, cored and cut lengthwise into ¼-inch-thick slices
4 thin slices prosciutto, cut crosswise into strips (about 2 ounces)
¾ cup shaved fresh Parmesan cheese (about 3 ounces)

4 tablespoons walnut halves, toasted
3 tablespoons white wine vinegar
2 tablespoons olive oil
¼ teaspoon salt
⅛ teaspoon black pepper

1. Combine first 5 ingredients in a large bowl.
2. Combine vinegar and next 3 ingredients in a small bowl, stirring with a whisk. Drizzle over salad, and toss gently to coat. Yield: 4 servings (serving size: about 2¾ cups).

CALORIES 251; FAT 19.1g (sat 5.4g, mono 6.9g, poly 6.5g); PROTEIN 13.2g; CARB 10.1g; FIBER 3.3g; CHOL 27mg; IRON 1mg; SODIUM 713mg; CALC 301mg

serve with

French Bread with Herbed Goat Cheese Spread

Prep: 6 minutes • Cook: 1 minute

2 ounces goat cheese, softened
½ teaspoon chopped fresh oregano
½ teaspoon chopped fresh thyme

¼ teaspoon freshly ground black pepper
8 (½-inch-thick) slices diagonally cut whole wheat baguette, toasted

1. Combine first 4 ingredients in a small bowl. Spread goat cheese mixture evenly on baguette slices. Yield: 4 servings (serving size: 2 slices).

CALORIES 134; FAT 4.8g (sat 3.1g, mono 0.8g, poly 0.8g); PROTEIN 6.4g; CARB 16.4g; FIBER 0.7g; CHOL 11mg; IRON 1.3mg; SODIUM 257mg; CALC 55mg

This satisfying pasta salad features three-cheese tortellini, which comes in a variety of flavors. Try either the chicken or mushroom version for a different variation. Freeze leftover tortellini in a zip-top plastic bag to use later in a soup or side dish.

Mediterranean Pasta Salad

Prep: 5 minutes • Cook: 10 minutes

½ (9-ounce) package refrigerated rainbow three-cheese tortellini
1 quart water
¼ pound asparagus spears, trimmed
⅓ cup bottled roasted red bell peppers, cut into 1-inch pieces
1 ounce Monterey Jack cheese with jalapeño peppers, cut into ¼-inch cubes (about ¼ cup)

6 drained canned quartered artichoke hearts
8 grape tomatoes
8 pitted kalamata olives
2 thin slices prosciutto, cut crosswise into strips (about 1 ounce)
1 tablespoon chopped fresh basil
3 tablespoons light balsamic vinaigrette

1. Cook pasta in 1 quart boiling water 6 minutes, omitting salt and fat. Add asparagus to boiling water, and cook 1 minute. Drain in a colander, and rinse with cold water until cooled. Drain.
2. While pasta and asparagus cook, combine roasted bell peppers and next 7 ingredients in a large bowl. Add tortellini and asparagus; toss gently. Yield: 3 servings (serving size: 1⅓ cups).

CALORIES 304; FAT 16.2g (sat 4.7g, mono 4g, poly 6.2g); PROTEIN 11.2g; CARB 29.7g; FIBER 2.2g; CHOL 28mg; IRON 0.6mg; SODIUM 876mg; CALC 82mg

choice ingredient

Prosciutto (pro-SHOO-toh), also known as Parma ham, is a salt-cured ham that is typically sliced thin and often eaten raw or lightly cooked, making it perfect to use in quick-cooking recipes. A little prosciutto offers a powerful punch of flavor in this dish, so you'll only need to use a small amount.

With a refreshing lemon vinaigrette, chickpeas, and spinach, this salad makes a great light lunch or dinner alternative to a traditional mixed greens salad. For heartier fare, stir in some chopped cooked chicken.

Lemony Fusilli with Chickpeas, Raisins, and Spinach

Prep: 2 minutes • Cook: 9 minutes

3 cups uncooked whole wheat fusilli (short twisted spaghetti)
2 lemons
1 tablespoon olive oil
½ teaspoon crushed red pepper
¼ teaspoon salt

2 garlic cloves, minced
1 (6-ounce) package fresh baby spinach
1 (15-ounce) can chickpeas (garbanzo beans), rinsed and drained
¾ cup golden raisins
¼ cup (1 ounce) shredded fontina cheese

1. Cook pasta according to package directions, omitting salt and fat.
2. While pasta cooks, grate rind and squeeze juice from lemon to measure 4 teaspoons and ¼ cup, respectively. Combine rind, juice, olive oil, and next 3 ingredients in a large bowl, stirring with a whisk. Add spinach, chickpeas, and raisins; toss well.
3. Drain pasta, and immediately add to spinach mixture, tossing until spinach wilts. Sprinkle with cheese. Serve immediately. Yield: 4 servings (serving size: 2 cups).

CALORIES 466; FAT 8.1g (sat 2g, mono 3.3g, poly 2.3g); PROTEIN 14.7g; CARB 87g; FIBER 10.8g; CHOL 8mg; IRON 4.4mg; SODIUM 376mg; CALC 145mg

serve with
Cheesy Crostini

Prep: 3 minutes • Cook: 5 minutes

8 (½-inch-thick) diagonally-cut baguette slices
2 garlic cloves, halved lengthwise

1 large plum tomato, cut diagonally into 8 slices
¼ cup freshly grated Parmesan cheese

1. Preheat oven to 450°.
2. Arrange baguette slices on a baking sheet. Rub cut surfaces of garlic over both sides of bread. Place 1 tomato slice on each; sprinkle evenly with cheese. Bake at 450° for 5 minutes or until cheese melts. Yield: 4 servings (serving size: 2 crostini).

CALORIES 91 (20% from fat); FAT 2.1g (sat 1g, mono 0.4g, poly 0.1g); PROTEIN 5.1g; CARB 13.9g; FIBER 0.6g; CHOL 5mg; IRON 0.8mg; SODIUM 265mg; CALC 104mg

Dressed with a simple vinaigrette made from fresh herbs and a good quality extra-virgin olive oil, this salad is as delicious as it is easy to prepare. The dressing will keep in the refrigerator for a couple of days, so consider doubling the recipe to keep some on hand.

Spinach, Tomato, and Fresh Mozzarella Pasta Salad with Italian Dressing

Prep: 10 minutes • Cook: 10 minutes

2½ cups multigrain rotini pasta (such as Barilla Plus)
Italian Dressing
2 cups grape tomatoes

1 (6-ounce) package baby spinach
4 ounces fresh mozzarella cheese, cubed

1. Cook pasta according to package directions, omitting salt and fat. Rinse with cold water; drain.
2. While pasta cooks, prepare Italian Dressing. Combine dressing and tomatoes in a large bowl. Add pasta and spinach; toss well, and top with cheese. Yield: 4 servings (serving size: 1½ cups).

CALORIES 450; FAT 15.9g (sat 5.1g, mono 6.6g, poly 3.3g); PROTEIN 19.9g; CARB 57g; FIBER 8g; CHOL 22mg; IRON 5.5mg; SODIUM 262mg; CALC 259mg

Italian Dressing

Prep: 5 minutes

¼ cup red wine vinegar
2 tablespoons chopped fresh flat-leaf parsley
1 tablespoon chopped fresh oregano or fresh basil

2 tablespoons extra-virgin olive oil
¼ teaspoon salt
¼ teaspoon freshly ground black pepper
2 garlic cloves, minced

1. Combine all ingredients, stirring with a whisk. Yield: 4 servings (serving size: 2 tablespoons).

CALORIES 67; FAT 7.1g (sat 1g, mono 5g, poly 1g); PROTEIN 0.2g; CARB 0.9g; FIBER 0.1g; CHOL 0mg; IRON 0.2mg; SODIUM 148mg; CALC 11mg

With orzo as its base, this salad makes a filling meal that highlights the fresh flavors of white beans, grape tomatoes, and arugula.

Grilled Pesto Salmon–Orzo Salad

Prep: 9 minutes • Cook: 14 minutes

2 (6-ounce) skinless salmon fillets
¼ cup commercial pesto, divided
¼ teaspoon kosher salt
¼ teaspoon freshly ground black pepper
2 (½-inch-thick) sweet onion slices

1½ cups grape tomatoes
Cooking spray
Orzo with Arugula and White Beans
⅛ teaspoon freshly ground black pepper

1. Brush fish evenly with 2 tablespoons pesto; sprinkle with salt and pepper. Brush 1 tablespoon pesto over onion slices. Toss tomatoes with remaining 1 tablespoon pesto, and place on a 12-inch square of heavy-duty foil. Fold edges of foil up around tomatoes to form a bowl, keeping tomatoes in a single layer. (Do not completely enclose.)
2. Place salmon, onion slices, and foil bowl with tomatoes on a grill rack coated with cooking spray. Grill 14 minutes or until salmon is desired degree of doneness, onion is tender, and tomatoes begin to burst, turning salmon and onion after 7 minutes.
3. Using a fork, gently break salmon into large chunks, and chop onion slices. Combine Orzo Salad with Arugula and White Beans, salmon, onion, tomatoes, and accumulated tomato juice. Toss gently; sprinkle with pepper. Yield: 6 servings (serving size: 1½ cups).

CALORIES 279; FAT 8.4g (sat 1.5g, mono 3.6g, poly 2.3g); PROTEIN 36.6g; CARB 12.4g; FIBER 2.5g; CHOL 89mg; IRON 2mg; SODIUM 673mg; CALC 51mg

Orzo with Arugula and White Beans

Prep: 13 minutes • Cook: 11 minutes

1 cup uncooked orzo (rice-shaped pasta)
1 (15.5-ounce) can cannellini beans, rinsed and drained

2 cups firmly packed arugula
2 tablespoons fresh lemon juice

1. Cook orzo according to package directions, omitting salt and fat. Drain.
2. Combine orzo, beans, arugula, and lemon juice in a large bowl. Yield: 6 servings (serving size: 1 cup).

CALORIES 140; FAT 0.7g (sat 0g, mono 0g, poly 0.2g); PROTEIN 5.3g; CARB 27.5g; FIBER 2.7g; CHOL 0mg; IRON 0.7mg; SODIUM 85mg; CALC 24mg

Soy, ginger, and garlic give this nutty noodle salad an extra dimension of tantalizing flavor. Look for rice noodles in the ethnic-food section of your supermarket.

Shrimp and Noodle Salad with Asian Vinaigrette Dressing

Prep: 9 minutes • Cook: 5 minutes

2 ounces dried rice noodles (such as Hokan)
Asian Vinaigrette Dressing
4 cups thinly sliced napa (Chinese) cabbage
¾ pound cooked peeled and deveined large shrimp
1 cup snow peas, trimmed and cut diagonally in half

3 cups fresh bean sprouts
3 tablespoons thinly sliced green onions (optional)
¼ cup chopped fresh cilantro (optional)

1. Cook noodles in boiling water 5 minutes, omitting salt and fat; drain and rinse with cold water. Drain.
2. While noodles cook, prepare Asian Vinaigrette Dressing; set aside.
3. Combine noodles, cabbage, and next 3 ingredients. Add dressing, and toss well. Sprinkle salad with green onions and cilantro, if desired. Yield: 4 servings (serving size: 2 cups).

CALORIES 243; FAT 6.2g (sat 0.9g, mono 2g, poly 2.9g); PROTEIN 26.9g; CARB 21.4g; FIBER 2g; CHOL 166mg; IRON 4.3mg; SODIUM 288mg; CALC 116mg

Asian Vinaigrette Dressing

Prep: 6 minutes

3 tablespoons lime juice
1½ teaspoons fish sauce
1½ tablespoons creamy peanut butter
2 teaspoons sugar

2 teaspoons grated peeled fresh ginger
2 teaspoons reduced-sodium soy sauce
2 teaspoons dark sesame oil
2 garlic cloves, minced

1. Combine all ingredients, stirring with a whisk until smooth. Yield: 4 servings (serving size: about 2 tablespoons).

CALORIES 71; FAT 5.4g (sat 1g, mono 2.4g, poly 1.8g); PROTEIN 2g; CARB 5.1g; FIBER 0.5g; CHOL 0mg; IRON 0.2mg; SODIUM 272mg; CALC 6.8mg

Like many Italian dishes, panzanella (pahn-zah-NEHL-lah) was probably first made out of necessity—combining stale bread with readily available fresh garden vegetables. This classic bread salad, full of juicy tomatoes, is like summer on a plate. For added color, we chose to use a combination of yellow and red heirloom tomatoes. If you prefer a drier panzanella, toast the bread before tossing it with the tomato mixture.

Whole Wheat Mediterranean Panzanella

Prep: 10 minutes

1 tablespoon vegetable oil	½ cup pitted kalamata olives
3 tablespoons white balsamic vinegar	½ cup fresh basil leaves, torn
⅛ teaspoon salt	6 ounces whole wheat country-style bread, torn into bite-size pieces (4 cups)
¼ teaspoon black pepper	
6½ cups chopped tomato (3 very large)	1 (4-ounce) package crumbled feta cheese
1½ cup cubed English cucumber	

1. Combine first 4 ingredients in a large bowl, stirring with a whisk. Stir in tomato and next 3 ingredients. Add bread and cheese; toss gently. Serve immediately. Yield: 4 servings (serving size: about 2⅔ cups).

CALORIES 362; FAT 20.4g (sat 5.7g, mono 9.2g, poly 4.2g); PROTEIN 13.7g; CARB 36.7g; FIBER 8.7g; CHOL 25mg; IRON 3.1mg; SODIUM 898mg; CALC 241mg

serve with
Prosciutto-Wrapped Melon Slices

Prep: 8 minutes

1 small cantaloupe, cut into 8 wedges	4 ounces thinly sliced prosciutto

1. Wrap melon slices evenly with prosciutto. Yield: 4 servings (serving size: 2 wedges).

CALORIES 88; FAT 2.8g (sat 0.9g, mono 1.3g, poly 0.5g); PROTEIN 7.3g; CARB 9g; FIBER 0g; CHOL 17mg; IRON 0.6mg; SODIUM 443mg; CALC 12mg

Beet, Bulgur, and Orange Salad with Parsley Vinaigrette

Prep: 7 minutes • Cook: 10 minutes • Other: 10 minutes

1¾ cups water
1 cup uncooked bulgur
1 medium beet, peeled
2 navel oranges

Parsley Vinaigrette, divided
½ cup (4 ounces) crumbled goat cheese
Fresh parsley leaves (optional)

1. Bring water to a boil in a medium saucepan; stir in bulgur. Cover, remove from heat; let stand 10 minutes. Rinse with cold water; drain.

2. While water for bulgur comes to a boil, place beet on a plate; cover with 3 layers of damp paper towels. Microwave at HIGH 6 minutes or until tender.

3. While beet cooks, peel oranges; cut crosswise into thin wagon wheel–shaped slices.

4. Cut beet in half lengthwise. Turn beet halves, cut side down, and cut into thin half moon–shaped slices; place in a bowl. Add 3 tablespoons Parsley Vinaigrette; toss until coated.

5. Stir remaining vinaigrette into bulgur. Spoon bulgur evenly onto each of 4 serving plates. Top evenly with beets and orange slices; sprinkle with cheese and parsley, if desired. Yield: 4 servings (serving size: 1 salad).

CALORIES 301; FAT 13.6g (sat 5.2g, mono 6.5g, poly 1.4g); PROTEIN 10.6g; CARB 37.8g; FIBER 8.6g; CHOL 13mg; IRON 1.8mg; SODIUM 274mg; CALC 89mg

Parsley Vinaigrette

Prep: 3 minutes

2 tablespoons coarsely chopped fresh parsley
2 tablespoons red wine vinegar
2 tablespoons olive oil

¼ teaspoon salt
¼ teaspoon freshly ground black pepper

1. Combine all ingredients in a small bowl, stirring with a whisk. Yield: 4 servings (serving size: about 4 teaspoons).

CALORIES 63; FAT 7g (sat 1g, mono 5g, poly 1g); PROTEIN 0.1g; CARB 0.2g; FIBER 0.1g; CHOL 0mg; IRON 0.2mg; SODIUM 147mg; CALC 4mg

shortcut kitchen tip

To quickly remove the peel from an orange, cut a thin slice from the top and bottom of the orange so the fruit will stand upright. Stand the orange vertically on the cutting board. Using a sharp knife, remove the skin in ½-inch slices. Be sure to remove the white pith, which can be very bitter.

We shaved minutes off the cook time of this meatless main-dish salad by microwaving the beets. Traditional cooking methods, such as baking, boiling, steaming, and roasting, can require 45 minutes or longer.

Tabbouleh is a Mediterranean grain salad that traditionally includes chopped cucumber. Instead of tossing the cucumber into the salad, we cut an English cucumber into thin planks and spooned the pilaf mixture over the planks for a crunchier variation. Toss the extra vinaigrette with salad greens or steamed vegetables.

Multigrain Tuna Tabbouleh with Creamy Black Olive Vinaigrette
Prep: 9 minutes

1 (8.5-ounce) package 7 whole-grain pilaf (such as Kashi)
1 (6-ounce) can albacore tuna in water, drained and flaked
1 cup chopped tomato
½ cup finely chopped fresh parsley
⅓ cup finely chopped red onion
⅓ cup Creamy Black Olive Vinaigrette
½ teaspoon coarsely ground black pepper
¼ teaspoon salt

1. Combine all ingredients in a large bowl; toss well. Serve immediately, or cover and chill until ready to serve. Yield: 4 servings (serving size: 1 cup).

CALORIES 275; FAT 15.9g (sat 2.2g, mono 10.8g, poly 2.6g); PROTEIN 12.3g; CARB 25.6g; FIBER 5.1g; CHOL 14mg; IRON 1.8mg; SODIUM 578mg; CALC 46mg

Creamy Black Olive Vinaigrette
Prep: 4 minutes

¾ cup drained large ripe olives
¼ cup fat-free, less sodium chicken broth
2 tablespoons red wine vinegar
2 teaspoons Dijon mustard
½ teaspoon black pepper
3 tablespoons extra-virgin olive oil

1. Place olives in a food processor; pulse 3 times until chopped. Add broth and next 3 ingredients; pulse 3 to 4 times or until blended. With processor on, slowly add oil though food chute. Yield: 8 servings (serving size: 2 tablespoons).

CALORIES 64; FAT 6.8g (sat 1g, mono 4.9g, poly 0.9g); PROTEIN 0.2g; CARB 1.3g; FIBER 0.5g; CHOL 0mg; IRON 0.5mg; SODIUM 122mg; CALC 13mg

The flavors of this salad meld as it chills. Be sure to prepare enough to have leftovers—it makes a great portable lunch.

Couscous Salad with Roasted Chicken

Prep: 8 minutes • Cook: 2 minutes • Other: 5 minutes

⅓ cup uncooked couscous
1½ cups chopped roasted chicken breast
1 cup chopped English cucumber
1 cup halved grape tomatoes
1 cup chopped fresh parsley
¼ cup chopped fresh mint

4 green onions, chopped
1 garlic clove, minced
¼ cup fresh lemon juice
2 tablespoons olive oil
¼ teaspoon salt

1. Prepare couscous according to package directions, omitting salt and fat. Fluff couscous with a fork.
2. Combine couscous, chicken, and next 6 ingredients in a large bowl. Set aside.
3. Combine lemon juice, olive oil, and salt in a small bowl; stir well with a whisk. Pour dressing over couscous mixture; toss gently. Yield: 4 servings (serving size: about 1 cup).

CALORIES 230; FAT 9.3g (sat 1.6g, mono 5.7g, poly 1.5g); PROTEIN 19.7g; CARB 17.7g; FIBER 2.8g; CHOL 45mg; IRON 2.7mg; SODIUM 356mg; CALC 66mg

serve with
Greek Pita Chips

Prep: 6 minutes • Cook: 15 minutes

2 (6-inch) pitas
Olive oil-flavored cooking spray

¼ teaspoon salt-free Greek seasoning
¼ teaspoon salt

1. Preheat oven to 350°.
2. Split pitas; cut into 8 wedges. Arrange pita wedges in a single layer on a large baking sheet; coat lightly with cooking spray. Sprinkle evenly with Greek seasoning and salt. Bake at 350° for 15 minutes or until crisp. Yield: 4 servings (serving size: 8 chips).

CALORIES 82; FAT 0.2g (sat 0g, mono 0g, poly 0g); PROTEIN 3.5g; CARB 16.5g; FIBER 0.5g; CHOL 0mg; IRON 1.4mg; SODIUM 225mg; CALC 20mg

Yucatecan cuisine combines Spanish, Mexican, and Caribbean flavors. In this spicy recipe, an authentic combination of turmeric, black beans, and olives accompanies the rice. Serve with lemon wedges, if desired.

Yucatecan Rice Salad

Prep: 7 minutes • Cook: 7 minutes • Other: 5 minutes

½ cup water
⅛ teaspoon ground turmeric
½ cup instant whole-grain brown rice (such as Minute)
1 (15-ounce) can black beans, rinsed and drained
½ cup jalapeño-stuffed green olives, coarsely chopped (about 11 olives)

⅓ cup prechopped red onion
3 (0.5-ounce) slices reduced-fat Monterey Jack cheese with jalapeño peppers, cut into ½-inch squares
¼ cup chopped fresh cilantro
1 tablespoon extra-virgin olive oil
Lemon wedges (optional)

1. Bring water and turmeric to a boil in a medium saucepan. Stir in rice; cover, reduce heat, and simmer 5 minutes. Remove from heat. Place rice in a wire mesh strainer; rinse rice with cold water, and drain well.
2. While rice cooks, combine beans and next 5 ingredients in a medium bowl. Add the cooled rice; toss gently until blended. Serve with lemon wedges, if desired. Yield: 4 servings (serving size: ¾ cup).

CALORIES 164; FAT 8.3g (sat 1.8g, mono 4.9g, poly 1.3g); PROTEIN 6.4g; CARB 20.9g; FIBER 4.1g; CHOL 8mg; IRON 1.2mg; SODIUM 430mg; CALC 102mg

serve with
Tomato-Avocado Wedges

Prep: 4 minutes

2 medium tomatoes, each cut into 8 wedges
1 medium avocado, thinly sliced
1½ tablespoons extra-virgin olive oil

1½ tablespoons cider vinegar
1 garlic clove, minced
⅛ teaspoon salt

1. Combine tomato and avocado in a medium bowl.
2. Combine olive oil and remaining ingredients in a small bowl, stirring with a whisk. Drizzle dressing over tomato mixture. Yield: 4 servings (serving size: ½ cup tomato mixture).

CALORIES 135; FAT 11.9g (sat 1.5g, mono 9g, poly 1.4g); PROTEIN 2.1g; CARB 7.5g; FIBER 2.4g; CHOL 0mg; IRON 0.7mg; SODIUM 77mg; CALC 9mg

Slivered almonds add just the right amount of crunch to this nourishing salad, which you can make up to a day ahead. To get a jump start on this dish, cook and chill the rice up to 2 days before making the salad.

Chicken and Wild Rice Salad with Orange-Mango Vinaigrette

Prep: 5 minutes • Cook: 15 minutes • Other: 30 minutes

1 (2.75-ounce) package quick-cooking wild rice (such as Gourmet House)
1 (3½-ounce) bag boil-in-bag brown rice (such as Success)

2 cups chopped cooked chicken breast (8 ounces)
Orange-Mango Vinaigrette
¼ cup slivered almonds, toasted

1. Cook wild rice and brown rice according to package directions, omitting salt and fat. Combine wild rice and brown rice, and spread rice mixture in a thin layer in a baking pan. Refrigerate 30 minutes or until cool, stirring occasionally. Combine chilled rice mixture, chicken, and Orange-Mango Vinaigrette in a large bowl; toss well. Spoon rice mixture evenly onto each of 4 serving plates; sprinkle evenly with almonds. Yield: 4 servings (serving size: 1½ cup rice mixture and 1 tablespoon almonds).

CALORIES 421; FAT 10.1g (sat 1.5g, mono 5.9g, poly 1.9g); PROTEIN 30.1g; CARB 45.6g; FIBER 4.2g; CHOL 60mg; IRON 2.7mg; SODIUM 352mg; CALC 80mg

Orange-Mango Vinaigrette

Prep: 7 minutes

½ cup refrigerated orange-mango juice
1 cup chopped green onions
¼ cup chopped fresh flat-leaf parsley
2 tablespoons white balsamic vinegar
2 tablespoons minced shallots

1 tablespoon chopped fresh thyme
1 tablespoon extra-virgin olive oil
½ teaspoon salt
½ teaspoon freshly ground black pepper

1. Combine all ingredients in a small bowl, stirring with a whisk. Yield: 8 servings (serving size: 2 tablespoons).

CALORIES 35; FAT 1.8g (sat 0.3g, mono 1.3g, poly 0.2g); PROTEIN 0.4g; CARB 4.5g; FIBER 0.5g; CHOL 0mg; IRON 0.4mg; SODIUM 149mg; CALC 14mg

meatless main

Falafel Patties with Tzatziki
Spaghetti with Zucchini and White Beans
Grilled Polenta with Tomatoes and White Beans
Southwestern Red Beans and Rice
Refried Beans and Rice Burritos
Sautéed Vegetables and Spicy Tofu
Samosas
Meatless Hash and Eggs
Meatless Meatballs over Herbed Spaghetti Squash
Cheese and Tomato Omelet
Zucchini-Potato Pancakes with Eggs
Spinach and Roasted Red Pepper Tart
Mini White Pizzas with Vegetables
Roasted Mushroom and Shallot Pizza
Whole Wheat Pita Pizzas with Spinach, Fontina, and Onions
Israeli Couscous with Moroccan-Roasted Butternut Squash
Mushroom Stroganoff
Grilled Stuffed Portobello Mushrooms
Potato and Jalapeño Cheese Bake

Falafel, a popular Middle Eastern food, consists of seasoned pureed chickpeas that are shaped into balls or patties and then deep fried and served stuffed inside pita bread. In our version, we've opted to lightly pan-fry the patties and serve them nestled in Boston lettuces leaves with a side of fresh, soft pita triangles. You'll need only one lemon for this meal so be sure to grate the lemon rind for the falafel before squeezing the juice for the Tzatziki.

Falafel Patties with Tzatziki

Prep: 6 minutes • Cook: 8 minutes

2 garlic cloves
1 (15-ounce) can chickpeas (garbanzo beans), rinsed and drained
¼ cup all-purpose flour
¼ cup fresh flat-leaf parsley leaves
2 tablespoons tahini (roasted sesame seed paste)

1 teaspoon baking powder
1 teaspoon ground cumin
1 teaspoon grated lemon rind
½ teaspoon salt
½ teaspoon black pepper
2 tablespoons olive oil
Tzatziki

1. With food processor on, drop garlic through food chute; process until minced. Add chickpeas and next 8 ingredients to garlic in food processor; process until chickpeas are finely ground. Shape mixture into 4 (3-inch) patties.
2. Heat oil in a large nonstick skillet over medium-high heat. Add patties to pan; cook 4 minutes on each side or until browned. Serve patties with Tzatziki. Yield: 4 servings (serving size: 1 patty and about ⅓ cup Tzatziki).

CALORIES 286; FAT 12.8g (sat 2.1g, mono 6.9g, poly 3.2g); PROTEIN 10.6g; CARB 33.8g; FIBER 7.1g; CHOL 5mg; IRON 18.7mg; SODIUM 573mg; CALC 291mg

Tzatziki

Prep: 3 minutes

1½ cups coarsely chopped English cucumber (½ medium)
¾ cup plain low-fat yogurt

½ cup chopped fresh mint
1 tablespoon fresh lemon juice

1. Combine all ingredients in a bowl. Yield: 4 servings (serving size: about ⅓ cup).

CALORIES 62; FAT 1.1g (sat 0.5g, mono 0.3g, poly 0.3g); PROTEIN 4.6g; CARB 9g; FIBER 3g; CHOL 5mg; IRON 16.6mg; SODIUM 54mg; CALC 223mg

Tender spaghetti noodles capture the fresh taste of the chunky bean and vegetable sauce, while a sprinkling of feta cheese adds a finishing touch.

Spaghetti with Zucchini and White Beans

Prep: 5 minutes • Cook: 10 minutes

6 ounces uncooked spaghetti
Olive oil-flavored cooking spray
3 cups (¼-inch) diced zucchini (2 medium)
⅓ cup water
1 tablespoon tomato paste (such as Amore)
¼ teaspoon kosher salt
⅛ teaspoon coarsely ground black pepper
1 (15.8-ounce) can Great Northern beans, rinsed and drained
1 (14.5-ounce) can diced tomatoes with basil, garlic, and oregano, undrained
½ cup (2 ounces) crumbled feta cheese

1. Cook spaghetti according to package directions, omitting salt and fat.
2. While pasta cooks, heat a large nonstick skillet over medium-high heat; coat pan with cooking spray. Add zucchini to pan; cook 5 minutes or until lightly browned, stirring occasionally. Stir in water and next 5 ingredients; cover and simmer 4 minutes.
3. Place pasta evenly on each of 4 plates. Top pasta evenly with zucchini mixture and cheese. Yield: 4 servings (serving size: about ⅔ cup pasta, 1 cup zucchini mixture, and 2 tablespoons cheese).

CALORIES 311; FAT 4.1g (sat 2.4g, mono 0.8g, poly 0.5g); PROTEIN 14.7g; CARB 55.3g; FIBER 7.5g; CHOL 13mg; IRON 3.3mg; SODIUM 452mg; CALC 147mg

serve with
Mixed Greens with Honey-Dijon Vinaigrette

Prep: 7 minutes

2 tablespoons balsamic vinegar
1 tablespoon extra-virgin olive oil
1 teaspoon honey
¼ teaspoon Dijon mustard
⅛ teaspoon coarsely ground black pepper
4 cups torn mixed salad greens
½ cup red seedless grape halves

1. Combine first 5 ingredients in a large bowl, stirring with a whisk. Add greens; toss gently. Divide greens mixture among 4 plates; top evenly with grape halves. Yield: 4 servings (serving size: about 1 cup salad and 2 tablespoons grapes).

CALORIES 66; FAT 3.7g (sat 0.5g, mono 2.5g, poly 0.6g); PROTEIN 1.1g; CARB 8.2g; FIBER 1.4g; CHOL 0mg; IRON 0.9mg; SODIUM 24mg; CALC 35mg

Grilled Polenta with Tomatoes and White Beans

Prep: 5 minutes • Cook: 10 minutes

1 (17-ounce) tube of basil and garlic-flavored
  polenta, cut into 9 slices
Cooking spray
2 teaspoons olive oil
2 cups halved grape tomatoes
2 garlic cloves, minced
1 (15-ounce) can cannellini beans, rinsed and
  drained

1 tablespoon white wine vinegar
1½ teaspoons chopped fresh rosemary
¼ teaspoon freshly ground black pepper
½ cup (2 ounces) grated Parmigiano-Reggiano
  cheese
Rosemary sprigs (optional)

1. Heat a grill pan or nonstick skillet over medium-high heat. Coat pan and polenta slices with cooking spray. Place polenta slices on grill pan or skillet; cook 2 minutes on each side or until golden brown. Remove from pan; keep warm.
2. While polenta cooks, heat oil in a large nonstick skillet over medium-high heat. Add tomatoes and garlic to skillet; sauté 4 minutes or until tomatoes soften and garlic is tender. Reduce heat to low. Stir in beans and next 3 ingredients. Cook, stirring constantly, 2 minutes or until thoroughly heated.
3. Place 3 polenta slices on each of 3 plates. Spoon tomato mixture evenly over polenta, and sprinkle evenly with cheese. Garnish with rosemary sprigs, if desired. Yield: 3 servings (serving size: 3 polenta slices, 1 cup tomato mixture, and about 2½ tablespoons cheese).

CALORIES 331; FAT 9g (sat 4.2g, mono 2.7g, poly 1.6g); PROTEIN 13.8g; CARB 43.5g; FIBER 5.7g; CHOL 19mg; IRON 2.2mg; SODIUM 993mg; CALC 296mg

shortcut kitchen tip

To quickly remove fresh rosemary leaves from the tough, woody stem, hold the top of the rosemary sprig with the leaves pointing upward over a cutting board. With the other hand, run your fingers along the stem against the direction of the leaves, pinching tightly. Your fingers will separate the leaves from the stem. Mound the leaves together on your cutting board, and then chop the leaves with a chef's knife.

The tomato-and-white bean mixture and the polenta cook in only a matter of minutes. To keep this recipe quick and easy yet deliver attractive grill marks, we used a grill pan instead of firing up an outdoor grill. If you don't have a grill pan, use a nonstick skillet.

Southwestern Red Beans and Rice

Prep: 4 minutes • Cook: 9 minutes

Cooking spray
1 (8-ounce) package presliced mushrooms
1 (8.8-ounce) package precooked whole-grain brown rice (such as Uncle Ben's Ready Rice)
1 (16-ounce) can light red kidney beans, rinsed and drained
1 (14.5-ounce) can diced tomatoes with zesty mild green chiles, undrained (such as Del Monte)

¼ teaspoon salt
⅛ teaspoon freshly ground black pepper
4 (7½-inch) flour tortillas
½ cup (2 ounces) reduced-fat shredded cheddar cheese
1 tablespoon chopped fresh cilantro

1. Heat a large nonstick skillet over medium-high heat; coat pan with cooking spray. Add mushrooms to pan; cook 6 minutes or until lightly browned, stirring occasionally. Stir in rice and next 4 ingredients. Cover and bring to a boil; reduce heat, and simmer 4 minutes or until thoroughly heated.

2. While rice mixture cooks, warm tortillas according to package directions. Sprinkle rice mixture with cheese and cilantro. Serve immediately with tortillas. Yield: 4 servings (serving size: about 1 cup rice mixture and 1 tortilla).

CALORIES 319; FAT 7g (sat 2.7g, mono 2.4g, poly 1.5g); PROTEIN 14.2g; CARB 52.1g; FIBER 8.4g; CHOL 11mg; IRON 2.6mg; SODIUM 794mg; CALC 144mg

choice ingredient

Kidney beans are a great pantry staple, and they provide an excellent low-fat source of fiber, protein, potassium, and magnesium. Rinsing and draining canned beans reduces the sodium by 40 percent.

Save some time by preparing the accompanying veggies while the burritos cook in the microwave.

Refried Beans and Rice Burritos
Prep: 10 minutes • Cook: 5 minutes

1 (10-ounce) package frozen Southwestern-style rice (such as Birds Eye Steamfresh)
1 cup canned fat-free refried beans
4 (8-inch) 96% fat-free whole wheat tortillas (such as Mission)
½ cup (2 ounces) reduced-fat shredded cheddar cheese

Thinly sliced iceberg lettuce (optional)
½ cup diced tomato
½ cup diced cucumber
½ cup fresh salsa
¼ cup light sour cream

1. Microwave rice according to package directions.
2. Spoon ¼ cup refried beans down center of each tortilla; top each with ⅓ cup rice and 2 tablespoons cheese.
3. Arrange burritos, seam side down, in a microwave-safe baking dish. Cover with plastic wrap, and microwave at HIGH 3 minutes or until thoroughly heated. Place lettuce on each of 4 plates, if desired, and top with burritos. Top each burrito with 2 tablespoons tomato, 2 tablespoons cucumber, 2 tablespoons salsa, and 1 table-spoon sour cream. Yield: 4 servings (serving size: 1 burrito).

CALORIES 379; FAT 9g (sat 3.3g, mono 3.2g, poly 2.2g); PROTEIN 15.1g; CARB 62.5g; FIBER 7.4g; CHOL 10mg; IRON 0.7mg; SODIUM 1190mg; CALC 148mg

serve with
Fruit Juice Coolers
Prep: 3 minutes

2 cups mango nectar (such as Jumex)
1 cup orange juice
1 (12-ounce) can diet citrus soda (such as original Fresca), chilled

2 cups ice cubes
4 lime wedges (optional)

1. Combine mango nectar and orange juice in a 1½-quart pitcher. Slowly add citrus soda. Serve over ice, and garnish with lime wedges, if desired. Yield: 4 servings (serving size: about 1 cup).

CALORIES 98; FAT 0.2g (sat 0g, mono 0g, poly 0.1g); PROTEIN 1g; CARB 23.4g; FIBER 0.1g; CHOL 0mg; IRON 0.5mg; SODIUM 36mg; CALC 26mg

Thanks to a seasoned packaged of tofu, this easy stir-fry comes together in a snap. This dish is delicious served alone, but for heartier fare serve it on top of rice noodles.

Sautéed Vegetables and Spicy Tofu

Prep: 5 minutes • Cook: 8 minutes

1 (16-ounce) package spicy tofu, drained
2 tablespoons olive oil, divided
2 tablespoons fresh lemon juice
½ teaspoon salt
¼ teaspoon crushed red pepper
2 large garlic cloves, pressed

1 large zucchini, halved lengthwise and cut crosswise into thin slices
1 cup thinly sliced red bell pepper
Lemon wedges (optional)

1. Place tofu on several layers of heavy-duty paper towels. Cover tofu with additional paper towels; gently press out moisture. Cut tofu into ½-inch cubes.
2. Combine 1 tablespoon oil and next 4 ingredients in a medium bowl. Set aside.
3. Heat remaining 1 tablespoon oil in a large nonstick skillet over medium-high heat. Add tofu, zucchini, and bell pepper; stir-fry 8 to 10 minutes or until tofu is browned and vegetables are crisp-tender. Add oil mixture; cook 1 minute, stirring gently. Serve with lemon wedges, if desired. Yield: 4 servings (serving size: 1 cup).

CALORIES 196; FAT 13.7g (sat 2.3g, mono 5g, poly 5g); PROTEIN 15g; CARB 7.9g; FIBER 3.2g; CHOL 0mg; IRON 3mg; SODIUM 302mg; CALC 154mg

make-it-faster

Reduce meal prep time by using jarred, prepeeled garlic cloves instead of peeling them yourself. Look for them in the refrigerated produce section at your supermarket.

Typically an appetizer, Indian samosas are little dough pockets filled with a spicy combination of potatoes, onion, and meat or fish. Here we've used meatless crumbles and made them larger to serve as a main dish. Serve with a mixed greens salad.

Samosas

Prep: 7 minutes • Cook: 12 minutes

1½ cups frozen vegetarian meatless crumbles (such as Morning Star Farms Meal Starters)
¾ cup country-style refrigerated mashed potatoes (such as Simply Potatoes)
⅓ cup frozen petite peas
Indian Spice Blend Mix
1 (8-ounce) can refrigerated reduced-fat crescent rolls (such as Pillsbury)
Cooking spray
Nonfat Greek yogurt (optional)

1. Preheat oven to 375°.
2. Combine first 4 ingredients in a medium microwave-safe bowl. Cover with plastic wrap; vent. Microwave at HIGH 2 minutes or until thoroughly heated.
3. While filling heats, unroll dough on work surface. Press diagonal perforations together. Cut dough along remaining perforated lines to create 4 (6½ x 3½-inch) rectangles. Spoon filling evenly on half of each rectangle. Fold dough over filling, pressing with a fork to seal. Coat a baking sheet with cooking spray, and place samosas on pan; coat samosas with cooking spray. Bake at 375° for 12 minutes. Serve with Greek yogurt, if desired. Yield: 4 servings (serving size: 1 samosa).

CALORIES 284; FAT 12.3g (sat 5.5g, mono 4.4g, poly 2.1g); PROTEIN 14.9g; CARB 35.1g; FIBER 3g; CHOL 6mg; IRON 3mg; SODIUM 964mg; CALC 56mg

Indian Spice Blend Mix

Prep: 3 minutes

1 teaspoon garam masala (such as McCormick)
1 teaspoon chili powder
¼ teaspoon crushed red pepper
¼ teaspoon garlic powder
¼ teaspoon ground cardamom
¼ teaspoon salt
¼ teaspoon freshly ground black pepper

1. Combine all ingredients in a small bowl. Yield: 4 servings (serving size: ¼ teaspoon).

CALORIES 2; FAT 0.1g (sat 0g, mono 0g, poly 0g); PROTEIN 0.1g; CARB 0.4g; FIBER 0.1g; CHOL 0mg; IRON 0.1mg; SODIUM 166mg; CALC 2mg

This meat-free dish, adapted from a traditional recipe for corned beef and hash, earned our Test Kitchens' highest rating.

Meatless Hash and Eggs

Prep: 3 minutes • Cook: 16 minutes

2½ cups frozen shredded hash brown potatoes
1½ cups frozen meatless crumbles
1½ cups prechopped tomato, green bell pepper, and onion mix
½ teaspoon salt
¼ teaspoon black pepper
1 tablespoon olive oil
Cooking spray
4 large eggs

1. Combine first 5 ingredients in a medium bowl.
2. Heat oil in a large nonstick skillet coated with cooking spray over medium heat. Add potato mixture, and cook 5 to 7 minutes or until potato mixture is thoroughly heated, stirring occasionally. Form 4 (3-inch) indentations in potato mixture using the back of a spoon. Break 1 egg into each indentation. Cover and cook 10 minutes or until eggs are done. Yield: 4 servings (serving size: 1 egg and 1 cup potato mixture).

CALORIES 271; FAT 10.8g (sat 2.3g, mono 4.7g, poly 3g); PROTEIN 15.2g; CARB 30.3g; FIBER 3.9g; CHOL 212mg; IRON 3.4mg; SODIUM 527mg; CALC 59mg

serve with
Citrus-Jicama Salad

Prep: 9 minutes

1 (24-ounce) jar red grapefruit sections
2 tablespoons fresh mint, chopped
⅛ teaspoon ground cinnamon
⅔ cup jicama, peeled and matchstick-cut

1. Drain red grapefruit sections, reserving ¼ cup juice. Combine juice, mint, and cinnamon in a medium bowl; stir with a whisk. Add grapefruit sections and jicama; toss gently. Yield: 4 servings (serving size: about ½ cup).

CALORIES 91; FAT 0g (sat 0g, mono 0g, poly 0g); PROTEIN 1.6g; CARB 21.1g; FIBER 2g; CHOL 0mg; IRON 1mg; SODIUM 22mg; CALC 9mg

Meatless Meatballs over Herbed Spaghetti Squash

Prep: 7 minutes • Cook: 14 minutes

Cooking spray
1 (8-ounce) container prechopped onion
1 (12-ounce) package frozen zesty Italian-flavored meatless meatballs (such as Nate's)
1 (26-ounce) jar fire roasted tomato-garlic pasta sauce (such as Classico)
2 tablespoons sun-dried tomato pesto (such as Classico)
Herbed Spaghetti Squash
Freshly shredded Parmesan cheese (optional)

1. Heat a large saucepan over medium-high heat; coat pan with cooking spray. Add onion; sauté 3 to 4 minutes or until tender. Add meatballs, pasta sauce, and pesto to pan; bring to a boil. Reduce heat; simmer 10 minutes or until meatballs are thoroughly heated. Spoon meatballs and sauce over Herbed Spaghetti Squash, and sprinkle with Parmesan cheese, if desired. Yield: 4 servings (serving size: about 1 cup meatball-sauce mixture and about 1 cup Herbed Spaghetti Squash).

CALORIES 272; FAT 10.6g (sat 1g, mono 4.8g, poly 4g); PROTEIN 15.5g; CARB 30.8g; FIBER 5.3g; CHOL 0mg; IRON 4mg; SODIUM 1082mg; CALC 167mg

Herbed Spaghetti Squash

Prep: 6 minutes • Cook: 13 minutes

1 (3¼-pound) spaghetti squash
½ cup water
1 tablespoon extra-virgin olive oil
2 tablespoons chopped fresh basil
½ teaspoon salt
¼ teaspoon freshly ground black pepper

1. Pierce squash several times with the tip of a sharp knife. Microwave at HIGH 3 minutes. Cut squash in half lengthwise, and remove seeds and membrane with a spoon.
2. Place squash halves in an 11 x 7–inch baking dish (squash halves will overlap); add ½ cup water. Cover with plastic wrap; vent. Microwave at HIGH 10 minutes or until tender. Using a fork, remove spaghettilike strands, and place in a large bowl. Add olive oil and remaining ingredients; toss well. Yield: 4 servings (serving size: about 1 cup).

CALORIES 76; FAT 3.3g (sat 0.5g, mono 1.9g, poly 1g); PROTEIN 0.6g; CARB 12.2g; FIBER 0.1g; CHOL 0mg; IRON 1mg; SODIUM 223mg; CALC 42mg

Reminiscent of classic spaghetti and meatballs, this meatless recipe will please both vegetarians and meat lovers. Spaghetti squash is a low-carb alternative to traditional pasta noodles, while soy meatballs stand in for the beef variety.

This veggie-packed omelet is perfect for brunch or a simple supper. For a delicious side, serve a medley of fresh fruit, such as Mandarin Oranges with Kiwifruit and Grapes.

Cheese and Tomato Omelet

Prep: 5 minutes • Cook: 7 minutes

2 large eggs
2 large egg whites
2 tablespoons water
1 tablespoon finely chopped fresh cilantro
¼ teaspoon salt
⅛ teaspoon coarsely ground black pepper

Cooking spray
¼ cup (1 ounce) reduced-fat shredded cheddar cheese
½ cup diced seeded tomato (1 small)
Fresh chopped cilantro

1. Combine first 6 ingredients in a medium bowl, stirring with a whisk.
2. Heat an 8-inch nonstick skillet over medium-high heat; coat pan with cooking spray. Add egg mixture, and cook until edges begin to set. Gently lift edges of egg mixture with a wide spatula, tilting pan to allow uncooked egg mixture to come in contact with pan. Cook 2 minutes or until egg mixture is almost set; sprinkle with cheese. Spoon tomato over half of omelet; fold in half.
3. Cut omelet in half crosswise, and slide one half onto each of 2 plates. Garnish with cilantro, if desired, and serve immediately. Yield: 2 servings (serving size: ½ omelet).

CALORIES 147; FAT 7.7g (sat 3.4g, mono 3g, poly 0.9g); PROTEIN 13.9g; CARB 3.8g; FIBER 0.5g; CHOL 190mg; IRON 1.4mg; SODIUM 510mg; CALC 132mg

serve with
Mandarin Oranges with Kiwifruit and Grapes

Prep: 4 minutes

2 tablespoons light syrup from mandarin oranges
¾ cup mandarin oranges in light syrup (such as Del Monte SunFresh), drained

½ cup cubed kiwifruit (about 1 kiwifruit)
¼ cup seedless red grape halves
1 teaspoon fresh lemon juice

1. Combine 2 tablespoons light syrup, oranges, and remaining ingredients. Yield: 2 servings (serving size: ¾ cup).

CALORIES 95; FAT 0.4g (sat 0g, mono 0.1g, poly 0.1g); PROTEIN 0.8g; CARB 24.1g; FIBER 1.9g; CHOL 0mg; IRON 0.5mg; SODIUM 6mg; CALC 19mg

These crispy pan-fried cakes showcase zucchini and potatoes topped with fried eggs.

Zucchini-Potato Pancakes with Eggs

Prep: 4 minutes • Cook: 13 minutes

2 cups refrigerated shredded hash brown potatoes (such as Simply Potatoes)
1 cup shredded zucchini (about 1 small)
¼ cup Italian-seasoned panko (Japanese breadcrumbs)
4 large egg whites, lightly beaten
¼ cup (1 ounce) shredded fresh Parmesan cheese
¼ teaspoon freshly ground black pepper
Cooking spray
4 large eggs
⅛ teaspoon freshly ground black pepper
Fresh salsa (optional)
Light sour cream (optional)

1. Combine first 6 ingredients in a large bowl.
2. Heat a large nonstick skillet over medium heat; heavily coat pan with cooking spray. Spoon about ½ cup potato mixture into 2 (5-inch) circles in pan. Cook 5 minutes; turn and cook 4 minutes or until potato is tender. Remove pancakes from pan, and keep warm. Repeat procedure with remaining potato mixture.
3. Reheat pan over medium-high heat; heavily recoat pan with cooking spray. Crack 4 eggs into pan; sprinkle with ⅛ teaspoon black pepper, and coat tops of eggs with cooking spray. Cover and cook 3 minutes or until whites have just set and yolks begin to thicken but are not hard or until desired degree of doneness. Slide 1 egg onto each pancake. Serve with salsa and sour cream, if desired. Yield: 4 servings (serving size: 1 pancake and 1 egg).

CALORIES 222; FAT 6.5g (sat 2.5g, mono 1.9g, poly 0.8g); PROTEIN 15.6g; CARB 24g; FIBER 1.6g; CHOL 186mg; IRON 1.4mg; SODIUM 392mg; CALC 120mg

serve with
Spinach Salad with Strawberries

Prep: 4 minutes

1 tablespoon olive oil
1 tablespoon fresh lemon juice
1 teaspoon honey
¼ teaspoon salt
⅛ teaspoon black pepper
3 cups bagged baby spinach leaves
1 cup quartered strawberries
⅓ cup (1.3 ounces) crumbled feta cheese (optional)

1. Combine first 5 ingredients in a large bowl, stirring well with a whisk. Add spinach and strawberries; toss well. Sprinkle with feta cheese, if desired. Yield: 2 servings (serving size: 2 cups).

CALORIES 108; FAT 7g (sat 0.9g, mono 5g, poly 0.8g); PROTEIN 1.5g; CARB 11.3g; FIBER 2.6g; CHOL 0mg; IRON 2mg; SODIUM 320mg; CALC 49mg

Pan-roasted potatoes make a hearty side dish for this savory tart. Take care not to stretch the dough while you are fitting it into the tart pan as this will cause it to shrink and fall away from the sides of the pan as it bakes.

Spinach and Roasted Red Pepper Tart

Prep: 4 minutes • Cook: 51 minutes

½ (15-ounce) package refrigerated piecrust
Cooking spray
1 (10-ounce) package frozen leaf spinach and butter sauce (such as Green Giant), thawed and drained
½ cup chopped drained bottled roasted red peppers

½ cup reduced-fat crumbled feta cheese with basil and sun-dried tomatoes
¾ cup egg substitute
¼ teaspoon salt
¼ teaspoon freshly ground black pepper

1. Preheat oven to 400°.
2. Unroll dough, and roll into a 12-inch circle. Fit dough into a 9-inch round removable bottom tart pan coated with cooking spray; press dough against sides of pan. Pierce bottom and sides of dough with a fork. Place pan on bottom rack in oven. Bake at 400° for 14 minutes or until golden.
3. While crust bakes, combine spinach, peppers, and cheese in a bowl. Combine egg substitute, salt, and pepper in another bowl.
4. Remove crust from oven; sprinkle spinach mixture over bottom of crust. Pour egg substitute mixture over spinach mixture. Return tart to bottom rack. Bake 37 additional minutes or until crust is golden brown and custard is set. Cut into 8 wedges. Yield: 4 servings (serving size: 2 wedges).

CALORIES 342; FAT 18.9g (sat 7.9g, mono 5g, poly 5g); PROTEIN 10g; CARB 31.8g; FIBER 1.5g; CHOL 21mg; IRON 2mg; SODIUM 908mg; CALC 138mg

serve now or later

This dish can easily be prepared the night you serve it or prepped up to a day ahead. To prep this recipe ahead of time, fit the dough in the tart pan, prepare the egg mixture, and store separately in the refrigerator.

We used whole wheat pita rounds to help with portion control and to speed up the cook time. For a Greek-inspired flavor variation, substitute hummus for the spreadable cheese.

Mini White Pizzas with Vegetables

Prep: 5 minutes • Cook: 9 minutes

4   (6-inch) whole wheat pitas
Olive oil-flavored cooking spray
1   medium zucchini, thinly sliced
¼   cup thinly sliced red onion, separated into rings
¼   teaspoon freshly ground black pepper
⅛   teaspoon salt
½   cup light garlic-and-herbs spreadable cheese (such as Alouette Light)
6   tablespoons shredded Asiago cheese

1. Preheat broiler.
2. Place pitas on a baking sheet; broil 3 minutes.
3. Heat a nonstick skillet over medium-high heat; coat pan with cooking spray. Add zucchini, onion, pepper, and salt; sauté 3 minutes or until vegetables are crisp-tender.
4. Remove pitas from oven, and spread 2 tablespoons garlic-and-herbs spreadable cheese over each pita. Top evenly with vegetables and Asiago cheese. Broil 3 minutes or until edges are lightly browned and cheese melts. Yield: 4 servings (serving size: 1 pizza).

CALORIES 272; FAT 8.7g (sat 4.6g, mono 1, poly 1g); PROTEIN 11.9g; CARB 40.2g; FIBER 5.5g; CHOL 24mg; IRON 2.2mg; SODIUM 505mg; CALC 137mg

serve with
Caesar Salad

Prep: 8 minutes

2   romaine hearts
2   tablespoons light Caesar dressing
2   tablespoons Parmesan cheese, grated
4   large-cut Caesar-flavored croutons, halved

1. Cut 2 romaine hearts in half lengthwise. Top each romaine half with 1 tablespoon light Caesar dressing, 1 tablespoon freshly grated Parmesan cheese, and 2 halved large-cut Caesar-flavored croutons. Yield: 4 servings (serving size: 1 salad).

CALORIES 102; FAT 6.1g (sat 1.5g, mono 2g, poly 2g); PROTEIN 5.1g; CARB 7.8g; FIBER 1.2g; CHOL 10mg; IRON 1.3mg; SODIUM 342mg; CALC 149mg

Lorraine cheese, which comes in long slices, is similar in flavor to Swiss cheese. If you don't have fresh oregano, you can substitute ½ teaspoon dried oregano.

Roasted Mushroom and Shallot Pizza
Prep: 5 minutes • Cook: 8 minutes

½ (8-ounce) tub light chive-and-onion cream cheese
1 (10-ounce) cheese-flavored thin pizza crust (such as Boboli)

2 cups Roasted Mushrooms and Shallots
3 (1-ounce) slices reduced-fat Lorraine cheese (such as Saputo)
2 tablespoons fresh oregano leaves

1. Preheat oven to 450°.
2. Spread cream cheese over pizza crust. Top with Roasted Mushrooms and Shallots and cheese slices.
3. Bake pizza directly on oven rack at 450° for 8 minutes or until crust is golden and cheese melts. Sprinkle with oregano, and serve immediately. Yield: 6 servings (serving size: 1 slice).

CALORIES 280; FAT 11.3g (sat 5.4g, mono 2.8g, poly 3g); PROTEIN 12.9g; CARB 32g; FIBER 2.5g; CHOL 19mg; IRON 2.7mg; SODIUM 520mg; CALC 302mg

Roasted Mushrooms and Shallots
Prep: 15 minutes • Cook: 15 minutes

1 tablespoon extra-virgin olive oil
¼ teaspoon salt
¾ teaspoon freshly ground black pepper
4 garlic cloves, minced
1 (8-ounce) package baby portobello mushrooms, quartered

1 (3.5-ounce) package shiitake mushrooms, stems removed and quartered
2 (3-ounce) packages small shallots, peeled and quartered lengthwise
Cooking spray

1. Preheat oven to 450°.
2. Combine first 4 ingredients in a large bowl. Add mushrooms and shallots; toss to coat. Spread mushroom mixture in a single layer in a jelly-roll pan coated with cooking spray.
3. Bake at 450° for 15 minutes (do not stir). Yield: 2 cups (serving size: ⅓ cup).

CALORIES 55; FAT 2.5g (sat 0.3g, mono 1.8g, poly 0.3g); PROTEIN 2g; CARB 6.4g; FIBER 1.2g; CHOL 0mg; IRON 0.7mg; SODIUM 105mg; CALC 15mg

Fontina, a creamy Italian cheese, has a nutty flavor. Its silky texture makes it the perfect topping for pizza because it melts so easily.

Whole Wheat Pita Pizzas with Spinach, Fontina, and Onions

Prep: 4 minutes • Cook: 11 minutes

3 teaspoons olive oil, divided
3 garlic cloves, minced
2 cups vertically sliced red onion
2 cups bagged baby spinach leaves
4 (7-inch) whole wheat pitas
¼ cup (2 ounces) shredded Fontina cheese

1. Preheat oven to 450°.
2. Heat 1 teaspoon olive oil in a medium nonstick skillet over medium-high heat. Add garlic and onion; sauté 5 minutes or until tender.
3. Add spinach and sauté 2 minutes or just until spinach begins to wilt. Remove from heat.
4. Place pitas on a large baking sheet; brush with remaining 2 teaspoons olive oil. Top pitas evenly with garlic-spinach mixture and cheese. Bake at 450° for 4 minutes or until cheese melts and pitas are brown. Yield: 4 servings (serving size: 1 pizza).

CALORIES 287; FAT 9.5g (sat 3.5g, mono 3.9g, poly 1.3g); PROTEIN 11g; CARB 42.6g; FIBER 6.2g; CHOL 16mg; IRON 2.6mg; SODIUM 466mg; CALC 118mg

serve with
Arugula Salad

Prep: 2 minutes

1 tablespoon balsamic vinegar
2 teaspoons olive oil
½ teaspoon freshly ground black pepper
¼ teaspoon salt
4 cups arugula leaves
1 cup cherry tomatoes, halved

1. Combine first 4 ingredients in a large bowl, stirring with a whisk. Add arugula and tomato halves; toss well. Yield: 4 servings (serving size: about 1 cup).

CALORIES 37; FAT 2.5g (sat 0.4g, mono 1.7g, poly 0.4g); PROTEIN 0.9g; CARB 3.3g; FIBER 0.8g; CHOL 0mg; IRON 0.5mg; SODIUM 155mg; CALC 36mg

Oil-cured olives pack a punch of flavor because they have been soaked in herb or spice-infused oil for several months. To save time, roast the squash while the couscous cooks.

Israeli Couscous with Moroccan-Roasted Butternut Squash

Prep: 5 minutes • Cook: 23 minutes

Cooking spray
1⅓ cups Israeli couscous
2 cups water
¼ teaspoon salt
¼ teaspoon black pepper
½ cup pitted oil-cured olives, halved
(about 12 olives)

¼ cup fresh mint leaves, coarsely chopped
3 tablespoons sliced almonds, toasted
Moroccan-Roasted Butternut Squash
Nonfat Greek yogurt (optional)
Fresh mint leaves (optional)

1. Heat a medium saucepan over medium-high heat; coat pan with cooking spray. Add couscous; sauté 1 minute. Stir in water, salt, and pepper. Bring to a boil; reduce heat, and simmer 12 minutes or until liquid is absorbed. Remove from heat. Add olives, mint, and almonds; toss well.
2. Divide couscous among 3 plates. Top evenly with Moroccan-Roasted Butternut Squash. Serve with yogurt, and garnish with mint leaves, if desired. Yield: 3 servings (serving size: 1 cup couscous and about 1 cup squash).

CALORIES 439; FAT 11.2g (sat 1.8g, mono 5.2g, poly 3.3g); PROTEIN 10.4g; CARB 80g; FIBER 11.2g; CHOL 0mg; IRON 9.4mg; SODIUM 620mg; CALC 132mg

Moroccan-Roasted Butternut Squash

Prep: 5 minutes • Cook: 20 minutes

1 small butternut squash (about 1¾ pounds)
1 tablespoon olive oil
⅛ teaspoon ground cinnamon
⅛ teaspoon ground red pepper

¼ teaspoon ground cumin
¼ teaspoon salt
Cooking spray

1. Preheat oven to 475°.
2. Peel squash, and cut into quarters; cut quarters crosswise into thin slices. Place squash in a large bowl; drizzle with oil. Combine cinnamon and next 3 ingredients in a small bowl. Sprinkle squash with spice mixture; toss well. Place squash on a large baking sheet coated with cooking spray. Bake at 475° for 20 minutes. Yield: 3 servings (serving size: about 1 cup).

CALORIES 160; FAT 4.8g (sat 0.7g, mono 3.3g, poly 0.6g); PROTEIN 2.7g; CARB 31.1g; FIBER 5.4g; CHOL 0mg; IRON 2mg; SODIUM 205mg; CALC 130mg

We used a blend of oyster, shiitake, and baby bella mushrooms in this superb vegetarian stroganoff. Browning the mushrooms over high heat ensures that they develop rich flavor.

Mushroom Stroganoff

Prep: 2 minutes • Cook: 13 minutes

3½ cups uncooked medium egg noodles
Butter-flavored cooking spay
5 (4-ounce) packages fresh gourmet-blend mushrooms
1 cup coarsely chopped onion
3 tablespoons all-purpose flour
1½ cups 2% reduced-fat milk

3 tablespoons dry sherry
2 tablespoons light butter, melted
½ teaspoon salt
½ teaspoon freshly ground black pepper
½ cup reduced-fat sour cream
1½ tablespoons finely chopped chives (optional)

1. Cook noodles according to package directions, omitting salt and fat; drain.
2. While noodles cook, heat a large Dutch oven over high heat; generously coat pan with cooking spray. Add mushrooms and onion; cook 10 minutes or until browned, stirring frequently.
3. While mushroom mixture cooks, place flour in a bowl. Gradually add milk, stirring with a whisk until smooth. Add sherry and next 3 ingredients, stirring with a whisk. Transfer cooked mushroom mixture to a large bowl. Gradually add milk mixture to hot pan, stirring with a whisk. Cook, whisking constantly, 3 minutes or until slightly thickened.
4. Stir sauce and cooked noodles into mushroom mixture. Stir in sour cream; sprinkle with chives, if desired. Serve immediately. Yield: 4 servings (serving size: 1¾ cups).

CALORIES 393); FAT 12.6g (sat 6.5g, mono 3.6g, poly 2g); PROTEIN 15g; CARB 55.2g; FIBER 3.5g; CHOL 83mg; IRON 3.8mg; SODIUM 400mg; CALC 162mg

shortcut kitchen tip

To chop chives quickly and safely, hold the chives in a bunch, and place them on a clean cutting board. With a sharp knife, chop the chives to the desired size. To prepare the chives ahead, chop them, and place in a zip-top plastic bag; store in the refrigerator until you need them.

A robust mixture of spinach, garlic, oregano, and Parmesan cheese fills juicy mushrooms in this recipe.

Grilled Stuffed Portobello Mushrooms

Prep: 5 minutes • Cook: 10 minutes

2 (4½-inch) portobello mushroom caps
2 teaspoons olive oil, divided
1 garlic clove, minced
¾ cup minced onion (1 small)
1½ teaspoons chopped fresh oregano
½ cup bagged baby spinach leaves
¼ cup grated Parmesan cheese
⅓ cup Italian-seasoned panko (Japanese breadcrumbs)
1½ teaspoons balsamic vinegar
½ teaspoon black pepper

1. Prepare grill.
2. Remove brown gills from undersides of mushrooms using a spoon; discard gills. Set mushroom caps aside.
3. Heat 1 teaspoon oil in a large nonstick skillet over medium-high heat. Add mushroom caps, garlic, and onion; sauté 2 minutes. Add oregano and spinach; sauté 1 minute or until spinach wilts.
4. Transfer spinach mixture to a medium bowl; stir in remaining 1 teaspoon oil, cheese, panko, vinegar, and pepper. Divide filling evenly among mushrooms, spooning onto gill sides.
5. Grill 7 minutes. Yield: 2 servings (serving size: 1 mushroom cap).

CALORIES 216; FAT 8.6g (sat 2.7g, mono 4.1g, poly 1g); PROTEIN 9.6g; CARB 25.3g; FIBER 3.2g; CHOL 9mg; IRON 1mg; SODIUM 300mg; CALC 146mg

serve with
Grilled Tomato Salad

Prep: 3 minutes • Cook: 6 minutes

2 plum tomatoes, quartered
Cooking spray
¼ cup small fresh basil leaves
1 teaspoon olive oil
1 teaspoon balsamic vinegar
⅛ teaspoon salt

1. Prepare grill.
2. Place tomatoes on a grill rack coated with cooking spray. Grill 3 minutes on each side. Place tomatoes in a bowl; add basil and remaining ingredients, tossing to coat. Yield: 2 servings (serving size: 4 tomato quarters).

CALORIES 36; FAT 2.4g (sat 0.4g, mono 1.6g, poly 0.4g); PROTEIN 0.6g; CARB 3.6g; FIBER 0.8g; CHOL 0mg; IRON 0.4mg; SODIUM 152mg; CALC 12mg

It takes about 5 seconds to shred the cheese for this casserole in the food processor—just make sure the cheese is cold before placing it in the food chute.

Potato and Jalapeño Cheese Bake

Prep: 13 minutes • Cook: 1 hour and 6 minutes

Butter-flavored cooking spray
2 (8-ounce) packages prechopped bell pepper-and-onion mix
4 garlic cloves, minced
1 (18-ounce) package refrigerated sliced potatoes (such as Simply Potatoes Homestyle Slices)

½ teaspoon salt
½ teaspoon freshly ground black pepper
1 (8-ounce) package 50% reduced-fat jalapeño cheddar cheese (such as Cabot), shredded
½ cup chopped fresh cilantro

1. Preheat oven to 400°.
2. Heat a large nonstick skillet over medium-high heat; coat pan with cooking spray. Add bell pepper mix; cook 5 minutes, stirring frequently. Add garlic; cook 1 additional minute.
3. While bell pepper mixture cooks, arrange half of potato slices in bottom of an 11 x 7-inch baking dish coated with cooking spray. Combine salt and pepper. Sprinkle potato slices with half of salt mixture.
4. Layer potato mixture with half of bell pepper mixture and one-third of cheese. Repeat procedure with remaining half of potato slices, salt mixture, bell pepper mixture, and remaining two-thirds of cheese.
5. Cover and bake at 400° for 40 minutes. Uncover and bake 10 additional minutes or until cheese is lightly browned and potatoes are tender. Sprinkle with cilantro. Yield: 6 servings (serving size: ⅙ of casserole).

CALORIES 186; FAT 6.3g (sat 4.1g, mono 1g, poly 1g); PROTEIN 12.9g; CARB 20.9g; FIBER 2.8g; CHOL 20mg; IRON 0.4mg; SODIUM 643mg; CALC 288mg

serve with
Romaine and Sweet Onion Salad

Prep: 8 minutes

1 cup vertically sliced sweet onion
1½ cups grape tomatoes, halved
1½ cups English cucumber slices (about 1 small)

⅓ cup Sweet Vidalia Onion Vinaigrette (such as Ken's Healthy Options)

1. Combine onion, tomato, and cucumber in a bowl. Add dressing; toss well. Yield: 4 servings (serving size: 1 cup).

CALORIES 93; FAT 3.1g (sat 0.4g, mono 1.5g, poly 1g); PROTEIN 1.6g; CARB 15.9g; FIBER 2.3g; CHOL 0mg; IRON 0.7mg; SODIUM 88mg; CALC 45mg

fish & shellfish

Fish

Grilled Amberjack with Country-Style Dijon Cream Sauce
Blackened Catfish
Baked Bayou Catfish with Spicy Sour Cream Sauce
Confetti Flounder Packets with Orange-Tarragon Butter
Pan-Seared Grouper with Sweet Ginger Relish
Meyer Lemon and Dill Fish Parcels
Pan-Fried Halibut with Cornichon Sauce
Pistou Halibut
Teriyaki Salmon with Mushrooms
Roasted Salmon with Tomatillo–Red Onion Salsa
Snapper Piccata
Snapper with Warm Italian-Style Salsa
Panko Pan-Fried Fish Strips
Grilled Thai-Spiced Tuna Steak
Seared Herbed Tuna

Shellfish

Chile-Crusted Scallops with Mango-Papaya Salsa
Seared Scallops with Sautéed Fennel, Orange, and Red Onion
Scallops with Lemon-Basil Sauce
Pan-Fried Shrimp
Shrimp with Capers, Garlic, and Rice
White Wine–Steamed Mussels

Prepare the cream sauce ahead, if you like—just be sure to reserve the lemon juice for the fish. Pick up a whole wheat baguette from the bakery at your supermarket, and steam fresh asparagus to make this meal quick and easy.

Grilled Amberjack with Country-Style Dijon Cream Sauce

Prep: 2 minutes • Cook: 7 minutes

2 teaspoons salt-free steak grilling blend (such as Mrs. Dash)
1½ teaspoons chopped fresh tarragon
Cooking spray

4 (6-ounce) amberjack fillets (about ¾ inch thick)
1 lemon
Country-Style Dijon Cream Sauce

1. Combine steak seasoning and tarragon in a small bowl; set aside.
2. Heat a grill pan over medium-high heat. Coat pan with cooking spray. Coat fillets with cooking spray, and rub with seasoning mixture. Add fish to pan. Cook 3 to 4 minutes on each side or until fillets flake easily when tested with a fork.
3. While fish cooks, grate 1 teaspoon rind from lemon; squeeze juice to measure 1 tablespoon. Reserve lemon rind for Country-Style Dijon Cream Sauce.
4. Place 1 fillet on each of 4 serving plates. Drizzle fillets evenly with lemon juice, and top with a dollop of cream sauce. Yield: 4 servings (serving size: 1 fillet, about ¾ teaspoon lemon juice, and 3 tablespoons cream sauce).

CALORIES 256; FAT 8g (sat 0.8g, mono 4g, poly 3g); PROTEIN 37.2g; CARB 6.3g; FIBER 0.6g; CHOL 83mg; IRON 0.1mg; SODIUM 473mg; CALC 39mg

Country-Style Dijon Cream Sauce

Prep: 4 minutes

¼ cup light mayonnaise
¼ cup fat-free sour cream
3 tablespoons water
1½ tablespoons country-style Dijon mustard

1½ teaspoons chopped fresh tarragon
1 teaspoon grated lemon rind
¼ teaspoon salt

1. Combine all ingredients in a small bowl. Yield: 4 servings (serving size: 3 tablespoons).

CALORIES 71; FAT 4.9g (sat 0.8g, mono 1g, poly 2.5g); PROTEIN 1.1g; CARB 5g; FIBER 0.1g; CHOL 8mg; IRON 0.1mg; SODIUM 413mg; CALC 33mg

A combination of a few pantry spices lends authentic Cajun flavor to catfish. The Sautéed Corn and Cherry Tomatoes are delicious served alone as a side dish or as a relish spooned over the catfish.

Blackened Catfish

Prep: 3 minutes • Cook: 9 minutes

1 tablespoon fresh thyme leaves, minced
1 teaspoon onion powder
1 teaspoon garlic powder
1 teaspoon paprika
1 teaspoon black pepper

½ teaspoon ground red pepper
¼ teaspoon salt
3 teaspoons olive oil, divided
4 (6-ounce) catfish fillets

1. Combine first 7 ingredients in a small bowl.
2. Heat a large nonstick skillet over medium-high heat. Add 2 teaspoons oil to pan. Brush fillets with remaining olive oil. Rub fillets with spice mixture, and add to pan; cook 3 minutes on each side or until fillets flake easily when tested with a fork. Yield: 4 servings (serving size: 1 fillet).

CALORIES 200; FAT 8.3g (sat 1.7g, mono 3.9g, poly 1.9g); PROTEIN 28.2g; CARB 1.9g; FIBER 0.5g; CHOL 99mg; IRON 0.9mg; SODIUM 220mg; CALC 37mg

serve with
Sautéed Corn and Cherry Tomatoes

Prep: 4 minutes • Cook: 6 minutes

2 teaspoons olive oil
1 garlic clove, minced
2 cups fresh corn kernels (about 3 ears)
1 cup cherry tomatoes, quartered (about 10)
3 tablespoons chopped green onions (about 2 large)

1 tablespoon sherry vinegar
2 teaspoons minced fresh thyme
½ teaspoon freshly ground black pepper
¼ teaspoon salt

1. Heat oil in a large nonstick skillet over medium heat. Add garlic to pan; sauté 1 minute. Add corn and tomatoes; cook 3 minutes or until vegetables are tender, stirring often. Remove from heat; stir in onions and remaining ingredients. Serve with Blackened Catfish. Yield: 4 servings (serving size: about ½ cup).

CALORIES 89; FAT 3.2g (sat 0.5g, mono 1.9g, poly 0.7g); PROTEIN 2.6g; CARB 15g; FIBER 2.4g; CHOL 0mg; IRON 0.7mg; SODIUM 158mg; CALC 12mg

Baked Bayou Catfish with Spicy Sour Cream Sauce

Prep: 5 minutes • Cook: 14 minutes

Cooking spray
2½ tablespoons hot sauce, divided
4 (6-ounce) catfish fillets
1 teaspoon Cajun seasoning (such as Luzianne)
½ cup yellow cornmeal
½ cup light sour cream
⅛ teaspoon salt
1 lemon, cut into wedges (optional)
Chopped fresh parsley (optional)

1. Preheat oven to 400°.
2. Line a large baking sheet with foil; coat foil with cooking spray.
3. Brush 1½ tablespoons hot sauce evenly on both sides of fillets; sprinkle with Cajun seasoning, and dredge in cornmeal, pressing gently. Place fillets on prepared pan. Coat fillets with cooking spray. Bake at 400° for 14 minutes or until fillets flake easily when tested with a fork.
4. While fillets bake, combine remaining 1 tablespoon hot sauce, sour cream, and salt in a small bowl, stirring with a whisk. Serve fillets with sauce and lemon wedges, if desired. Sprinkle with parsley, if desired. Yield: 4 servings (serving size: 1 fillet and 2 tablespoons sauce).

CALORIES 322; FAT 15.7g (sat 4.6g, mono 6.2g, poly 4.9g); PROTEIN 28.7g; CARB 15.7g; FIBER 1.3g; CHOL 90mg; IRON 2.1mg; SODIUM 524mg; CALC 77mg

serve with
Sweet-and-Sour Broccoli Slaw

Prep: 4 minutes

1 tablespoon sugar
2 tablespoons cider vinegar
1 tablespoon canola oil
¼ teaspoon poppy seeds
⅛ teaspoon salt
⅛ teaspoon freshly ground black pepper
Dash of ground red pepper
2½ cups packaged broccoli coleslaw

1. Combine first 7 ingredients in a medium bowl, stirring with a whisk. Add coleslaw; toss well. Serve immediately. Yield: 4 servings (serving size: about ⅔ cup).

CALORIES 62; FAT 3.6g (sat 0.3g, mono 2.1g, poly 1.1g); PROTEIN 1.3g; CARB 5.7g; FIBER 1.3g; CHOL 0mg; IRON 0.4mg; SODIUM 88mg; CALC 13.5mg

For a crisp texture similar to fried fish, coat the fillets with cornmeal and bake them at a high temperature. Try squeezing a lemon wedge over the fillets to enhance the flavor.

Cooking the fish in parchment paper infuses the fish with flavor. Serve with precooked rice tossed with orange rind and chopped fresh tarragon.

Confetti Flounder Packets with Orange-Tarragon Butter

Prep: 6 minutes • Cook: 12 minutes • Other: 5 minutes

8 fresh snow peas, trimmed	¼ teaspoon salt
1 cup matchstick-cut carrots	¼ teaspoon black pepper
½ cup diced yellow bell pepper	Orange-Tarragon Butter
2 tablespoons water	Orange wedges (optional)
4 (6-ounce) flounder fillets (¼ inch thick)	

1. Preheat oven to 400°.
2. Cut snow peas lengthwise into strips and in half crosswise. Place snow pea strips, carrots, bell pepper, and water in a microwave-safe bowl. Cover with plastic wrap; vent. Microwave at HIGH 2 minutes.
3. Sprinkle fillets with salt and pepper. Cut 4 (15 x 12-inch) squares of parchment paper. Fold each square in half. Open folded parchment paper; place 1 fillet near fold on each square. Top each fillet with one-fourth of carrot mixture; crumble or spread 1 tablespoon Orange-Tarragon Butter over carrot mixture. Fold paper; seal edges with narrow folds. Place packets on a large baking sheet.
4. Bake at 400° for 10 minutes. Let stand 5 minutes. Place 1 packet on each of 4 plates; cut open, and serve immediately. Garnish with orange wedges, if desired. Yield: 4 servings (serving size: 1 packet).

CALORIES 291; FAT 13.5g (sat 7.7g, mono 3.4g, poly 2g); PROTEIN 33.7g; CARB 5.8g; FIBER 1.8g; CHOL 112mg; IRON 1.5mg; SODIUM 442mg; CALC 72mg

Orange-Tarragon Butter

Prep: 3 minutes

¼ cup butter, softened	⅛ teaspoon salt
1 tablespoon finely chopped fresh tarragon	⅛ teaspoon ground red pepper
1½ teaspoons grated orange rind	

1. Combine all ingredients in a bowl. Stir with a spoon until blended. Cover and chill until ready to serve. Yield: 4 servings (serving size: 1 tablespoon).

CALORIES 105; FAT 11.5g (sat 7.2g, mono 3g, poly 0.5g); PROTEIN 0.4g; CARB 0.9g; FIBER 0.2g; CHOL 30mg; IRON 0.4mg; SODIUM 154mg; CALC 18mg

Ginger and red bell pepper add a burst of spicy, fresh flavor to this Asian-inspired dish. Make a quick side by heating precooked jasmine rice in the microwave and tossing it with fresh chopped mint.

Pan-Seared Grouper with Sweet Ginger Relish

Prep: 2 minutes • Cook: 13 minutes

1 tablespoon reduced-sodium soy sauce
1 tablespoon chili oil
¼ teaspoon freshly ground black pepper
2 garlic cloves, pressed

4 (6-ounce) grouper fillets
   (about 1 inch thick)
Cooking spray
Sweet Ginger Relish

1. Combine first 4 ingredients; brush mixture over fillets.
2. Heat a large nonstick skillet over medium-high heat. Coat pan with cooking spray. Add fillets; cook 6 to 7 minutes on each side or until fillets flake easily when tested with a fork. Serve with Sweet Ginger Relish. Yield: 4 servings (serving size: 1 fillet and ¼ cup Sweet Ginger Relish).

CALORIES 211; FAT 5.4g (sat 0.9g, mono 1.1g, poly 2.9g); PROTEIN 33.8g; CARB 5.5g; FIBER 0.8g; CHOL 63mg; IRON 2mg; SODIUM 225mg; CALC 60mg

Sweet Ginger Relish

Prep: 10 minutes

½ cup finely chopped red bell pepper
¼ cup chopped fresh mint
¼ cup finely chopped red onion

1 tablespoon grated peeled fresh ginger
1 tablespoon fresh lime juice
1 teaspoon sugar

1. Combine all ingredients in a small bowl. Toss gently. Yield: 4 servings (serving size: ¼ cup).

CALORIES 19; FAT 0.2g (sat 0g, mono 0g, poly 0.1g); PROTEIN 0.5g; CARB 4.5g; FIBER 0.7g; CHOL 0mg; IRON 0.4mg; SODIUM 2mg; CALC 11mg

Orange-yellow Meyer lemons are a hybrid of the mandarin orange and lemon, which gives them a sweeter flavor than their run-of-the-mill counterparts. If you have difficulty finding them, you can use regular lemons, such as Eurekas, instead.

Meyer Lemon and Dill Fish Parcels

Prep: 4 minutes • Cook: 15 minutes

4 (6-ounce) halibut fillets (¾ inch thick)
½ teaspoon salt
½ teaspoon freshly ground black pepper

8 (¼-inch-thick) Meyer lemon slices (2 lemons)
1 tablespoon butter, quartered
4 teaspoons chopped fresh dill

1. Preheat oven to 375°.
2. Cut 4 (15-inch) squares of parchment paper. Fold each square in half. Open folded parchment paper; place 1 fillet near fold on each square. Sprinkle fillets evenly with salt and pepper. Top evenly with lemon slices, butter quarters, and dill. Fold paper; seal edges with narrow folds. Place packets on a large baking sheet.
3. Bake at 375° for 15 minutes or until paper is puffy and lightly browned. Place 1 packet on each of 4 serving plates, and cut open. Serve immediately. Yield: 4 servings (serving size: 1 packet).

CALORIES 221; FAT 6.7g (sat 2.4g, mono 2g, poly 1.4g); PROTEIN 35.5g; CARB 2.7g; FIBER 1.1g; CHOL 62mg; IRON 1.5mg; SODIUM 403mg; CALC 92mg

serve with
Sweet Potato Salad

Prep: 7 minutes • Cook: 6 minutes • Other: 30 minutes

3 medium sweet potatoes (1½ pounds)
2 tablespoons chopped green onions
2 tablespoons fresh lime juice

1 tablespoon olive oil
¼ teaspoon salt
¼ teaspoon black pepper

1. Scrub potatoes; place in a single layer in a microwave-safe casserole dish (do not pierce potatoes with a fork). Cover bowl with plastic wrap (do not allow plastic wrap to touch food); vent. Microwave at HIGH 6 minutes or until tender. Let stand 30 minutes or until cool to the touch.
2. Peel potatoes, and cut into 1-inch cubes. Place in a medium bowl. Sprinkle with onions and remaining ingredients; toss gently. Yield: 4 servings (serving size: ¾ cup).

CALORIES 164; FAT 3.4g (sat 0.5g, mono 2.5g, poly 0.4g); PROTEIN 2.7g; CARB 31.1g; FIBER 5.4g; CHOL 0mg; IRON 1.1mg; SODIUM 238mg; CALC 30mg

Cornichon Sauce is an easy variation on classic tartar sauce and is also delicious on crab cakes and fish sandwiches. Cornichons are sour pickles that are made from tiny gherkin cucumbers. You can find them next to the pickles at your supermarket.

Pan-Fried Halibut with Cornichon Sauce

Prep: 5 minutes • Cook: 6 minutes

4 (6-ounce) skinless halibut fillets
    (about ½ inch thick)
¼ teaspoon salt
½ cup all-purpose flour
2 teaspoons dried thyme

1 teaspoon grated lemon rind
½ teaspoon black pepper
Olive oil-flavored cooking spray
Cornichon Sauce

1. Rinse fillets; pat dry, and sprinkle with salt. Combine flour and next 3 ingredients in a shallow bowl. Dredge fillets in flour mixture, shaking off excess flour.
2. Heat a large nonstick skillet over medium heat. Coat pan with cooking spray. Add fillets; cook 3 minutes on each side or until fillets are golden brown. Serve with Cornichon Sauce. Yield: 4 servings (serving size: 1 fillet and 3 tablespoons sauce).

CALORIES 321; FAT 14.6g (sat 2.8g, mono 6g, poly 5.3g); PROTEIN 37.5g; CARB 8.5g; FIBER 1.2g; CHOL 64mg; IRON 2.6mg; SODIUM 737mg; CALC 124mg

Cornichon Sauce

Prep: 6 minutes

½ cup light mayonnaise
¼ cup finely chopped cornichon pickles
    (such as Maille; about 6 pickles)
1 tablespoon thinly sliced green onions
    (about 1 small)

2 teaspoons drained capers
2 teaspoons fresh lemon juice
1 teaspoon country-style Dijon mustard
⅛ teaspoon salt
Dash of freshly ground black pepper

1. Combine all ingredients in a small bowl. Yield: 4 servings (serving size: 3 tablespoons).

CALORIES 105; FAT 10.1g (sat 2g, mono 4g, poly 4g); PROTEIN 0.2g; CARB 3g; FIBER 0.2g; CHOL 10mg; IRON 0.1mg; SODIUM 496mg; CALC 4mg

Like Italian pesto, French *pistou* (pee-TOO), is made of basil, garlic, and olive oil. Here we use pistou to season fish, but it is also delicious when tossed with potatoes and pasta, so make an extra batch or two to freeze or keep on hand to use later in the week.

Pistou Halibut

Prep: 4 minutes • Cook: 6 minutes

⅓ cup minced fresh basil
1 tablespoon olive oil
½ teaspoon salt
¼ teaspoon freshly ground black pepper
2 garlic cloves, minced

4 (6-ounce) skinless halibut fillets (1 inch thick)
Cooking spray
4 lemon wedges

1. Combine first 5 ingredients in a small bowl; rub over both sides of fillets.
2. Heat a large nonstick skillet over medium heat. Coat pan with cooking spray. Add fillets; cook 2 to 3 minutes on each side or until fillets flake easily when tested with a fork. Serve with lemon wedges. Yield: 4 servings (serving size: 1 fillet and 1 lemon wedge).

CALORIES 223; FAT 7.3g (sat 1g, mono 3.7g, poly 1.6g); PROTEIN 35.7g; CARB 1.4g; FIBER 0.4g; CHOL 54mg; IRON 1.6mg; SODIUM 383mg; CALC 91mg

serve with
Sautéed Garlicky Spinach

Prep: 2 minutes • Cook: 3 minutes

1 tablespoon olive oil
3 garlic cloves, thinly sliced
2 (6-ounce) packages baby spinach

¼ teaspoon salt
¼ teaspoon freshly ground black pepper

1. Heat oil in a large deep skillet or Dutch oven over medium heat. Add garlic; cook 1 minute or until golden. Add half of spinach; cook, 1 minute, turning with tongs. Add remaining half of spinach, cook 1 minute, turning with tongs, until spinach wilts. Stir in salt and pepper. Yield: 4 servings (serving size: ½ cup).

CALORIES 54; FAT 3.4g (sat 0.5g, mono 2.5g, poly 0.4g); PROTEIN 2.2g; CARB 3.8g; FIBER 2.1g; CHOL 0mg; IRON 2.8mg; SODIUM 211mg; CALC 85mg

Get a healthy dose of omega-3 fatty acids, the fatty acids that lower the risk of heart disease, from this pan-seared salmon served with a rich mushroom sauce. You can substitute chicken broth for the sherry, if you prefer.

Teriyaki Salmon with Mushrooms

Prep: 3 minutes • Cook: 15 minutes

¼ cup dry sherry
¼ cup low-sodium teriyaki sauce
2 tablespoons light brown sugar
1 teaspoon canola oil

1 (8-ounce) package presliced baby portobello mushrooms
4 (6-ounce) skinless salmon fillets (about 1 to 1½ inches thick)

1. Combine first 3 ingredients in a small bowl; stir to dissolve sugar.
2. Heat oil in a large nonstick skillet over medium-high heat; add mushrooms, and sauté 4 minutes or until tender. Add ⅓ cup sherry mixture to mushrooms. Reduce heat, and simmer 1 to 2 minutes or until liquid almost evaporates. Spoon mushroom mixture into a bowl; set aside.
3. Heat pan over medium-high heat; add fillets. Cook 3 to 4 minutes on each side or until browned on all sides. Add mushrooms and remaining sherry mixture to pan; cook 2 minutes. Transfer fillets to a serving platter, and top with sauce and mushrooms. Yield: 4 servings (serving size: 1 fillet and 2 tablespoons mushroom mixture).

CALORIES 335; FAT 14.3g (sat 3.2g; mono 5g; poly 5g); PROTEIN 37.6g; CARB 9.5g; FIBER 0.9g; CHOL 87mg; IRON 1.2mg; SODIUM 346mg; CALC 32mg

serve with

Orange-Ginger Sugar Snaps

Prep: 4 minutes • Cook: 5 minutes

1 teaspoon dark sesame oil
2 green onions, sliced
½ teaspoon grated peeled fresh ginger
1 (8-ounce) package sugar snap peas

1 teaspoon grated orange rind
¼ teaspoon salt

1. Heat oil in a nonstick skillet over medium heat; add onions and ginger. Sauté 2 minutes; add sugar snap peas, and sauté 2 minutes or just until crisp-tender. Remove from heat; stir in orange rind and salt. Yield: 4 servings (serving size: ½ cup).

CALORIES 40; FAT 1.2g (sat 0.2g; mono 0.5; poly 0.5); PROTEIN 1.5g; CARB 5.4g; FIBER 1.6g; CHOL 0mg; IRON 0.8mg; SODIUM 153mg; CALC 46mg

Roasted Salmon with Tomatillo–Red Onion Salsa

Prep: 3 minutes • Cook: 20 minutes

Cooking spray
4 (6-ounce) salmon fillets (1 inch thick)
2 teaspoons ground cumin
1½ teaspoons smoked paprika

1½ teaspoons coarsely ground black pepper
¼ teaspoon salt
Tomatillo-Red Onion Salsa
1 lemon, cut into 4 wedges

1. Preheat oven 350°.
2. Line a baking sheet with foil; coat foil with cooking spray. Arrange fillets on prepared pan.
3. Combine cumin and next 3 ingredients. Rub spice mixture over tops of fillets. Coat fillets with cooking spray.
4. Bake at 350° for 20 minutes or until desired degree of doneness. Place 1 fillet on each of 4 individual plates. Spoon Tomatillo–Red Onion Salsa evenly over fillets. Serve with lemon wedges. Yield: 4 servings (serving size: 1 fillet, ¼ cup salsa, and 1 lemon wedge).

CALORIES 257; FAT 10g (sat 1.5g, mono 4.3g, poly 1.8g); PROTEIN 34.7g; CARB 6g; FIBER 2.1g; CHOL 88mg; IRON 2.1mg; SODIUM 408mg; CALC 46mg

Tomatillo–Red Onion Salsa

Prep: 6 minutes

⅔ cup chopped tomatillos (3 medium)
⅓ cup finely chopped red onion
2 teaspoons grated lemon rind

2 tablespoons fresh lemon juice
1 tablespoon extra-virgin olive oil
¼ teaspoon salt

1. Combine all ingredients in a small bowl. Yield: 4 servings (serving size: ¼ cup).

CALORIES 46; FAT 3.7g (sat 0.5g, mono 2.7g, poly 0.4g); PROTEIN 0.4g; CARB 3.4g; FIBER 0.8g; CHOL 0mg; IRON 0.2mg; SODIUM 146mg; CALC 7mg

flavorful combinations

This Latin-inspired salsa, which is primarily made of chopped red onion, chopped tomatillos, lemon juice, and extra-virgin olive oil, takes little time and effort to prepare. It's tasty and versatile enough to serve over grilled chicken and steak or with tacos and fajitas. For a tropical variation, try substituting chopped pineapple for the tomatillo.

Although they look like small green tomatoes, tomatillos, also known as husk tomatoes, are actually related to gooseberries. In this recipe, their tart-yet-subtle apple and lemon-like flavors cut the richness of the salmon. Remove the papery skin from the tomatillos, wash them well, and pat them dry before chopping them. Round out your meal with fresh corn on the cob.

The wine and lemon juice are used to deglaze the skillet, capturing the flavorful browned bits that remain after the fish is cooked. You can substitute fat-free, less-sodium chicken broth for the wine, if desired. Cook the pasta while you prepare the fish so that both dishes will be ready at the same time.

Snapper Piccata

Prep: 5 minutes • Cook: 9 minutes

1 tablespoon olive oil	½ cup dry white wine
4 (6-ounce) snapper fillets (about ¾ inch thick)	2 tablespoons fresh lemon juice
¼ teaspoon salt	2 tablespoons capers
¼ teaspoon freshly ground black pepper	2 tablespoons chopped fresh parsley

1. Heat oil in a large nonstick skillet over medium-high heat. Sprinkle fillets evenly with salt and pepper. Add fillets to pan, and cook 3 to 4 minutes on each side or until fillets flake easily when tested with a fork. Remove fillets from pan; keep warm.

2. Add wine and juice to pan; bring to a boil. Reduce heat, and simmer 2 minutes or until slightly thick, scraping pan to loosen browned bits. Stir in capers and parsley. Spoon sauce evenly over fillets. Yield: 4 servings (serving size: 1 fillet and about 1½ tablespoons sauce).

CALORIES 205; FAT 5.8g (sat 1g; mono 3.6; poly 1); PROTEIN 35.4g; CARB 1.4g; FIBER 0.1g; CHOL 63mg; IRON 0.6mg; SODIUM 416mg; CALC 63mg

serve with
Parsley-Buttered Pasta

Prep: 3 minutes • Cook: 10 minutes

4 ounces angel hair pasta	2 teaspoons chopped fresh parsley
1 (8-ounce) slice light whole wheat bread	¼ teaspoon salt
1 tablespoon light stick butter	⅛ teaspoon freshly ground black pepper

1. Cook pasta according to package directions, omitting salt and fat.

2. While pasta cooks, place bread in a food processor; pulse 10 times or until coarse crumbs measure ½ cup. Combine cooked pasta, breadcrumbs, butter, parsley, salt, and pepper; toss gently. Serve immediately. Yield: 4 servings (serving size: ½ cup).

CALORIES 125; FAT 2.3g (sat 1g; mono 0.8; poly 0.5); PROTEIN 4.4g; CARB 23.3g; FIBER 1.6g; CHOL 4mg; IRON 1.2mg; SODIUM 196mg; CALC 17mg

Three words describe this dependable weeknight dish: quick, easy, and delicious. This tangy salsa complements the sweet, mild flavor of the red snapper. If red snapper is unavailable, use halibut or sea bass. Serve the fish over a bed of rice tossed with garlic, green onions, and, if desired, fresh herbs.

Snapper with Warm Italian-Style Salsa

Prep: 2 minutes • Cook: 11 minutes

Warm Italian-Style Salsa
1½ teaspoons extra-virgin olive oil
4 (6-ounce) snapper fillets
¼ teaspoon black pepper

Cooking spray
2 tablespoons crumbled reduced-fat feta cheese

1. Prepare Warm Italian-Style Salsa. Cover and keep warm.
2. Heat oil in a large nonstick skillet over medium-high heat. Sprinkle fillets with pepper; coat with cooking spray. Add fillets to pan. Cook 5 minutes on each side or until fillets flake easily when tested with a fork.
3. Place 1 fillet on each of 4 serving plates; top evenly with Warm Italian-Style Salsa. Sprinkle evenly with cheese. Yield: 4 servings (serving size: 1 fillet, ¼ cup salsa, and 1½ teaspoons cheese).

CALORIES 240; FAT 8.2g (sat 1.6g, mono 4.4g, poly 1.4g); PROTEIN 36.4g; CARB 3.2g; FIBER 1g; CHOL 64mg; IRON 0.4mg; SODIUM 392mg; CALC 86mg

Warm Italian-Style Salsa

Prep: 5 minutes • Cook: 3 minutes

1 tablespoon extra-virgin olive oil
1½ cups grape tomatoes, halved
2 tablespoons fresh oregano leaves
2 tablespoons drained capers

1 medium garlic clove, minced
¼ teaspoon crushed red pepper (optional)
2 tablespoons water
¼ teaspoon salt

1. Heat a large nonstick skillet over medium-high heat; add oil. Add tomatoes, next 3 ingredients, and red pepper, if desired. Sauté 1 to 2 minutes or until tomato begins to soften. Stir in water and salt. Yield: 4 servings (serving size: ¼ cup).

CALORIES 46; FAT 3.6g (sat 0.5g, mono 2.7g, poly 0.3g); PROTEIN 0.6g; CARB 3g; FIBER 0.9g; CHOL 0mg; IRON 0.1mg; SODIUM 225mg; CALC 22mg

flavorful combinations

For a quick and tasty side dish, stir 2 tablespoons chopped green onions; 1½ teaspoons extra-virgin olive oil; 1 garlic clove, minced; ¼ teaspoon dried rosemary leaves; and ¼ teaspoon salt into 1½ cups cooked rice. Fluff with a fork until blended.

The delightful crunchy crust in this family-friendly dish comes from panko, Japanese breadcrumbs. Reminiscent of fried fish fingers, this recipe will please even the pickiest of eaters.

Panko Pan-Fried Fish Strips

Prep: 8 minutes • Cook: 12 minutes

½ teaspoon garlic powder
½ teaspoon salt
¼ teaspoon black pepper
4 (6-ounce) tilapia fillets, cut in half lengthwise

¾ cup low-fat buttermilk
1½ cups panko (Japanese breadcrumbs)
1½ tablespoons olive oil, divided

1. Combine first 3 ingredients; sprinkle evenly over fish.
2. Place buttermilk in a shallow dish. Place panko in another shallow dish. Working with 1 piece of fish at a time, dip fish into buttermilk, and dredge in panko.
3. Heat a large nonstick skillet over medium-high heat. Add half of oil to pan; add half of fish. Reduce heat to medium; cook 4 minutes on each side or until fish flakes easily when tested with a fork. Repeat procedure with remaining oil and fish. Yield: 4 servings (serving size: 2 fish strips).

CALORIES 311; FAT 9.1g (sat 1.9g, mono 4.6g, poly 2.2g); PROTEIN 38.8g; CARB 17.5g; FIBER 0.8g; CHOL 87mg; IRON 1mg; SODIUM 491mg; CALC 71mg

serve with
Dijon Green Beans

Prep: 2 minutes • Cook: 5 minutes

1 (12-ounce) package trimmed fresh green beans
1 tablespoon light butter, melted
2 teaspoons Dijon mustard

1 tablespoon finely chopped fresh parsley
½ teaspoon grated lemon rind
¼ teaspoon salt

1. Microwave beans according to package directions.
2. While beans cook, combine butter and remaining ingredients in a small bowl. Place beans in a serving bowl. Add butter mixture; toss well. Serve immediately. Yield: 4 servings (serving size: ¾ cup).

CALORIES 36; FAT 1.5g (sat 0.9g, mono 0g, poly 0g); PROTEIN 1.1g; CARB 6g; FIBER 3.1g; CHOL 4mg; IRON 0.4mg; SODIUM 230mg; CALC 43mg

Red curry paste gives this tuna dish spiciness and depth of flavor. The sweetness from the vibrantly colored accompanying salad balances the heat and adds a burst of fresh flavor to the meal. Use less curry paste, if you prefer.

Grilled Thai-Spiced Tuna Steak

Prep: 3 minutes • Cook: 4 minutes

4 (6-ounce) sushi-grade tuna steaks (1 inch thick)
½ teaspoon salt
1 tablespoon olive oil

1 tablespoon red curry paste (such as Thai Kitchen)
Cooking spray
4 lime wedges

1. Prepare grill.
2. Sprinkle fish with salt. Combine olive oil and curry paste; brush over fish.
3. Place fish on a grill rack coated with cooking spray. Grill 2 minutes on each side or until desired degree of doneness. Serve with lime wedges. Yield: 4 servings (serving size: 1 tuna steak and 1 lime wedge).

CALORIES 224; FAT 3.4g (sat 0.5g, mono 2.5g, poly 0.4g); PROTEIN 42.1g; CARB 2.3g; FIBER 0.5g; CHOL 78mg; IRON 1.1mg; SODIUM 436mg; CALC 361mg

serve with
Edamame and Roasted Red Pepper Salad

Prep: 8 minutes

1 cup chopped bottled roasted red bell peppers
¼ cup chopped fresh cilantro
2 tablespoons sesame ginger dressing (such as Newman's Own)

1 tablespoon minced peeled fresh ginger
1 (10-ounce) package refrigerated ready-to-eat shelled edamame (such as Marjon)

1. Combine all ingredients in a medium bowl, toss to coat. Yield: 4 servings (serving size: about ⅔ cup).

CALORIES 123; FAT 3.7g (sat 0.1g, mono 2.4g, poly 1.2g) ; PROTEIN 8.4g; CARB 13.1g; FIBER 4.2g; CHOL 0mg; IRON 2mg; SODIUM 333mg; CALC 54mg

In this recipe, meaty tuna cooks up in no time. The side salad capitalizes on filling ingredients such as potatoes and green beans.

Seared Herbed Tuna

Prep: 5 minutes • Cook: 4 minutes

2 teaspoons herbs de Provence
¼ teaspoon salt
¼ teaspoon freshly ground black pepper
4 (6-ounce) sushi-grade tuna steaks
(about ½ inch thick)

1 teaspoon olive oil
4 lemon wedges

1. Combine first 3 ingredients in a small bowl. Brush fish with oil; sprinkle with herb mixture.
2. Heat a large nonstick skillet over medium heat. Add fish; cook 2 minutes on each side or until desired degree of doneness. Garnish with lemon wedges. Yield: 4 servings (serving size: 1 tuna steak and 1 lemon wedge).

CALORIES 196; FAT 2.8g (sat 0.6g, mono 1.1g, poly 0.9g); PROTEIN 40g; CARB 0.7g; FIBER 0.2g; CHOL 77mg; IRON 1mg; SODIUM 368mg; CALC 30mg

serve with
Niçoise Salad

Prep: 15 minutes

4 small red potatoes (about 8 ounces), halved
8 ounces fresh green beans
1 (5-ounce) package gourmet salad greens
⅓ cup pitted kalamata olive halves (about 12 olives)

½ cup light balsamic salad dressing (such as Newman's Own)
2 precooked peeled eggs (such as Eggland's Best), quartered
Freshly ground black pepper (optional)

1. Place potato halves in a single layer in a microwave-safe casserole dish. Cover bowl with plastic wrap (do not allow plastic wrap to touch food); vent. Microwave at HIGH 2 minutes or until tender.
2. While potatoes cook, trim green beans. Add beans to potatoes. Re-cover and microwave at HIGH 2 minutes or until vegetables are tender; drain. Rinse with cold water until cool; drain.
3. While vegetables cook, combine salad greens, olives, and salad dressing; toss well. Place about 1½ cups greens mixture on each of 4 plates. Place 2 potato halves, ¾ cup green beans, and 2 egg quarters on each plate. Sprinkle with pepper, if desired. Yield: 4 servings (serving size: 1 salad).

CALORIES 172; FAT 9g (sat 1.4g, mono 4.3g, poly 3.3g); PROTEIN 5.8g; CARB 17.8g; FIBER 2.4g; CHOL 106mg; IRON 1.8mg; SODIUM 736mg; CALC 59mg

Mango-Papaya Salsa tames the heat of the chipotle chile powder on these scallops. Serve over jasmine or basmati rice flavored with fresh chopped green onions.

Chile-Crusted Scallops with Mango-Papaya Salsa

Prep: 2 minutes • Cook: 6 minutes

1½ pounds large sea scallops
1 teaspoon chipotle chile powder
  (such as McCormick)
½ teaspoon salt

2 teaspoons olive oil
Mango-Papaya Salsa
4 lime wedges

1. Pat scallops dry with paper towels. Sprinkle scallops with chile powder and salt.
2. Heat oil in a large nonstick skillet. Add scallops; cook 3 to 4 minutes on each side or until done. Serve with Mango-Papaya Salsa and lime wedges. Yield: 4 servings (serving size: about 5 ounces scallops, ¼ cup salsa, and 1 lime wedge).

CALORIES 212; FAT 4.8g (sat 0.6g, mono 2.6g, poly 0.8g); PROTEIN 29g; CARB 12.8g; FIBER 1.3g; CHOL 56mg; IRON 0.7mg; SODIUM 732mg; CALC 51mg

Mango-Papaya Salsa

Prep: 6 minutes

½ cup coarsely chopped peeled papaya
½ cup coarsely chopped ripe mango
2 tablespoons fresh lime juice
1 tablespoon minced shallot (about 1 small)

1 tablespoon chopped fresh cilantro
1 teaspoon olive oil
¼ teaspoon salt

1. Combine all ingredients in a bowl. Yield: 4 servings (serving size: ¼ cup).

CALORIES 34; FAT 1.2g (sat 0.2g, mono 0.9g, poly 0.1g); PROTEIN 0.3g; CARB 6.3g; FIBER 0.7g; CHOL 0mg; IRON 0.1mg; SODIUM 147mg; CALC 9mg

choice ingredient

Large sea scallops are great for a fast and filling protein source any night of the week. They can be seared or sautéed and then added to salads and pastas or served solo as an entrée. Their mild taste and universal appeal make them a good host for complex flavors.

The secret to getting a beautiful brown sear is to pat the scallops dry, sear them in a hot skillet, and move them only to turn them over.

Seared Scallops with Sautéed Fennel, Orange, and Red Onion

Prep: 6 minutes • Cook: 9 minutes

1½ pounds large sea scallops
½ teaspoon salt, divided
¼ teaspoon black pepper, divided
1 tablespoon extra-virgin olive oil, divided
⅓ cup orange juice
1 tablespoon butter

3 cups thinly sliced fennel bulb
1 cup vertically sliced red onion
¼ cup fennel fronds
1 cup peeled, halved orange slices (1 large orange)

1. Pat scallops dry with paper towels. Sprinkle scallops with ¼ teaspoon salt and ⅛ teaspoon pepper. Heat 1½ teaspoons oil in a large nonstick skillet over medium-high heat. Add scallops; cook 3 minutes on each side. Remove scallops from pan; keep warm. Add orange juice to pan; cook 2 minutes. Add butter, stirring to melt.
2. Heat remaining 1½ teaspoons oil in a large nonstick skillet over medium-high heat. Add fennel slices and onion; sauté 3 minutes. Stir in fennel fronds, remaining ¼ teaspoon salt, remaining ⅛ teaspoon pepper, and orange slices. Serve immediately. Yield: 4 servings (serving size: 5 ounces scallops and ⅓ cup sauce).

CALORIES 277; FAT 14g (sat 3.3g, mono 8.4g, poly 1.3g); PROTEIN 13.5g; CARB 25.7g; FIBER 4.6g; CHOL 27mg; IRON 1.5mg; SODIUM 659mg; CALC 88mg

serve with
Whole Wheat Bread with Caper-Mint Dipping Sauce

Prep: 4 minutes • Cook: 5 minutes

2 tablespoons chopped fresh mint
2 tablespoons rinsed capers, chopped
2 tablespoons fresh lemon juice

2 tablespoons extra-virgin olive oil
16 (0.2-ounce) diagonally-cut whole wheat baguette slices, toasted

1. Combine first 4 ingredients in a small bowl. Serve with toasts. Yield: 4 servings (serving size: about 1 tablespoon sauce and 4 slices).

CALORIES 182; FAT 7.5g (sat 1g, mono 5.4g, poly 0.7g); PROTEIN 4.3g; CARB 23.3g; FIBER 1.1g; CHOL 0mg; IRON 1.3mg; SODIUM 384mg; CALC 4.2mg

Look for dry-packed sea scallops at your local seafood market. They haven't been soaked in a liquid solution, which increases their weight and sodium content.

Scallops with Lemon-Basil Sauce
Prep: 3 minutes • Cook: 12 minutes

1 large lemon	1 tablespoon butter, divided
1½ pounds large sea scallops	¾ cup dry white wine
¼ teaspoon salt, divided	1 tablespoon water
¼ teaspoon freshly ground black pepper, divided	½ teaspoon cornstarch
	1 tablespoon finely chopped fresh basil

1. Finely grate lemon rind, reserving ¼ teaspoon. Squeeze lemon, reserving 2 tablespoons juice. Pat scallops dry with paper towels.
2. Sprinkle scallops with ⅛ teaspoon each salt and pepper. Melt 2 teaspoons butter in a large nonstick skillet over medium heat. Add scallops; cook 3 to 4 minutes on each side or until done. Remove scallops from pan; keep warm.
3. Add wine and reserved lemon juice to pan, and bring to a boil. Reduce heat, and simmer 2 minutes, stirring to loosen browned bits from bottom of pan. Combine water and cornstarch; add to pan. Cook, stirring constantly, 2 minutes or until sauce begins to thicken. Add reserved lemon rind, remaining 1 teaspoon butter, remaining ⅛ teaspoon each salt and pepper, and basil. Remove from heat. Serve over scallops. Yield: 4 servings (serving size: 5 ounces scallops and about 1 tablespoon sauce).

CALORIES 185; FAT 4.1g (sat 1.9g; mono 1; poly 0.9g); PROTEIN 28.9g; CARB 7g; FIBER 0.7g; CHOL 64mg; IRON 0.8mg; SODIUM 447mg; CALC 51mg

serve with
Buttery Angel Hair Pasta with Parmesan Cheese
Prep: 3 minute • Cook: 5 minutes

4 ounces angel hair pasta	1 tablespoons butter
¼ cup grated Parmesan cheese	

1. Cook pasta according to package directions, omitting salt and fat. Drain. Combine cooked pasta, cheese, and butter; toss well. Yield: 4 servings (serving size: about ½ cup).

CALORIES 161; FAT 5.5g (sat 3g; mono 0.8g; poly 0.2g); PROTEIN 6.6g; CARB 21.8g; FIBER 0.5g; CHOL 13mg; IRON 1mg; SODIUM 145mg; CALC 101m

Processing the panko and cilantro creates fine crumbs that adhere well to the shrimp. To save time, buy a peeled, cored fresh pineapple and presliced mango for the slaw. Enjoy the rest of it later in the week as part of a fresh fruit salad.

Pan-Fried Shrimp
Prep: 4 minutes • Cook: 8 minutes

1 cup panko (Japanese breadcrumbs)
2 tablespoons chopped fresh cilantro
1 pound extra-large shrimp, peeled and deveined (about 15)
¼ teaspoon salt
¼ teaspoon black pepper
1 large egg, beaten
2 teaspoon water
2 tablespoons canola oil

1. Combine panko and cilantro in a food processor; pulse 2 to 3 times or until cilantro is finely minced. Transfer to a shallow dish.
2. Sprinkle shrimp with salt and pepper. Combine egg and water in a shallow dish. Dip half of shrimp in egg mixture; dredge in crumb mixture, and place in a single layer on a plate. Repeat procedure with remaining shrimp, egg mixture, and crumb mixture.
3. Heat oil in a large nonstick skillet over medium-high heat. Add shrimp, and cook 2 minutes on each side or until done. Drain shrimp on paper towels. Yield: 3 servings (serving size: about 5 shrimp).

CALORIES 295; FAT 12.6g (sat 1.4g, mono 6.4g, poly 3.5g); PROTEIN 28.8g; CARB 13.9g; FIBER 0.7g; CHOL 284mg; IRON 3.9mg; SODIUM 532mg; CALC 55mg

serve with
Tropical Slaw
Prep: 5 minutes • Other: 15 minutes

3¼ cups packaged coleslaw
¾ cup chopped fresh mango
½ cup chopped fresh pineapple
2 tablespoons light mayonnaise
¼ teaspoon salt
¼ teaspoon black pepper
1 tablespoon finely chopped fresh cilantro

1. Combine first 6 ingredients in a large bowl; toss well. Cover and chill 15 minutes. Stir in cilantro. Yield: 3 servings (serving size: 1 cup).

CALORIES 87; FAT 3.5g (sat 0.1g, mono 1.7g, poly 1g); PROTEIN 0.9g; CARB 14.4g; FIBER 2.2g; CHOL 3mg; IRON 0.4mg; SODIUM 287mg; CALC 30mg

The clean tastes of fresh lemon juice and thyme complement the saltiness of the capers in this shrimp and rice dish. Starting with peeled and deveined shrimp from the fish counter and a package of precooked rice makes this a fast and satisfying meal after a busy day.

Shrimp with Capers, Garlic, and Rice

Prep: 7 minutes • Cook: 5 minutes

2 teaspoons olive oil
2 tablespoons chopped fresh thyme
2 tablespoons drained capers
3 garlic cloves

1½ pounds large shrimp, peeled and deveined
1 tablespoon fresh lemon juice
1 (8.8-ounce) package precooked long-grain rice (such as Uncle Ben's Ready Rice)

1. Heat oil in a large nonstick skillet over medium-high heat. Add thyme, capers, and garlic; sauté 1 minute. Add shrimp and lemon juice; sauté 4 minutes or until shrimp are done.
2. Microwave rice according to package directions. Serve shrimp mixture over rice. Yield: 4 servings (serving size: ¾ cup shrimp mixture and about ⅓ cup rice).

CALORIES 296; FAT 6.4g (sat 0.9g, mono 2.1g, poly 1.4g); PROTEIN 36.7g; CARB 20.9g; FIBER 0.8g; CHOL 259mg; IRON 5.2mg; SODIUM 333mg; CALC 126mg

serve with
Greek-Style Green Beans

Prep: 5 minutes • Cook: 4 minutes

1 (12-ounce) package trimmed fresh green beans
¼ cup (⅛-inch) sliced shallots (about 2)
¼ cup crumbled feta cheese

2 tablespoons fresh lemon juice
1 tablespoon olive oil
2 tablespoons fresh lemon juice
⅛ teaspoon black pepper

1. Microwave green beans according to package directions. Plunge beans into ice water; drain. Place in a large bowl. Add shallots and remaining ingredients; toss well. Yield: 4 servings (serving size: ¾ cup)

CALORIES 93; FAT 5.6g (sat 1.9g, mono 2.9g, poly 0.5g); PROTEIN 3.2g; CARB 9.3g; FIBER 2.8g; CHOL 8mg; IRON 0.8mg; SODIUM 107mg; CALC 87mg

Mussels make any meal a special occasion, but they're so easy and quick to cook that they're perfect for an impromptu casual dinner party. Serve them with a garden salad and Garlic Bread for sopping up the sauce.

White Wine–Steamed Mussels

Prep: 5 minutes • Cook: 10 minutes

1 tablespoon butter
¼ cup minced shallots (2 medium)
1 serrano chile, finely chopped
¼ teaspoon salt
¼ teaspoon black pepper

2 pounds mussels, scrubbed and debearded (about 60)
½ cup dry white wine
¼ cup chopped fresh parsley

1. Melt butter in a Dutch oven over medium heat. Add shallots and chile to pan, and sauté 3 minutes or until tender. Stir in salt and pepper.
2. Add mussels and wine; cover and cook 7 minutes or until shells open; discard any unopened shells. Divide mussels evenly among 4 shallow bowls. Sprinkle evenly with parsley. Yield: 4 servings (serving size: 15 mussels and ¾ cup wine mixture).

CALORIES 250; FAT 8g (sat 2.8g, mono 2.9g, poly 1.9g); PROTEIN 27.5g; CARB 14.1g; FIBER 0.3g; CHOL 71mg; IRON 9.7mg; SODIUM 998mg; CALC 72mg

serve with
Garlic Bread

Prep: 4 minutes • Cook: 10 minutes

2 tablespoons butter, softened
3 garlic cloves, minced
¼ teaspoon dried thyme

¼ teaspoon black pepper
1 (8-ounce) loaf sourdough French bread

1. Preheat oven to 350°.
2. Combine first 4 ingredients in a small bowl.
3. Using a serrated knife, cut bread diagonally into 4 equal pieces, cutting to, but not through loaf. Spread butter mixture on cut sides of bread. Wrap loaf in foil.
4. Bake at 350° for 10 minutes or until thoroughly heated. Yield: 4 servings (serving size: 1 piece).

CALORIES 207; FAT 7.2g (sat 3.6g, mono 1.5g, poly 1.2g); PROTEIN 5.3g; CARB 30.4g; FIBER 1.2g; CHOL 15mg; IRON 1.9mg; SODIUM 304mg; CALC 51mg

meats

Beef
Cowboy Flank Steak
Grilled Flank Steak with Balsamic Glaze and Orange Gremolata
Edamame and Steak Stir-Fry
Skirt Steak with Green Olive Tapenade
Mojito Strip Steaks with Pico de Gallo
Coffee-Marinated Beef Tenderloin Steaks
Grilled Beef Tenderloin with Horseradish-Walnut Sauce
Italian Beef and Polenta Casserole
Pasta Bolognese
Stuffed Peppers

Lamb
Lamb Chops with Minted Yogurt Sauce
Grilled Lamb Chops with Cherry Port Sauce
Lamb with Couscous and Roasted Eggplant

Pork
Pork Chops with Mustard Cream Sauce
Pork Chops with Tarragon-Onion Gravy
Slow-Cooker Pork Loin Carnita Tacos with Chimichurri Sauce
Hoisin Pork Steak
Seared Pork Tenderloin Medallions with Shallot-Mushroom Pan Gravy
Teriyaki Pork Medallions
Smoked Paprika Pork

Cowboy Flank Steak

Prep: 3 minutes • Cook: 12 minutes • Other: 5 minutes

2 teaspoons chili powder
1 teaspoon instant coffee granules
½ teaspoon ground cumin
½ teaspoon brown sugar

1 (1-pound) flank steak, trimmed
½ teaspoon salt
¼ teaspoon black pepper
Cooking spray

1. Preheat broiler.
2. Combine first 4 ingredients in a bowl, stirring with a small whisk until blended. Sprinkle steak with salt and pepper; rub steak with spice mixture. Place steak on a broiler pan coated with cooking spray.
3. Broil steak 4 inches from heat 12 minutes or until desired degree of doneness (do not turn steak). Remove steak from oven; loosely cover with foil, and let stand 5 minutes.
4. Cut steak diagonally across the grain into thin slices. Yield: 4 servings (serving size: 3 ounces steak).

CALORIES 181; FAT 8.2g (sat 3.4g, mono 3.3g, poly 1.3g); PROTEIN 24.2g; CARB 0.9g; FIBER 0.1g; CHOL 40mg; IRON 1.9mg; SODIUM 393mg; CALC 32mg

serve with
Mini Cheddar Potato Skins

Prep: 5 minutes • Cook: 7 minutes • Other: 5 minutes

1 pound red fingerling potatoes (about 20)
1 tablespoon butter, melted
¼ teaspoon salt
¼ teaspoon black pepper

3 tablespoons reduced-fat shredded extra-sharp cheddar cheese
2 tablespoons thinly sliced green onion tops

1. Preheat broiler.
2. Scrub potatoes; place in a single layer in a microwave-safe bowl (do not pierce potatoes with a fork). Cover bowl with plastic wrap (do not allow plastic wrap to touch food); vent. Microwave at HIGH 5 to 6 minutes or until tender. Let stand 5 minutes or until cool enough to touch. Cut potatoes in half; drizzle evenly with butter, and sprinkle evenly with salt and pepper. Top evenly with cheese. Broil 2 minutes or until cheese melts, and sprinkle evenly with green onions. Yield: 4 servings (serving size: about 5 potato halves).

CALORIES 149; FAT 4.2g (sat 2.6g, mono 1g, poly 0.2g); PROTEIN 3.9g; CARB 24.4g; FIBER 2.5g; CHOL 12mg; IRON 0.8mg; SODIUM 174mg; CALC 55mg

Instant coffee granules may seem like an odd ingredient to use in a meat rub, but we found that it actually deepens the flavor. The coffee also helps caramelize the steak's surface, sealing in its natural juices and creating a tastier, more tender bite.

Gremolata, a zesty Italian garnish traditionally made of minced parsley, lemon rind, and garlic, is simple to prepare and great for adding a burst of fresh flavor to a variety of dishes. Here, we've substituted orange rind for the lemon rind. Serve with mashed sweet potatoes.

Grilled Flank Steak with Balsamic Glaze and Orange Gremolata

Prep: 2 minutes • Cook: 12 minutes • Other: 5 minutes

1 (1-pound) flank steak, trimmed
½ teaspoon salt
¼ teaspoon black pepper
1 medium-size red onion, cut into 8 wedges

Cooking spray
½ cup balsamic vinegar
¼ cup finely chopped shallots
Orange Gremolata

1. Prepare grill.

2. Sprinkle steak with salt and pepper. Place steak and onion wedges on a grill rack coated with cooking spray. Grill 5 minutes on each side or until desired degree of doneness. Let stand 5 minutes. Cut steak diagonally across grain into thin slices.

3. While steak grills, combine balsamic vinegar and shallots in a small saucepan. Bring to a boil; reduce heat, and simmer 7 minutes or until reduced to ¼ cup. Drizzle balsamic mixture over steak slices, and sprinkle with Orange Gremolata. Yield: 4 servings (serving size: 3 ounces steak, 1 tablespoon glaze, and 1 tablespoon Orange Gremolata).

CALORIES 236; FAT 8.3g (sat 3.4g, mono 3.6g, poly 0.8g); PROTEIN 25.6g; CARB 12.2g; FIBER 1.6g; CHOL 40mg; IRON 3.4mg; SODIUM 378mg; CALC 86mg

Orange Gremolata

Prep: 5 minutes

¼ cup minced fresh parsley
1 tablespoon grated orange rind

2 garlic cloves, minced

1. Combine all ingredients in a small bowl. Yield: 4 servings (serving size: 1 tablespoon).

CALORIES 5; FAT 0.1g (sat 0g, mono 0g, poly 0g); PROTEIN 0.2g; CARB 1.1g; FIBER 0.3g; CHOL 0mg; IRON 0.3mg; SODIUM 2mg; CALC 10mg

flavorful combinations

Add a bit of zing to meats, poultry, fish, and vegetables with this Orange Gremolata—a lively topping of fresh minced garlic, parsley, and orange rind. If you have a minichopper, use it to mince the parsley and garlic. A large chef's knife will work well, too.

You will enjoy the tantalizing aroma as you prepare this colorful stir-fry. It's a snap to fix when you use prechopped bell peppers and frozen shelled edamame. Serve this dish over hot cooked jasmine rice to soak up the sweet and savory sauce.

Edamame and Steak Stir-Fry

Prep: 2 minutes • Cook: 13 minutes

Cooking spray
8 ounces boneless sirloin steak, trimmed and cut into thin strips
1 cup frozen shelled edamame (green soybeans)
3 tablespoons water

1 (5-ounce) package prechopped tricolor bell pepper mix
1 teaspoon minced garlic
3 tablespoons teriyaki basting sauce (such as Iron Chef Baste and Glaze)

1. Heat a large nonstick skillet over medium-high heat. Coat pan with cooking spray; add steak strips. Stir-fry 5 minutes or until steak is done; transfer to a plate.
2. Add edamame and water to pan; stir-fry 2 minutes or until thoroughly heated. Add bell pepper mix; stir-fry 2 to 3 minutes. Add garlic; stir-fry 1 minute. Stir in basting sauce; cook, stirring constantly, 1 minute or until thoroughly heated. Return beef to vegetable mixture; toss to coat. Yield: 2 servings (serving size: 1½ cups).

CALORIES 345; FAT 10.2g (sat 2.4g, mono 4.4g, poly 2.7g); PROTEIN 35.8g; CARB 24.3g; FIBER 5.3g; CHOL 67mg; IRON 5mg; SODIUM 652mg; CALC 52mg

serve with
Orange-Pineapple Spritzer

Prep: 3 minutes

½ cup blood orange sorbet, softened
⅓ cup unsweetened pineapple juice

½ cup diet tonic water, chilled
Unpeeled fresh pineapple wedges (optional)

1. Combine sorbet and juice; pour evenly into 2 tall glasses. Pour tonic water evenly into pineapple mixture in each glass, and garnish with pineapple wedges, if desired. Serve immediately. Yield: 2 servings (serving size: about ⅔ cup).

CALORIES 67; FAT 0.1g (sat 0g, mono 0g, poly 0g); PROTEIN 0.2g; CARB 14.9g; FIBER 0.1g; CHOL 0mg; IRON 0.1mg; SODIUM 10mg; CALC 5mg

This topping capitalizes on bold-tasting olives and capers to deliver a huge amount of flavor. To make this meal even quicker, use a store-bought tapenade instead of making your own. If you can't find skirt steak, you can use flank steak. Serve with an arugula and tomato salad.

Skirt Steak with Green Olive Tapenade

Prep: 3 minutes • Cook: 6 minutes • Other: 8 hours and 5 minutes

1½ pounds skirt steak, cut in half crosswise
¼ teaspoon black pepper
⅛ teaspoon salt
¼ cup balsamic vinegar

2 tablespoons olive oil
1 garlic clove, minced
Cooking spray
Green Olive Tapenade

1. Sprinkle steak on both sides with pepper and salt. Combine vinegar, olive oil, and garlic in a large heavy-duty zip-top plastic bag. Add steak to bag; seal. Marinate in refrigerator 8 hours, turning occasionally.
2. Prepare grill.
3. Remove steak from bag, discarding marinade. Place steak on a grill rack coated with cooking spray. Grill 6 to 8 minutes or until desired degree of doneness. Remove steak from grill; cover and let stand 5 minutes. Cut diagonally across the grain into thin slices. Serve with Green Olive Tapenade. Yield: 6 servings (serving size: 3 ounces steak and 2 tablespoons Green Olive Tapenade).

CALORIES 287; FAT 19.3g (sat 4.9g, mono 12g, poly 1.9g); PROTEIN 21.6g; CARB 3g; FIBER 0.3g; CHOL 60mg; IRON 2.9mg; SODIUM 335mg; CALC 22mg

Green Olive Tapenade

Prep: 3 minutes

1 lemon
12 large garlic-stuffed green olives
1 tablespoon drained capers

1 tablespoon chopped fresh flat-leaf parsley
2 tablespoons olive oil

1. Grate rind and squeeze juice from lemon to equal 1 tablespoon and 2½ tablespoons, respectively. Process lemon rind, juice, olives, and remaining ingredients in a food processor until coarsely chopped. Yield: 6 servings (serving size: 2 tablespoons).

CALORIES 51; FAT 5.4g (sat 0.7g, mono 3.9g, poly 0.6g); PROTEIN 0.2g; CARB 1g; FIBER 0.3g; CHOL 0mg; IRON 0.2mg; SODIUM 208mg; CALC 8mg

Strip steaks are tender and full of flavor, so they're a great choice for broiling or grilling. One steak will generally weigh about 8 ounces when purchased raw because it's a long, thick cut of meat. For portion control, we've called for 2 (8-ounce) steaks cut in half. Serve with grilled corn on the cob.

Mojito Strip Steaks with Pico de Gallo

Prep: 3 minutes • Cook: 4 minutes • Other: 33 minutes

1 lime
¼ cup chopped fresh mint
2 tablespoons light rum
2 (½-inch-thick) beef strip steaks, trimmed and cut in half crosswise (about 1 pound)

Pico de Gallo
½ teaspoon salt
½ teaspoon freshly ground black pepper
Cooking spray

1. Grate rind and squeeze juice from lime to measure 1 teaspoon and 1 tablespoon, respectively. Combine rind, juice, mint, and rum in a large zip-top plastic bag. Add steak to bag, and seal bag. Marinate in refrigerator 30 minutes, turning occasionally.
2. While steak marinates, prepare Pico de Gallo.
3. Prepare grill.
4. Remove steaks from marinade, discarding marinade. Sprinkle steaks with salt and pepper. Place steaks on a grill rack coated with cooking spray. Grill 2 minutes on each side or until desired degree of doneness. Let stand 3 minutes. Cut steak into slices. Serve with Pico de Gallo. Yield: 4 servings (serving size: 3 ounces steak and ½ cup Pico de Gallo).

CALORIES 217; FAT 7.6g (sat 2.8g, mono 3.2g, poly 1.4g); PROTEIN 22.4g; CARB 7.2g; FIBER 1.7g; CHOL 76mg; IRON 2.4mg; SODIUM 506mg; CALC 24mg

Pico de Gallo

Prep: 8 minutes

2 cups chopped seeded tomato (2 medium)
⅓ cup chopped red onion
⅓ cup chopped fresh cilantro
2 tablespoons fresh lime juice (2 limes)

1½ tablespoons chopped seeded jalapeño (about 1)
¼ teaspoon salt
¼ teaspoon freshly ground black pepper

1. Combine all ingredients in a medium bowl; toss well. Yield: 4 servings (serving size: ½ cup).

CALORIES 28; FAT 0.4g (sat 0.1g, mono 0.1g, poly 0.1g); PROTEIN 1g; CARB 6.4g; FIBER 1.4g; CHOL 0mg; IRON 0.5mg; SODIUM 155mg; CALC 11mg

Coffee-Marinated Beef Tenderloin Steaks

Prep: 5 minutes • Cook: 4 minutes • Other: 8 hours

 1 cup strong brewed coffee
1½ tablespoons dark brown sugar
 ½ teaspoon salt
 ½ teaspoon pepper
 ¼ teaspoon ground red pepper

 2 garlic cloves, minced
 4 (4-ounce) beef tenderloin steaks, trimmed (½ inch thick)
Cooking spray

1. Combine first 6 ingredients in a large zip-top plastic bag. Add steaks; seal bag. Marinate in refrigerator 8 hours, turning occasionally.
2. Prepare grill.
3. Remove steaks from marinade, discarding marinade. Place steaks on a grill rack coated with cooking spray. Grill 2 minutes on each side or until desired degree of doneness. Yield: 4 servings (serving size: 1 steak).

CALORIES 174; FAT 6.3g (sat 2.4g, mono 2.5g, poly 1.2g); PROTEIN 22g; CARB 5.8g; FIBER 0.1g; CHOL 59mg; IRON 1.5mg; SODIUM 339mg; CALC 24mg

serve with
Grilled Asparagus and Tomatoes

Prep: 2 minutes • Cook: 6 minutes

 1 pound fresh asparagus, trimmed
 4 plum tomatoes, halved
 1 tablespoon olive oil
Cooking spray

 ¼ teaspoon salt
 ⅛ teaspoon black pepper
 ½ teaspoon grated lemon rind

1. Prepare grill.
2. Place asparagus and tomato halves in an 11 x 7–inch baking dish. Drizzle vegetables with oil; toss gently to coat. Place vegetables on a grill rack coated with cooking spray. Grill asparagus 3 minutes on each side; grill tomato 1 minute on each side. Return asparagus and tomato to dish. Sprinkle vegetables with salt, pepper, and lemon rind. Yield: 4 servings (serving size: ¼ of asparagus and 2 tomato halves).

CALORIES 62; FAT 3.7g (sat 0.5g, mono 2.5g, poly 0.4g); PROTEIN 3.8g; CARB 5.7g; FIBER 1.3g; CHOL 0mg; IRON 0.9mg; SODIUM 151mg; CALC 27mg

It takes about 5 seconds to shred the cheese for this casserole in the food processor—just make sure the cheese is cold before placing it in the food chute.

Potato and Jalapeño Cheese Bake

Prep: 13 minutes • Cook: 1 hour and 6 minutes

Butter-flavored cooking spray
2 (8-ounce) packages prechopped bell pepper-and-onion mix
4 garlic cloves, minced
1 (18-ounce) package refrigerated sliced potatoes (such as Simply Potatoes Homestyle Slices)

½ teaspoon salt
½ teaspoon freshly ground black pepper
1 (8-ounce) package 50% reduced-fat jalapeño cheddar cheese (such as Cabot), shredded
½ cup chopped fresh cilantro

1. Preheat oven to 400°.
2. Heat a large nonstick skillet over medium-high heat; coat pan with cooking spray. Add bell pepper mix; cook 5 minutes, stirring frequently. Add garlic; cook 1 additional minute.
3. While bell pepper mixture cooks, arrange half of potato slices in bottom of an 11 x 7-inch baking dish coated with cooking spray. Combine salt and pepper. Sprinkle potato slices with half of salt mixture.
4. Layer potato mixture with half of bell pepper mixture and one-third of cheese. Repeat procedure with remaining half of potato slices, salt mixture, bell pepper mixture, and remaining two-thirds of cheese.
5. Cover and bake at 400° for 40 minutes. Uncover and bake 10 additional minutes or until cheese is lightly browned and potatoes are tender. Sprinkle with cilantro. Yield: 6 servings (serving size: ⅙ of casserole).

CALORIES 186; FAT 6.3g (sat 4.1g, mono 1g, poly 1g); PROTEIN 12.9g; CARB 20.9g; FIBER 2.8g; CHOL 20mg; IRON 0.4mg; SODIUM 643mg; CALC 288mg

serve with
Romaine and Sweet Onion Salad

Prep: 8 minutes

1 cup vertically sliced sweet onion
1½ cups grape tomatoes, halved
1½ cups English cucumber slices (about 1 small)

⅓ cup Sweet Vidalia Onion Vinaigrette (such as Ken's Healthy Options)

1. Combine onion, tomato, and cucumber in a bowl. Add dressing; toss well. Yield: 4 servings (serving size: 1 cup).

CALORIES 93; FAT 3.1g (sat 0.4g, mono 1.5g, poly 1g); PROTEIN 1.6g; CARB 15.9g; FIBER 2.3g; CHOL 0mg; IRON 0.7mg; SODIUM 88mg; CALC 45mg

If you look in your pantry, you'll probably find the staple items needed to make this marinade. Make an extra cup of joe the morning you plan to prepare the marinade. Store the marinade in the refrigerator until you're ready to use it.

Even on the nights when you don't feel like cooking, a restaurant-quality meal is still within reach. These quick-cooking steaks rubbed with fresh thyme and garlic and topped with a creamy sauce will delight your palate and leave you satisfied. Grill zucchini strips with the steak for a super-simple side.

Grilled Beef Tenderloin with Horseradish-Walnut Sauce

Prep: 6 minutes • Cook: 6 minutes

1 tablespoon chopped fresh thyme
2 teaspoons olive oil
½ teaspoon salt
¼ teaspoon freshly ground black pepper
4 garlic cloves, minced

4 (4-ounce) beef tenderloin steaks (about ¾ inch thick)
Cooking spray
Horseradish-Walnut Sauce

1. Prepare grill.
2. Combine first 5 ingredients in a small bowl; rub herb mixture over steaks. Place steaks on a grill rack coated with cooking spray. Grill 3 minutes on each side or until desired degree of doneness. Serve with Horseradish-Walnut Sauce. Yield: 4 servings (serving size: 1 steak and 1½ tablespoons sauce).

CALORIES 246; FAT 14.9g (sat 4.2g, mono 4.5g, poly 5.8g); PROTEIN 23.3g; CARB 3.5g; FIBER 0.4g; CHOL 62mg; IRON 1.9mg; SODIUM 419mg; CALC 34mg

Horseradish-Walnut Sauce

Prep: 4 minutes

2½ tablespoons light sour cream
2½ tablespoons light mayonnaise
2 tablespoons finely chopped walnuts, toasted

1 tablespoon finely chopped green onions
2 teaspoons prepared horseradish
¼ teaspoon freshly ground black pepper

1. Combine all ingredients in a small bowl. Yield: 4 servings (serving size: 1½ tablespoons).

CALORIES 70; FAT 6.3g (sat 1.5g, mono 1.3g, poly 3.3g); PROTEIN 1.3g; CARB 2.2g; FIBER 0.3g; CHOL 3mg; IRON 0.2mg; SODIUM 83mg; CALC 7mg

You can make this casserole up to two days in advance, cover it, and store it in the refrigerator—but you'll need to bake it an additional 10 minutes. If you're cooking for one or two, the leftovers make great lunches and dinners throughout the week. Serve with a mixed greens salad.

Italian Beef and Polenta Casserole

Prep: 4 minutes • Cook: 38 minutes

2 medium zucchini
1 (17-ounce) tube of basil and garlic-flavored polenta (such as Marjon)
Olive oil-flavored cooking spray
1 pound ground sirloin
1 (24-ounce) jar fire-roasted tomato-garlic pasta sauce (such as Classico)

¼ teaspoon black pepper
1 cup (4 ounces) shredded reduced-fat 4-cheese Italian blend cheese (such as Sargento)

1. Preheat oven to 375°.
2. Cut zucchini in half lengthwise; cut diagonally crosswise into ¼-inch slices. Cut polenta crosswise into 8 slices; coat both sides of each slice with cooking spray.
3. Heat a large nonstick skillet over medium-high heat. Add polenta slices; cook 3 minutes on each side or until lightly browned. Arrange polenta slices in an 11 x 7–inch baking dish coated with cooking spray.
4. Reheat pan over medium-high heat. Add beef to pan. Cook 4 to 5 minutes, stirring to crumble; remove from pan, and drain, if necessary. Add zucchini to pan; sauté 3 to 4 minutes or until tender. Add beef, pasta sauce, and pepper; cook 1 to 2 minutes or until thoroughly heated, stirring occasionally. Spoon beef mixture over polenta; sprinkle with cheese.
5. Bake at 375° for 18 to 20 minutes or until bubbly and cheese melts. Yield: 6 servings (serving size: ⅙ of casserole).

CALORIES 266; FAT 7.6g (sat 3.4g, mono 2.2g, poly 1.6g); PROTEIN 24g; CARB 24.7g; FIBER 3.3g; CHOL 50mg; IRON 2.4mg; SODIUM 891mg; CALC 157mg.

choice ingredient

As a shortcut to making polenta from scratch in a saucepan, use precooked polenta. Look for flavored or plain 17-ounce tubes in the produce section of your supermarket. This precooked polenta works well in recipes that call for it to be cut into slices or cubes and sautéed, baked, or grilled.

This tastes-like-you-cooked-it-all-day sauce is perfect tossed with linguine. It also freezes well and can be ready in minutes with a quick thaw in the microwave.

Pasta Bolognese

Prep: 3 minutes • Cook: 12 minutes

1 (13.25-ounce) package whole-grain linguine (such as Ronzoni Healthy Harvest)
2 (4-ounce) links hot turkey Italian sausage
Olive oil-flavored cooking spray
1 pound 93% lean ground beef
1 cup chopped onion
1 (8-ounce) package button mushrooms, chopped
1 tablespoon finely chopped fresh rosemary
1 (28-ounce) can petite diced tomatoes, undrained
½ cup fat-free evaporated milk
¼ teaspoon freshly ground black pepper
⅛ teaspoon salt
Grated Parmesan cheese (optional)

1. Cook pasta in a large Dutch oven according to package directions, omitting salt and fat; drain, return to pan, and keep warm.
2. While pasta cooks, remove casings from sausage. Heat a large nonstick skillet over medium-high heat. Coat pan with cooking spray. Add sausage, beef, and onion; cook 2 minutes, stirring to crumble; drain, if necessary. Add mushrooms and rosemary. Cook 5 minutes or until browned.
3. Stir in tomatoes; reduce heat, and simmer, uncovered, 3 minutes. Stir in milk, pepper, and salt; cook 2 minutes. Add sauce to pasta, tossing well. Sprinkle with cheese, if desired. Yield: 8 servings (serving size: 1½ cups).

CALORIES 324; FAT 9.4g (sat 2g, mono 4g, poly 3.1g); PROTEIN 23.9g; CARB 43.6g; FIBER 7.2g; CHOL 47.3mg; IRON 3.7mg; SODIUM 444mg; CALC 81mg

serve with
Shaved Fennel Salad

Prep: 8 minutes

3 tablespoons olive oil
3 tablespoons fresh lemon juice
¼ teaspoon salt
¼ teaspoon freshly ground black pepper
8 cups thinly sliced fennel bulb (about 2 bulbs)
1 (10-ounce) package Italian-blend salad greens (about 8 cups)
⅓ cup loosely packed celery leaves, coarsely chopped
½ cup shaved fresh Parmesan cheese

1. Combine first 4 ingredients in a large bowl, stirring with a whisk. Add fennel, greens, and celery leaves; toss well. Add cheese, and toss gently. Yield: 8 servings (serving size: 1½ cups).

CALORIES 110; FAT 7.3g (sat 1.7g, mono 4.1g, poly 1.2g); PROTEIN 4.6g; CARB 8.3g; FIBER 3.2g; CHOL 5mg; IRON 1mg; SODIUM 251mg; CALC 154mg

Beef and rice seasoned with herbs and a robust pasta sauce fill these tender, flavorful peppers. If you don't have dried Italian seasoning, use ½ teaspoon dried basil and ½ teaspoon dried oregano. Make sure the bell peppers are 10 ounces or larger so the beef stuffing will fit.

Stuffed Peppers

Prep: 4 minutes • Cook: 10 minutes

2 large green bell peppers (about 10 ounces each)
¾ pound ground sirloin
¼ cup chopped onion
1 teaspoon dried Italian seasoning
¼ teaspoon salt

¼ teaspoon black pepper
1 (8.8-ounce) package precooked whole-grain brown rice (such as Uncle Ben's)
1 cup tomato-basil pasta sauce (such as Classico)
1 cup shredded part-skim mozzarella cheese

1. Cut bell peppers in half lengthwise; discard seeds and membranes. Place bell pepper halves, cut sides up, in an 11 x 7–inch baking dish. Microwave at HIGH 6 to 7 minutes or until tender.
2. While bell peppers cook, heat a large nonstick skillet over medium-high heat. Cook beef and onion until browned, stirring to crumble beef. Drain, if necessary; return to pan. Stir in dried Italian seasoning, salt, black pepper, brown rice, and pasta sauce. Cook 1 to 2 minutes or until warm, stirring occasionally.
3. Fill bell pepper halves with beef mixture; sprinkle evenly with cheese. Microwave at HIGH 2 to 3 minutes or until cheese melts. Yield: 4 servings (serving size: ½ pepper).

CALORIES 312; FAT 9.8g (sat 4.6g, mono 3.3g; poly 1.5g); PROTEIN 27.4g; CARB 29.9g; FIBER 4.1g; CHOL 61mg; IRON 2.4mg; SODIUM 543mg; CALC 242mg

choice ingredient

Microwaveable precooked rice, such as whole-grain brown, long-grain white, jasmine, or basmati, is a great shortcut instead of cooking rice from scratch. Precooked rice can be used as a stuffing, stirred into soups, or served as a healthy ninety-second side. It comes in an assortment of flavors, but be sure to look at each one's nutrition label—some seasoned varieties can be high in sodium.

Tender lamb loin chops dressed up with a tangy, yogurt dipping sauce and served with Couscous Salad offer a mouthwatering meal with minimal effort.

Lamb Chops with Minted Yogurt Sauce

Prep: 4 minutes • Cook: 6 minutes

½ cup plain fat-free yogurt
1 tablespoon chopped fresh mint
1 teaspoon lemon juice
1 small garlic clove, minced
½ teaspoon salt, divided

½ teaspoon freshly ground black pepper, divided
8 (4-ounce) lamb loin chops, trimmed
Cooking spray

1. Prepare grill.

2. Combine yogurt and next 3 ingredients. Stir in ⅛ teaspoon salt and ⅛ teaspoon pepper. Chill.

3. Sprinkle lamb evenly with remaining ⅜ teaspoon each salt and pepper. Place lamb on grill rack coated with cooking spray; grill 3 minutes on each side or until desired degree of doneness. Serve with yogurt sauce. Yield: 4 servings (serving size: 2 chops and 2 tablespoons sauce).

CALORIES 221; FAT 9.3g (sat 3.3g; mono 4.4g; poly 1.6g); PROTEIN 29.9g; CARB 3g; FIBER 0.1g; CHOL 91mg; IRON 2mg; SODIUM 388mg; CALC 59mg

serve with
Couscous Salad

Prep: 6 minutes • Cook: 3 minutes • Other: 5 minutes

½ cup water
½ cup uncooked wheat couscous (such as Near East)
¾ cup chopped seeded plum tomato
⅓ cup minced fresh parsley

⅓ cup minced fresh mint
2 tablespoons lemon juice
1 tablespoon olive oil
⅛ teaspoon salt

1. Bring water to a boil in a small saucepan. Stir in couscous. Cover, remove from heat, and let stand 5 minutes.

2. While couscous stands, combine tomato, parsley, mint, lemon juice, oil, and salt in a small bowl. Add couscous, and stir to combine. Serve at room temperature or chilled. Yield: 4 servings (serving size: ½ cup).

CALORIES 110; FAT 4.2g (sat 0.5g; mono 3.2g; poly 0.5g); PROTEIN 3.2g; CARB 16.6g; FIBER 1.9g; CHOL 0mg; IRON 0.7mg; SODIUM 78mg; CALC 16mg

Grilled Lamb Chops with Cherry Port Sauce

Prep: 3 minutes • Cook: 16 minutes

8 (4-ounce) lamb loin chops, trimmed
½ teaspoon salt, divided
½ teaspoon freshly ground black pepper
⅔ cup tawny port
1 teaspoon cornstarch
1 teaspoon water
¾ cup frozen pitted dark sweet cherries
1 teaspoon minced fresh thyme
Cooking spray

1. Prepare grill.
2. Sprinkle lamb evenly with ¼ teaspoon salt and pepper; set aside.
3. Bring port to a boil in a medium skillet over high heat. Boil, uncovered, 2 to 3 minutes or until reduced to ⅓ cup. Reduce heat to medium. Combine cornstarch and water in a separate bowl, stirring until smooth. Add cornstarch mixture and cherries to pan. Simmer 1 minute or until sauce is slightly thick. Remove from heat; stir in thyme and remaining ¼ teaspoon salt.
4. Coat lamb with cooking spray; place on grill rack. Grill 5 minutes on each side or until desired degree of doneness. Serve cherry sauce over lamb. Yield: 4 servings (serving size: 2 chops and about 2½ tablespoons sauce).

CALORIES 295; FAT 9.3g (sat 3.3g; mono 4.3g; poly 1.6g); PROTEIN 28.9g; CARB 11.2g; FIBER 0.9g; CHOL 91mg; IRON 2.1mg; SODIUM 374mg; CALC 28mg

serve with
Grilled Red Onion and Zucchini

Prep: 2 minutes • Cook: 10 minutes

3 tablespoons balsamic vinegar
2 teaspoons olive oil
¾ teaspoon Greek seasoning
1 large red onion, cut into 4 (½-inch thick) slices
2 large zucchini, halved lengthwise
Cooking spray

1. Prepare grill.
2. Combine first 3 ingredients in a large bowl. Add onion and zucchini, and toss to coat.
3. Place vegetables on grill rack coated with cooking spray; cover and grill 10 to 12 minutes or until vegetables are tender. Yield: 4 servings (serving size: 1 zucchini half and 1 onion slice).

CALORIES 68; FAT 2.7g (sat 0.4g; mono 1.8g; poly 0.5g); PROTEIN 2.4g; CARB 10.4g; FIBER 2.4g; CHOL 0mg; IRON 0.6mg; SODIUM 202mg; CALC 33mg

We used port, a sweet fortified wine, to create a vibrant sauce for the lamb. The unique flavor of port is hard to match, but if you need a substitute, use a fruity red wine or ⅔ cup pomegranate-cherry juice and ½ teaspoon sugar.

The distinct flavor of lamb stands up to assertive feta cheese in this Mediterranean-inspired meal. Prepare the couscous and lamb while the eggplant roasts.

Lamb with Couscous and Roasted Eggplant

Prep: 5 minutes • Cook: 8 minutes • Other: 5 minutes

½ cup uncooked couscous
1 pound lean lamb, cut into 1-inch pieces
¼ teaspoon salt
¼ teaspoon freshly ground black pepper
Cooking spray

1 (14.5-ounce) can diced tomatoes with basil, garlic, and oregano, drained
⅓ cup crumbled feta cheese
Fresh rosemary leaves (optional)
Roasted Eggplant

1. Prepare couscous according to package directions, omitting salt and fat. Keep warm.
2. Sprinkle lamb with salt and pepper. Heat a large nonstick skillet over medium-high heat; coat pan with cooking spray. Add lamb; cook 5 minutes or until browned, turning after 3 minutes. Stir in couscous, tomatoes, cheese, and rosemary, if desired; cook 1 additional minute or until thoroughly heated. Serve over Roasted Eggplant. Yield: 4 servings (serving size: about ⅔ cup lamb mixture and ¾ cup eggplant slices).

CALORIES 375; FAT 13.4g (sat 5.2g, mono 6g, poly 2g); PROTEIN 30.8g; CARB 33g; FIBER 7.5g; CHOL 84mg; IRON 3.9mg; SODIUM 717mg; CALC 137mg

Roasted Eggplant

Prep: 4 minutes • Cook: 15 minutes

4 (6-ounce) baby eggplants, cut into ¼-inch slices
Cooking spray
1 tablespoon olive oil

¼ teaspoon salt
¼ teaspoon freshly ground black pepper
1 teaspoon minced fresh rosemary

1. Preheat oven to 450°.
2. Place eggplant slices on a large baking sheet coated with cooking spray. Drizzle with oil, and sprinkle with salt and pepper. Bake at 450° for 15 to 18 minutes or until tender. Sprinkle with rosemary. Yield: 4 servings (serving size: about ¾ cup).

CALORIES 71; FAT 3.7g (sat 0.5g, mono 2.5g, poly 0.5g); PROTEIN 1.7g; CARB 9.8g; FIBER 5.8g; CHOL 0mg; IRON 0.5mg; SODIUM 149mg; CALC 17mg

Using fat-free half-and-half gives this dish a creamy, rich flavor that fat-free milk can't. Sprinkle the finished dish with chopped fresh parsley, if desired.

Pork Chops with Mustard Cream Sauce

Prep: 3 minutes • Cook: 14 minutes

4 (4-ounce) boneless center-cut loin pork chops (½ inch thick)
½ teaspoon salt
¼ teaspoon black pepper
Cooking spray

½ cup fat-free, less-sodium chicken broth
⅔ cup fat-free half-and-half
1 tablespoon Dijon mustard
2 teaspoons lemon juice
Chopped fresh parsley (optional)

1. Sprinkle both sides of pork with salt and pepper.
2. Heat a large nonstick skillet over medium-high heat. Coat pan with cooking spray. Add pork, and cook 4 to 5 minutes on each side or until lightly browned and done. Transfer pork to a serving plate, and keep warm.
3. Add broth to pan, scraping pan to loosen browned bits. Stir in half-and-half, mustard, and lemon juice. Reduce heat, and simmer, uncovered, 6 minutes or until sauce is slightly thick. Spoon sauce over pork; sprinkle with parsley, if desired. Yield: 4 servings (serving size: 1 pork chop and 2 tablespoons sauce).

CALORIES 193; FAT 6.4g (sat 2.3g; mono 2.7g; poly 1.2g); PROTEIN 24.3g; CARB 5.2g; FIBER 0g; CHOL 65mg; IRON 0.7mg; SODIUM 539mg; CALC 52mg

serve with
Roasted Potato Wedges

Prep: 3 minutes • Cook: 20 minutes

1 pound red small potatoes, quartered
2 teaspoons olive oil
¼ cup panko (Japanese breadcrumbs) with Italian seasoning

2 tablespoons grated Parmesan-Romano cheese blend
Cooking spray

1. Preheat oven to 475°.
2. Combine potatoes and oil in a medium bowl, tossing to coat. Combine panko and cheese in a large zip-top plastic bag; add potatoes, tossing to coat. Place potatoes on a jelly-roll pan coated with cooking spray; discard remaining breadcrumb mixture. Bake at 475° for 20 minutes or until browned and crispy. Yield: 4 servings (serving size: about ¾ cup).

CALORIES 123; FAT 3.7g (sat 1.1g; mono 2g; poly 0.6g); PROTEIN 3.9g; CARB 19.9g; FIBER 2.2g; CHOL 4mg; IRON 0.9mg; SODIUM 88mg; CALC 56mg

Pork Chops with Tarragon-Onion Gravy

Prep: 2 minutes • Cook: 14 minutes

8 (2-ounce) boneless center-cut loin pork chops (¼ inch thick)
½ teaspoon salt
¼ teaspoon black pepper
¼ cup all-purpose flour

1 tablespoon olive oil
½ cup thinly sliced onion
¾ cup fat-free, less sodium beef broth
1 tablespoon chopped fresh tarragon

1. Sprinkle pork chops evenly with salt and pepper. Dredge pork in flour. Heat oil in a large skillet over medium-high heat. Add half of pork to pan; cook 1 to 2 minutes on each side or until pork is browned. Transfer pork to a plate. Repeat procedure with remaining pork. Reduce heat to medium. Add onion to pan, and cook 3 minutes or until tender.

2. Stir in broth, scraping to loosen browned bits. Return pork and any accumulated juices to pan. Bring to a boil; reduce heat, cover, and cook 4 minutes or until pork is done. Stir in tarragon. Yield: 4 servings (serving size: 2 pork chops and ½ cup gravy).

CALORIES 259; FAT 14.4g (sat 4.6g, mono 7.6g, poly 1.9g); PROTEIN 22.7g; CARB 9g; FIBER 0.6g; CHOL 59mg; IRON 1.1mg; SODIUM 803mg; CALC 25mg

serve with
Homestyle Smashed Potatoes

Prep: 2 minutes • Cook: 8 minutes

1 pound red potatoes (about 5)
1 cup nonfat buttermilk
¼ cup grated Parmigiano-Reggiano cheese
2 tablespoons yogurt-based spread (such as Brummel & Brown)

¼ teaspoon salt
¼ teaspoon freshly ground black pepper

1. Scrub potatoes; place in a single layer in a microwave-safe bowl (do not pierce potatoes with a fork). Cover bowl with plastic wrap (do not allow plastic wrap to touch food); vent. Microwave at HIGH 8 minutes or until tender.

2. Add buttermilk and remaining ingredients to potatoes. Mash potato mixture with a potato masher until creamy. Yield: 4 servings (serving size: about ½ cup).

CALORIES 169; FAT 4.8g (sat 2g, mono 1.2g, poly 1.3g); PROTEIN 7.9g; CARB 23.6g; FIBER 1.4g; CHOL 8mg; IRON 1mg; SODIUM 385mg; CALC 166mg

When your family tastes these tender pork chops smothered in a homestyle gravy, they'll never suspect you made dinner at the last minute. Because the chops are very thin, they cook quickly so be careful not to overcook them, which will make them tough.

These make-ahead tacos are an ideal way to showcase slow-cooked pork. Browning the pork roast before adding it to the slow cooker adds rich flavor.

Slow-Cooker Pork Loin Carnita Tacos with Chimichurri Sauce

Prep: 6 minutes • Cook: 8 hours and 13 minutes

1 (1½-pound) boneless pork loin roast, trimmed
½ teaspoon salt
½ teaspoon black pepper
8 garlic cloves, minced
Cooking spray
2 cups chicken stock (such as Swanson)
½ cup water
12 (6-inch) corn tortillas
6 tablespoons light sour cream (optional)
Chimichurri Sauce

1. Rub pork with salt, pepper, and garlic. Heat a large nonstick skillet over medium-high heat. Coat pan with cooking spray. Add pork; cook 3 minutes on each side or until browned. Transfer pork to a 5-quart round electric slow cooker coated with cooking spray. Add stock to pan, scraping to loosen browned bits; cook 2 minutes. Pour stock mixture over pork; add water. Cover and cook on LOW 8 hours or until tender.
2. Remove pork from slow cooker, and place in a medium bowl. Pour broth into a medium skillet. Bring to a boil over high heat; boil 5 minutes or until reduced to ⅔ cup.
3. While broth reduces, shred pork using 2 forks. Stir in broth reduction.
4. Warm tortillas according to package directions. Serve pork with tortillas, sour cream, if desired, and Chimichurri Sauce. Yield: 6 servings (serving size: ½ cup pork mixture, 2 tortillas, and about 2 tablespoons Chimichurri Sauce).

CALORIES 320; FAT 12.6g (sat 3g, mono 6.7g, poly 2.7g); PROTEIN 29.4g; CARB 23.4g; FIBER 2.3g; CHOL 62mg; IRON 1.5mg; SODIUM 506mg; CALC 71mg

Chimichurri Sauce

Prep: 7 minutes

3 garlic cloves
3 small shallots, peeled and quartered
½ cup fresh flat-leaf parsley leaves
¼ cup white wine vinegar
3 tablespoons fresh oregano leaves
2 tablespoons extra-virgin olive oil
½ teaspoon crushed red pepper
¼ teaspoon kosher salt

1. With processor on, drop garlic through food chute; process until minced. Add shallots and remaining ingredients; pulse 8 times or until finely chopped, scraping sides as necessary. Yield: 6 servings (serving size: about 2 tablespoons).

CALORIES 58; FAT 4.8g (sat 0.7g, mono 3.6g, poly 0.4g); PROTEIN 0.8g; CARB 3.6g; FIBER 0.1g; CHOL 0mg; IRON 0.5mg; SODIUM 81mg; CALC 19mg

Butterflying the pork tenderloin and pounding it to a ¼-inch thickness helps these pork steaks cook fast and ensures a fork-tender bite. If you can't find baby bok choy, use a large bok choy, but chop it into large pieces.

Hoisin Pork Steak

Prep: 3 minutes • Cook: 9 minutes • Other: 3 minutes

1 (1-pound) pork tenderloin, trimmed
¼ teaspoon salt
Cooking spray
¼ cup rice wine vinegar

3 tablespoons honey
1 tablespoon hoisin sauce
¼ teaspoon crushed red pepper

1. Slice pork tenderloin lengthwise, cutting to, but not through, other side. Open halves, laying pork flat. Place plastic wrap over pork; pound to ¼-inch thickness using a meat mallet or small heavy skillet. Cut pork crosswise into 4 steaks; sprinkle with salt.

2. Heat a large nonstick skillet over medium-high heat. Coat pan with cooking spray. Add pork; cook 3 to 4 minutes on each side or until done. Transfer pork to a plate. Reduce heat to low.

3. Combine vinegar and remaining ingredients in a small bowl, stirring with a whisk. Stir vinegar mixture into pan drippings; cook 1 minute. Return pork to skillet; remove from heat. Let stand 2 to 3 minutes or until thoroughly heated, turning often. Yield: 4 servings (serving size: 3 ounces pork and about 1 tablespoon sauce).

CALORIES 214; FAT 4.6g (sat 1.5g, mono 1.8g, poly 1g); PROTEIN 23.9g; CARB 18.8g; FIBER 0.1g; CHOL 74mg; IRON 1.5mg; SODIUM 399mg; CALC 7mg

serve with
Sesame Bok Choy

Prep: 2 minutes • Cook: 12 minutes

6 baby bok choy
Cooking spray
2 teaspoon dark sesame oil
¼ teaspoon salt

⅛ teaspoon black pepper
1 teaspoon sesame seeds
1 teaspoon black sesame seeds

1. Cut bok choy in half lengthwise, leaving core intact. Steam bok choy, covered, 4 minutes or until tender; drain well.

2. Heat a large nonstick skillet over medium-high heat. Coat pan with cooking spray. Drizzle cut sides of bok choy with oil; sprinkle with salt and pepper. Place bok choy, cut sides down, in pan; cook 6 minutes or until lightly browned. Turn bok choy over; cook an additional 1 to 2 minutes or until lightly browned. Sprinkle with sesame seeds. Yield: 4 servings (serving size: 3 bok choy halves).

CALORIES 52; FAT 3.1g (sat 0.4g, mono 1.2g, poly 1.3g); PROTEIN 2.6g; CARB 4.9g; FIBER 2.5g; CHOL 0mg; IRON 0.2mg; SODIUM 225mg; CALC 15mg

Combine the cornstarch with the stock and sherry before adding it to the hot pan to keep the gravy smooth.

Seared Pork Tenderloin Medallions with Shallot-Mushroom Pan Gravy

Prep: 4 minutes • Cook: 10 minutes

1 (1-pound) pork tenderloin, trimmed
½ teaspoon salt
½ teaspoon freshly ground black pepper
3 garlic cloves, minced
Cooking spray
1 teaspoon olive oil

1 (8-ounce) package sliced baby bella mushrooms
⅓ cup chopped shallots (about 4)
2 teaspoons cornstarch
1 cup beef stock (such as Swanson)
1 tablespoon dry sherry

1. Cut pork diagonally into thin slices. Sprinkle pork with salt and pepper; rub with garlic. Heat a large nonstick skillet over medium-high heat. Coat pan with cooking spray; add oil. Add pork; cook 1 to 2 minutes on each side or until done. Transfer pork to a platter; keep warm.
2. Recoat skillet with cooking spray. Add mushrooms and shallots; cook, stirring often, 5 minutes.
3. While mushroom mixture cooks, place cornstarch in a small bowl. Gradually add stock and sherry, stirring with a whisk until smooth. Stir stock mixture into mushroom mixture, scraping to loosen browned bits. Bring to a boil; cook, stirring constantly with a whisk, 1 minute or until thickened. Return pork and accumulated juices to pan; cook 1 to 2 minutes or until thoroughly heated. Yield: 4 servings (serving size: 3 ounces pork and about ¾ cup mushroom gravy).

CALORIES 199; FAT 5.2g (sat 1.5g, mono 2.6g, poly 0.8g); PROTEIN 27.4g; CARB 10.1g; FIBER 1.2g; CHOL 74mg; IRON 2.2mg; SODIUM 490mg; CALC 26mg

serve with
Balsamic-Glazed Green Beans

Prep: 2 minutes • Cook: 6 minutes

1 (12-ounce) package trimmed green beans
1 tablespoon butter
3 tablespoons minced shallots (about 2)
2 garlic cloves, minced

¼ cup balsamic vinegar
½ teaspoon salt
¼ teaspoon freshly ground black pepper

1. Microwave green beans according to package directions.
2. While beans cook, melt butter in a large skillet over medium heat. Add shallots and garlic; cook, stirring constantly, 2 minutes. Stir in vinegar, salt, and pepper; cook 1 minute. Add beans, tossing to coat. Yield: 4 servings (serving size: ¾ cup).

CALORIES 76; FAT 3.1g (sat 1.9g, mono 0.8g, poly 0.2g); PROTEIN 2g; CARB 11.1g; FIBER 2.8g; CHOL 8mg; IRON 0.8mg; SODIUM 515mg; CALC 48mg

Mirin, a rice wine with a low alcohol content, is the key ingredient to this teriyaki sauce's authentic flavor. The wine's high sugar content allows it to reduce into a syrup glaze. Look for mirin in the Asian foods section of your local supermarket. Serve with Pineapple Salsa and precooked white rice.

Teriyaki Pork Medallions

Prep: 5 minutes • Cook: 11 minutes

6   tablespoons mirin (sweet rice wine)
2   tablespoons low-sodium soy sauce
1½ teaspoons brown sugar
1   teaspoon dark sesame oil

1   (1-pound) pork tenderloin
Cooking spray
Pineapple Salsa

1. Combine first 4 ingredients, stirring with a whisk.
2. Cut pork crosswise into 8 pieces. Place pork pieces between 2 sheets of heavy-duty plastic wrap; pound each piece to ½-inch thickness using a meat mallet or small heavy skillet.
3. Heat a large nonstick skillet over medium-high heat. Coat pork generously with cooking spray; add to pan. Cook 3 minutes on each side or until done. Remove pork from pan; place on a serving platter. Add mirin mixture to pan. Cook 2 minutes or until mixture thickens slightly.
4. Return pork and accumulated juices to pan. Cook 2 minutes, turning pork to coat. Serve pork with sauce and Pineapple Salsa. Yield: 4 servings (serving size: 3 ounces pork, 1 tablespoon sauce, and ⅓ cup Pineapple Salsa).

CALORIES 284; FAT 8.3g (sat 2.7g, mono 3.4g, poly 1.9g); PROTEIN 35.1g; CARB 9.5g; FIBER 0.1g; CHOL 107mg; IRON 1.9mg; SODIUM 374mg; CALC 11mg

Pineapple Salsa

Prep: 8 minute

1   cup diced fresh pineapple
¼   cup diced red onion
½   medium jalapeño pepper, minced

2   tablespoons chopped fresh cilantro
1   tablespoon fresh lime juice

1. Combine all ingredients in a medium bowl. Yield: 4 servings (serving size: ⅓ cup).

CALORIES 25; FAT 0.1g (sat 0g, mono 0g, poly 0g); PROTEIN 0.4g; CARB 6.5g; FIBER 0.7g; CHOL 0mg; IRON 0.1mg; SODIUM 1mg; CALC 8mg

Infusing the oil with smoked paprika elevates the flavor of the marinade.

Smoked Paprika Pork

Prep: 4 minutes • Cook: 15 minutes • Other: 8 hours and 10 minutes

¼ cup canola oil
1½ teaspoons smoked paprika
1 tablespoon sherry vinegar
½ teaspoon finely chopped fresh rosemary (optional)

¼ teaspoon salt
2 garlic cloves, minced
2 (1-pound) pork tenderloins, trimmed
Cooking spray

1. Combine oil and paprika in a small saucepan, stirring with a whisk. Cook over low heat 2 minutes or until thoroughly heated. Add vinegar, rosemary, if desired, salt, and garlic, stirring with a whisk. Remove from heat.
2. Place pork in a large zip-top plastic bag. Add oil mixture; seal bag. Marinate in refrigerator 8 hours, turning bag occasionally.
3. Prepare grill.
4. While grill heats, remove pork from marinade, discarding marinade. Place pork on a grill rack coated with cooking spray. Grill 20 minutes or until a thermometer registers 155° (slightly pink), turning every 5 minutes. Remove from grill. Let stand 10 minutes before slicing. Cut pork diagonally into ½-inch slices. Yield: 8 servings (serving size: 3 ounces pork).

CALORIES 170; FAT 7.4g (sat 1.6g, mono 3.8g, poly 1.7g); PROTEIN 23.9g; CARB 0.5g; FIBER 0.2g; CHOL 74mg; IRON 1.5mg; SODIUM 130mg; CALC 8mg

serve with
Fragrant Saffron Rice

Prep: 5 minutes • Cook: 5 minutes

2 (8.5-ounce) packages microwaveable precooked basmati rice (such as Uncle Ben's Ready Rice)
Cooking spray
½ cup chopped red onion
2 garlic cloves, minced

½ cup frozen petite green peas
1 (.035-ounce) envelope flavoring and coloring for yellow rice (such as Vigo)
¼ teaspoon salt
¼ teaspoon crushed red pepper
¼ cup sliced almonds, toasted

1. Microwave rice according to package directions.
2. While rice cooks, heat a medium nonstick skillet over medium-high heat. Coat pan with cooking spray. Add onion and garlic; sauté 3 minutes. Add green peas; sauté 1 minute or until peas are thoroughly heated.
3. Place rice in a large bowl; stir in sautéed vegetables, rice flavoring and coloring, salt, and crushed red pepper. Toss well. Sprinkle with almonds. Yield: 8 servings (serving size: ½ cup).

CALORIES 120; FAT 1.8g (sat 0.1g, mono 1g, poly 0.4g); PROTEIN 3.2g; CARB 22.7g; FIBER 1.4g; CHOL 0mg; IRON 1.2mg; SODIUM 83mg; CALC 14mg

poultry

Rotini with Chicken, Asparagus, and Tomatoes
Skillet Barbecue Chicken
Herb-Crusted Chicken with Feta Sauce
Green Salsa Chicken
Chicken Scaloppini
Grilled Chicken and Veggies with Chimichurri Sauce
Roasted Chicken Breasts and Butternut Squash with Herbed Wine Sauce
Grilled Sun-Dried Tomato Chicken Breast
Grilled Rosemary Chicken with Chunky Tomato-Avocado Salsa
Chicken Thighs with Chipotle-Peach Sauce
Spicy Chicken Fajitas
Moroccan-Spiced Chicken Thighs
Chicken Thighs with Orange-Ginger Glaze
Chicken Under a Brick
Thai Green Curry Chicken
Roasted Chicken and White Beans with Greek Dressing
Sage Turkey Meat Loaves with Onion and Cider Gravy
Seared Turkey Cutlets with Cranberry–Caramelized Onion Salsa
Two-Tomato Turkey Sausage Pizza

Reminiscent of pasta salad, this recipe calls for mixing rotini with tender, garden-fresh vegetables and a basil-flecked balsamic vinaigrette. This dish is delicious served warm or chilled, which makes it a great lunch-box option. Serve with a side of fresh bread from the bakery.

Rotini with Chicken, Asparagus, and Tomatoes

Prep: 7 minutes • Cook: 8 minutes

- 8 ounces uncooked rotini (corkscrew pasta)
- Cooking spray
- 1 pound skinless, boneless chicken breast, cut into ¼-inch strips
- ½ teaspoon kosher salt
- ½ teaspoon freshly ground black pepper
- 1 cup (1-inch) slices asparagus

- 2 cups cherry tomatoes, halved
- 2 garlic cloves, minced
- 2 tablespoons chopped fresh basil
- 2 tablespoons balsamic vinegar
- 1 tablespoon extra-virgin olive oil
- ¼ cup (1 ounce) crumbled goat cheese

1. Cook pasta according to package directions, omitting salt and fat.
2. While pasta cooks, heat a large nonstick skillet over medium-high heat; coat with cooking spray. Sprinkle chicken with salt and pepper. Add chicken and asparagus to pan; sauté 5 minutes. Add tomatoes and garlic to pan; sauté 1 minute. Remove from heat. Stir in pasta, basil, vinegar, and oil to chicken mixture in pan. Top with cheese. Yield: 4 servings (serving size: 2 cups).

CALORIES 419; FAT 9.5g (sat 3.2g, mono 4.1g, poly 1.6g); PROTEIN 33.9g; CARB 48.5g; FIBER 3.4g; CHOL 70mg; IRON 3.2mg; SODIUM 324mg; CALC 105mg

serve with
Spinach Salad with Balsamic Vinaigrette

Prep: 3 minutes

- 2 tablespoons minced shallots
- 1 tablespoon olive oil
- 1 tablespoon balsamic vinegar

- ⅛ teaspoon salt
- Dash of black pepper
- 6 cups baby spinach

1. Combine first 5 ingredients in a large bowl, stirring with a whisk. Add spinach; toss well. Yield: 4 servings (serving size: about 1½ cups).

CALORIES 52; FAT 3.5g (sat 0.5g, mono 2.5g, poly 0.5g); PROTEIN 1g; CARB 5.4g; FIBER 1.8g; CHOL 0mg; IRON 1.3mg; SODIUM 132mg; CALC 29mg

With this dish, you'll get the flavor of barbecue without having to fire up the grill. Two of the best features of this easy chicken dish are that it dresses up a store-bought barbecue sauce and everything is cooked in the same skillet. Use presliced onion and bell pepper to make preparing this meal even faster.

Skillet Barbecue Chicken

Prep: 6 minutes • Cook: 9 minutes

4 (6-ounce) chicken breast halves
3 garlic cloves, minced
1 tablespoon salt-free Southwest chipotle seasoning blend (such as Mrs. Dash)
¼ teaspoon kosher salt

1 tablespoon olive oil
½ cup honey-roasted garlic barbecue sauce (such as Kraft)
¼ cup water

1. Place chicken between 2 sheets of plastic wrap; pound to ½-inch thickness using a meat mallet or small heavy skillet. Rub garlic over chicken, and sprinkle evenly with seasoning blend and salt.
2. Heat oil in a large nonstick skillet over medium-high heat. Add chicken; cook 3 to 4 minutes on each side. Add barbecue sauce and water, scraping pan to loosen browned bits; cook 1 to 2 minutes or until chicken is done. Yield: 4 servings (serving size: 1 chicken breast half and ¼ cup sauce).

CALORIES 266; FAT 7.3g (sat 1.6g, mono 3.8g, poly 1.5g); PROTEIN 34.4g; CARB 11.7g; FIBER 0.1g; CHOL 94mg; IRON 1.2mg; SODIUM 580mg; CALC 21mg

serve with
Sweet-and-Sour Slaw

Prep: 5 minutes • Other: 10 minutes

¼ cup cider vinegar
1 tablespoon olive oil
2 tablespoons honey
½ teaspoon salt

½ teaspoon freshly ground black pepper
4 cups packaged coleslaw
1 cup thinly sliced red bell pepper
⅓ cup thinly vertically sliced red onion

1. Combine first 5 ingredients in a large bowl, stirring with a whisk. Add coleslaw, bell pepper, and onion, tossing to coat. Cover and chill 10 minutes. Toss well before serving. Yield: 4 servings (serving size: 1 cup).

CALORIES 93; FAT 3.5g (sat 0.5g, mono 2.5g, poly 0.4g); PROTEIN 1.1g; CARB 14.9g; FIBER 2g; CHOL 0mg; IRON 0.5mg; SODIUM 301mg; CALC 28mg

A tangy Greek sauce made of mint, lemon, and feta cheese is a welcome addition to succulent breaded chicken breast. Serve it over a bed of orzo combined with chopped fresh basil. Use leftover sauce as a dressing spooned over Romaine lettuce or tossed with fresh veggies such as tomatoes and cucumbers.

Herb-Crusted Chicken with Feta Sauce

Prep: 2 minutes • Cook: 11 minutes

⅔ cup whole wheat panko (Japanese breadcrumbs)
2 tablespoons Italian seasoning
4 (6-ounce) skinless, boneless chicken breast halves

½ teaspoon salt
¼ teaspoon black pepper
4 teaspoons olive oil
6 tablespoons Feta Sauce

1. Combine panko and Italian seasoning in a shallow bowl. Sprinkle chicken with salt and pepper; dredge in panko mixture.
2. Heat oil in a large nonstick skillet over medium-high heat. Add chicken; cook 5 minutes or until browned. Turn chicken over; reduce heat to medium, and cook 5 minutes or until done. Place 1 chicken breast half on each of 4 plates, and spoon 1½ tablespoons Feta Sauce over each serving. Yield: 4 servings (serving size: 1 chicken breast and 1½ tablespoons sauce).

CALORIES 323; FAT 13.3g (sat 3.4g, mono 6.7g, poly 2.8g); PROTEIN 39.3g; CARB 10.3g; FIBER 1.6g; CHOL 98mg; IRON 1.8mg; SODIUM 584mg; CALC 51mg

Feta Sauce

Prep: 4 minutes

1 lemon
1 tablespoon chopped fresh mint
4 teaspoons extra-virgin olive oil

Dash of black pepper
1 (3.5-ounce) package reduced-fat feta cheese

1. Grate rind and squeeze juice from lemon to measure ½ teaspoon and 2 tablespoons, respectively. Combine rind, juice, mint, oil, and pepper in a small bowl, stirring with a whisk. Add cheese, stirring with a whisk. Yield: 7 servings (serving size: about 1½ tablespoons).

CALORIES 55; FAT 4.5g (sat 1.6g, mono 2.1g, poly 0.5g); PROTEIN 2.9g; CARB 0.8g; FIBER 0.3g; CHOL 4mg; IRON 0mg; SODIUM 196mg; CALC 34mg

You'll only need to purchase one package of prechopped green, yellow, and red bell pepper to use in the salsa and the corn.

Green Salsa Chicken

Prep: 5 minutes • Cook: 18 minutes

1 lime
4 tomatillos, husks and stems removed
¼ cup prechopped tricolor bell pepper mix
2 tablespoons chopped fresh cilantro

2 (6-ounce) skinless, boneless chicken breast halves
Cooking spray

1. Prepare grill.
2. Grate rind from lime and squeeze juice to measure ⅛ teaspoon and 1 tablespoon, respectively. Place rind and juice in a medium bowl. Cut tomatillos in half.
3. Heat a medium nonstick skillet over medium-high heat. Add tomatillo halves, skin side down; cook 4 minutes or until lightly charred on edges. Turn tomatillos over, and move to one side of pan; add bell pepper on the other side. Cook 2 minutes or until bell pepper is lightly charred, stirring occasionally (do not stir tomatillos). Remove pan from heat; remove tomatillos from pan, and coarsely chop. Add tomatillo, bell pepper, and cilantro to lime juice mixture; toss well.
4. Place chicken on a grill rack coated with cooking spray. Grill 6 minutes on each side or until done. Spoon tomatillo salsa over chicken. Yield: 2 servings (serving size: 1 chicken breast half and about ⅓ cup salsa).

CALORIES 309; FAT 4.7g (sat 1.2g, mono 1.5g, poly 1.6g); PROTEIN 35g; CARB 31.1g; FIBER 2.3g; CHOL 94mg; IRON 1.6mg; SODIUM 437mg; CALC 22mg

serve with
Cumin Corn

Prep: 5 minutes • Cook: 10 minutes

2 ears corn
2 teaspoons butter
¼ cup finely chopped onion
¼ cup prechopped tricolor bell pepper mix

¼ teaspoon ground cumin
⅛ teaspoon salt
⅛ teaspoon black pepper

1. Remove husks from corn; scrub silks from corn. Cut kernels from ears of corn; set corn aside. Discard cobs.
2. Melt butter in a nonstick skillet over medium heat. Add onion and bell pepper mix; cook, stirring constantly, 3 to 4 minutes until crisp-tender. Stir in cumin, salt, and pepper; cook 1 minute. Stir in corn; cook 5 minutes or until corn is crisp-tender, stirring frequently. Yield: 2 servings (serving size: ½ cup).

CALORIES 122; FAT 5g (sat 2.6g, mono 1.3g, poly 0.7g); PROTEIN 3.3g; CARB 19.6g; FIBER 3.1g; CHOL 10mg; IRON 0.7mg; SODIUM 187mg; CALC 10mg

Scallopini are cuts of meat that are pounded thin and then cooked to perfection in about 6 minutes. For a beautifully browned crust, make sure the pan and oil are hot—the chicken should hiss as it hits the pan.

Chicken Scaloppini

Prep: 10 minutes • Cook: 15 minutes

4 (6-ounce) skinless, boneless chicken breast halves
1 large egg white
2 teaspoons water

½ cup Italian-seasoned breadcrumbs
2 teaspoons olive oil, divided
½ cup fat-free, less-sodium chicken broth
1 tablespoon fresh lemon juice

1. Place chicken between 2 sheets of plastic wrap. Pound to ¼-inch thickness using a meat mallet or small heavy skillet.
2. Combine egg white and water in a shallow dish, stirring with a whisk. Place breadcrumbs in another shallow dish. Dip each chicken breast half in egg mixture; dredge in breadcrumbs.
3. Heat 1 teaspoon oil in a large nonstick skillet over medium-high heat. Add half of chicken to pan. Cook 3 minutes on each side or until golden. Transfer to a plate; cover and keep warm. Repeat procedure with remaining oil and chicken.
4. Add broth and lemon juice to pan, stirring to loosen browned bits. Cook, uncovered, over high heat 2 to 3 minutes or until reduced to ⅓ cup. Drizzle sauce over chicken. Yield: 4 servings (serving size: 1 chicken breast half and about 1 tablespoon sauce).

CALORIES 265; FAT 7g (sat 1.4g, mono 3g, poly 2.1g); PROTEIN 37.4g; CARB 10.5g; FIBER 0.5g; CHOL 94mg; IRON 1.9mg; SODIUM 380mg; CALC 38mg

serve with
Pan-Roasted Asparagus and Tomatoes

Prep: 5 minutes • Cook: 6 minutes

1 pound asparagus spears, trimmed
1 tablespoon olive oil
2 cups grape tomatoes

¼ teaspoon salt
¼ teaspoon freshly ground black pepper

1. Rinse asparagus (do not dry). Heat oil in a large nonstick skillet over medium-high heat. Add asparagus; cook 3 minutes. Add tomatoes; cook 2 minutes or until asparagus is crisp-tender and tomatoes just begin to burst, turning asparagus occasionally with tongs. Sprinkle with salt and pepper. Yield: 4 servings (serving size: ¼ of asparagus-tomato mixture).

CALORIES 72; FAT 3.5g (sat 0.5g, mono 2.5g, poly 0.4g); PROTEIN 3g; CARB 7.5g; FIBER 3.4g; CHOL 0mg; IRON 2.5mg; SODIUM 151mg; CALC 40mg

Chimichurri is a very flavorful and vinegary condiment made from parsley, garlic, and olive oil that is served in Argentina with grilled meats. You can make the sauce up to a day ahead and store it in the refrigerator.

Grilled Chicken and Veggies with Chimichurri Sauce

Prep: 8 minutes • Cook: 12 minutes

4 (6-ounce) skinless, boneless chicken breast halves
2 yellow squash, cut into ¼-inch slices
1 red bell pepper, cut into 2-inch-squares
1 red onion, cut into ¼-inch slices

Cooking spray
½ teaspoon salt
½ teaspoon black pepper
Chimichurri Sauce

1. Prepare grill.
2. Coat chicken and vegetables with cooking spray; sprinkle with salt and pepper.
3. Place chicken and vegetables on a grill rack coated with cooking spray. Grill chicken 6 minutes on each side or until done; grill vegetables 3 minutes on each side. Serve chicken with Chimichurri Sauce. Yield: 4 servings (serving size: 3 ounces chicken, about 1 cup vegetables, and ⅓ cup sauce).

CALORIES 351; FAT 14.9g (sat 2.6g, mono 8.9g, poly 2.5g); PROTEIN 37.8g; CARB 17g; FIBER 3.7g; CHOL 94mg; IRON 3.5mg; SODIUM 542mg; CALC 140mg

Chimichurri Sauce

Prep: 13 minutes

10 garlic cloves
2 cups fresh flat-leaf parsley leaves
1 cup chopped onion
½ cup chopped fresh oregano
½ cup white wine vinegar

3 tablespoons olive oil
2 tablespoons fresh lemon juice
1 teaspoon grated lemon rind
½ teaspoon freshly ground black pepper
¼ teaspoon salt

1. With food processor on, drop garlic through food chute; process until minced. Add parsley and remaining ingredients; process 1 minute or until finely minced. Yield: 4 servings (serving size: about ⅓ cup sauce).

CALORIES 138; FAT 10.7g (sat 1.5g, mono 7.5g, poly 1.1g); PROTEIN 2.1g; CARB 10.2g; FIBER 2g; CHOL 0mg; IRON 2.2mg; SODIUM 166mg; CALC 104mg

Roasted Chicken Breasts and Butternut Squash with Herbed Wine Sauce

Prep: 9 minutes • Cook: 38 minutes

4 bone-in chicken breast halves (about 2 pounds), skinned
Cooking spray
1 tablespoon olive oil, divided
½ teaspoon salt, divided
½ teaspoon freshly ground black pepper, divided

5 cups (½-inch) cubed peeled butternut squash (2¼ pounds)
1 teaspoon fine herbs
3 tablespoons dry white wine

1. Preheat oven to 450°.
2. Place chicken in a large roasting pan coated with cooking spray. Brush chicken with 1½ teaspoons olive oil; sprinkle with ¼ teaspoon salt and ¼ teaspoon pepper.
3. Place squash in a large bowl. Drizzle with remaining olive oil, and sprinkle with fine herbs, remaining salt, and remaining pepper; toss well. Add squash to pan. Bake at 450° for 38 minutes or until chicken is done. Transfer chicken and squash to a serving platter; keep warm.
4. Add wine to pan drippings; bring to a boil over high heat, scraping pan to loosen browned bits. Reduce heat; cook 2 minutes or until reduced to ¼ cup. Place 1 chicken breast half on each of 4 plates. Spoon 1 tablespoon sauce over each chicken breast. Serve with squash. Yield: 4 servings (serving size: 1 chicken breast half, 1 cup squash, and 1 tablespoon sauce).

CALORIES 370; FAT 7.9g (sat 1.7g, mono 4g, poly 1.4g); PROTEIN 40.1g; CARB 36.5g; FIBER 6.1g; CHOL 102mg; IRON 3mg; SODIUM 539mg; CALC 164mg

make it faster

Peeling and cubing a butternut squash isn't difficult, but it will require a few extra minutes of your time. We peeled and cubed a butternut squash for this dish. To prepare this recipe even quicker, look for precubed butternut squash in the produce section of your supermarket. It may cost a little extra, but the trade-off is time saved in prepping this meal.

Butternut squash's natural sugars caramelize during roasting. When paired with fine herbs and wine, they create a flavor explosion that rivals any bistro specialty.

Chicken cutlets are a great convenience because they adapt to a variety of quick-cooking techniques, such as grilling, searing, and baking. Dress them up with jarred sun-dried tomato pesto embellished with fresh herbs and garlic.

Grilled Sun-Dried Tomato Chicken Breast

Prep: 7 minutes • Cook: 6 minutes

2 tablespoons sun-dried tomato pesto (such as Classico)
2 tablespoons chopped fresh basil
1 tablespoon chopped fresh oregano
2 garlic cloves, minced

4 (4-ounce) chicken breast cutlets
¼ teaspoon salt
¼ teaspoon freshly ground black pepper
Cooking spray

1. Prepare grill.
2. Combine first 4 ingredients. Sprinkle chicken with salt and pepper; coat with cooking spray.
3. Place chicken on a grill rack coated with cooking spray. Grill 3 minutes on each side or until done. Spoon pesto mixture evenly over chicken. Yield: 4 servings (serving size: 1 chicken cutlet and about 1 tablespoon pesto mixture).

CALORIES 137; FAT 3.3g (sat 0.9g, mono 0.9g, poly 0.8g); PROTEIN 23.4g; CARB 1.8g; FIBER 0.2g; CHOL 63mg; IRON 1mg; SODIUM 279mg; CALC 21mg

serve with
Warm Cannellini Bean Salad

Prep: 3 minutes • Cook: 10 minutes

1 tablespoon olive oil
1 red onion, vertically cut into thin slices
3 garlic cloves, minced
1 (19-ounce) can cannellini beans, rinsed and drained

1 (12-ounce) jar roasted red bell peppers
4 cups baby arugula
4 teaspoons balsamic glaze (such as Monari Federzoni)

1. Heat oil in a large nonstick skillet over medium heat. Add onion; cook 6 minutes or until lightly browned and tender, stirring occasionally.
2. Add garlic; sauté 1 minute. Add beans, peppers, and arugula; cook 1 to 2 minutes or just until arugula begins to wilt. Spoon salad evenly onto 4 serving plates. Drizzle with balsamic glaze. Yield: 4 servings (serving size: about 1 cup salad and 1 teaspoon glaze).

CALORIES 134; FAT 3.9g (sat 0.5g, mono 2.5g, poly 0.7g); PROTEIN 4g; CARB 20.3g; FIBER 3.9g; CHOL 0mg; IRON 1.5mg; SODIUM 347mg; CALC 67mg

Assertive feta cheese pairs well with acidic tomatoes and rich avocados in this 5-minute salsa. Make this salsa right before serving, and avoid refrigerating it—the texture of the tomato will soften. Serve this dish with a side of grilled vegetables.

Grilled Rosemary Chicken with Chunky Tomato-Avocado Salsa

Prep: 3 minutes • Cook: 6 minutes • Other: 30 minutes

2 tablespoons olive oil
2 tablespoons red wine vinegar
1 tablespoon chopped fresh rosemary
1 tablespoon minced garlic
4 (4-ounce) chicken cutlets

¼ teaspoon salt
¼ teaspoon black pepper
Cooking spray
Chunky Tomato-Avocado Salsa

1. Combine first 4 ingredients in a large heavy-duty zip-top plastic bag. Place chicken between 2 sheets of plastic wrap; pound to ¼-inch thickness using a meat mallet or small heavy skillet. Sprinkle chicken with salt and pepper, and add to bag; seal. Marinate in refrigerator 30 minutes.
2. Prepare grill.
3. Remove chicken from marinade, discarding marinade. Place chicken on a grill rack coated with cooking spray. Grill 3 minutes on each side or until done. Yield: 4 servings (serving size: 1 chicken cutlet).

CALORIES 393; FAT 21.8g (sat 4.5g, mono 12.3g, poly 3.9g); PROTEIN 39.4g; CARB 7.3g; FIBER 3.1g; CHOL 101mg; IRON 1.7mg; SODIUM 430mg; CALC 84mg

Chunky Tomato-Avocado Salsa

Prep: 5 minutes

1 tablespoon chopped fresh oregano
1 tablespoon extra-virgin olive oil
2 tablespoons red wine vinegar
1 garlic clove, minced

2 cups grape tomatoes, halved
½ cup (2 ounces) crumbled reduced-fat feta cheese with basil and sun-dried tomatoes
1 ripe peeled avocado, chopped

1. Combine first 4 ingredients in a large bowl, stirring with a whisk. Add tomato halves, cheese, and avocado; toss gently. Yield: 4 servings (serving size: ¾ cup).

CALORIES 132; FAT 10.6g (sat 2.4g, mono 5.9g, poly 1.9g); PROTEIN 4.2g; CARB 6.3g; FIBER 3g; CHOL 4mg; IRON 0.4mg; SODIUM 199mg; CALC 64mg

Juicy, ripe peaches in peak season are key for this recipe. If your peaches are firm, let them stand on the kitchen counter for a few days until they're soft to the touch and have an enticing aroma. While the chicken and vegetables grill, prepare the chipotle-peach sauce.

Chicken Thighs with Chipotle-Peach Sauce

Prep: 3 minutes • Cook: 12 minutes

1½ pounds skinless, boneless chicken thighs (about 8 thighs)
½ teaspoon salt, divided
½ teaspoon freshly ground black pepper
Olive oil-flavored cooking spray

2 medium peaches, peeled, pitted, and quartered
2 tablespoons honey
1 chipotle chile in adobo sauce

1. Prepare grill.
2. Sprinkle chicken with ¼ teaspoon salt and ½ teaspoon pepper; coat with cooking spray. Place chicken on a grill rack coated with cooking spray. Grill 12 minutes or until done, turning chicken once.
3. While chicken cooks, puree peaches, honey, chile, and remaining ¼ teaspoon salt in a food processor. Reserve ¾ cup chipotle-peach sauce to serve with chicken; brush remaining ½ cup sauce over chicken during last 2 minutes of cooking. Yield: 4 servings (serving size: about 2 thighs and 3 tablespoons sauce).

CALORIES 307; FAT 13.2g (sat 3.6g; mono 4.9g; poly 4.3g); PROTEIN 31.1g; CARB 15.1g; FIBER 1.2g; CHOL 112mg; IRON 1.8mg; SODIUM 423mg; CALC 20mg

serve with
Grilled Corn and Red Pepper Salad

Prep: 7 minutes • Cook: 12 minutes

2 ears corn, shucked
2 red bell peppers, seeded and halved
Olive oil-flavored cooking spray
2 green onions, chopped

2 tablespoons fresh lime juice
¼ teaspoon salt
¼ teaspoon freshly ground black pepper

1. Prepare grill.
2. Coat corn and bell peppers with cooking spray. Place on a grill rack coated with cooking spray. Grill 6 minutes on each side or until slightly charred.
3. Cut corn from cob; cut bell pepper into strips. Place in a bowl with green onions and remaining ingredients. Toss well. Yield: 4 servings (serving size: about ⅔ cup).

CALORIES 57; FAT 0.9g (sat 0.1g; mono 0.1g; poly 0.3g); PROTEIN 2.1g; CARB 12.7g; FIBER 2.8g; CHOL 0mg; IRON 0.6mg; SODIUM 155mg; CALC 13mg

Simple to prepare and packed with flavor, this recipe is one you'll turn to every time you get a craving for sizzling Mexican fare. Serve with sour cream or chopped avocado, if desired.

Spicy Chicken Fajitas

Prep: 7 minutes • Cook: 8 minutes

6 skinless, boneless chicken thighs (1 pound)
2 teaspoons fajita seasoning (such as McCormick)
Cooking spray
2 cups vertically sliced onion
2 cups red bell pepper strips

4 (7½-inch) 96% fat-free whole wheat tortillas
½ cup fresh salsa
Chopped avocado (optional)
Chopped fresh cilantro (optional)
Reduced-fat sour cream (optional)

1. Cut chicken into ½-inch-wide strips. Place chicken in a small bowl; sprinkle with fajita seasoning, tossing to coat. Heat a large nonstick skillet over medium-high heat. Coat pan with cooking spray. Add chicken and onion; stir-fry 3 minutes. Add bell pepper; stir-fry 5 minutes or until chicken is done.
2. Place 1 tortilla on each of 4 plates. Top each evenly with chicken mixture and salsa. Top with avocado and cilantro, if desired. Fold tortillas over filling, and top with sour cream, if desired. Serve immediately. Yield: 4 servings (serving size: 1 tortilla, 1 cup chicken mixture, and 2 tablespoons salsa).

CALORIES 341; FAT 10.7g (sat 2.4g, mono 4.3g, poly 3.5g); PROTEIN 25.4g; CARB 34.8g; FIBER 4.6g; CHOL 74mg; IRON 1.4mg; SODIUM 747mg; CALC 27mg

serve with
Chili-Dusted Mango

Prep: 8 minutes

2 ripe mangoes, peeled, seeded, and cut into ½-inch slices
2 teaspoons fresh lime juice

¼ teaspoon chili powder
1 teaspoon fresh cilantro

1. Arrange mango slices evenly on 4 plates; sprinkle evenly with lime juice, chili powder, and cilantro. Yield: 4 servings (serving size: ¼ of mango slices).

CALORIES 72; FAT 0.3g (sat 0.1g, mono 0.1g, poly 0.1g); PROTEIN 0.6g; CARB 18.9g; FIBER 2g; CHOL 0mg; IRON 0.2mg; SODIUM 7mg; CALC 11mg

Chicken thighs cooked in a smoky, acidic tomato sauce combine seamlessly with a sweet, nutty couscous to create a hearty North African–inspired meal. While the chicken simmers, prepare the couscous so both dishes will be ready at the same time.

Moroccan-Spiced Chicken Thighs

Prep: 8 minutes • Cook: 15 minutes

¼ teaspoon salt
½ teaspoon smoked paprika
½ teaspoon ground cumin
½ teaspoon dried thyme
8 skinless, boneless chicken thighs (1½ pounds)

Cooking spray
1 (14.5-ounce) can fire-roasted diced tomatoes with garlic, undrained
Chopped fresh cilantro (optional)

1. Combine first 4 ingredients. Rub chicken thighs with spice mixture.
2. Heat a large nonstick skillet over medium-high heat. Coat pan with cooking spray. Add chicken; cook 2 minutes. Turn chicken over; stir in tomatoes. Bring to a boil; cover, reduce heat, and simmer 10 minutes. Uncover and cook 1 minute or until liquid is reduced by half. Sprinkle with cilantro, if desired. Yield: 4 servings (serving size: 2 chicken thighs and ¼ cup tomato sauce).

CALORIES 273; FAT 12.9g (sat 3.6g, mono 4.9g, poly 3.6g); PROTEIN 31.4g; CARB 5.4g; FIBER 1.2g; CHOL 112mg; IRON 3mg; SODIUM 479mg; CALC 42mg

serve with
Whole Wheat Couscous and Apricots

Prep: 5 minutes • Cook: 5 minutes • Other: 5 minutes

2 teaspoons olive oil
¾ cup whole wheat couscous
1 cup fat-free, less-sodium chicken broth

⅓ cup diced dried apricots
⅓ cup slivered almonds, toasted

1. Heat oil in a medium saucepan over medium heat. Add couscous; sauté 1 minute. Stir in broth and apricots. Bring to a boil; remove from heat. Let stand 5 minutes or until liquid is absorbed. Add almonds; fluff with a fork. Yield: 4 servings (serving size: about ⅔ cup).

CALORIES 196; FAT 7.6g (sat 0.8g, mono 4.7g, poly 1.4g); PROTEIN 6.6g; CARB 27.7g; FIBER 4.4g; CHOL 0mg; IRON 1.7mg; SODIUM 19mg; CALC 39mg

Chicken Thighs with Orange-Ginger Glaze

Prep: 1 minute • Cook: 14 minutes

8   skinless, boneless chicken thighs (about 1½ pounds)
½   teaspoon salt
¼   teaspoon black pepper
⅛   teaspoon garlic powder

1½   teaspoons olive oil
1   navel orange
3   tablespoons honey
1   teaspoon grated peeled fresh ginger
Chopped green onions (optional)

1. Sprinkle chicken with salt, pepper, and garlic powder. Heat oil in a large nonstick skillet over medium-high heat. Add chicken; cook 3 to 4 minutes on each side or until browned.
2. While chicken cooks, grate rind and squeeze juice from orange to measure 1 teaspoon and ¼ cup, respectively. Add orange rind, juice, honey, and ginger to chicken, scraping to loosen browned bits. Bring to a boil; reduce heat, and simmer, uncovered, 7 minutes or until chicken is done and orange mixture is syrupy. Sprinkle with green onions, if desired. Yield: 4 servings (serving size: 2 chicken thighs and about 1½ tablespoons sauce).

CALORIES 327; FAT 14.5g (sat 3.8g, mono 6.4g, poly 3.6g); PROTEIN 30.9g; CARB 17.7g; FIBER 0.9g; CHOL 112mg; IRON 1.7mg; SODIUM 395mg; CALC 31mg

serve with
Roasted Broccoli with Almonds

Prep: 6 minutes • Cook: 14 minutes

1¼   pounds fresh broccoli crowns (about 3)
Cooking spray
1   tablespoon olive oil
1   garlic clove, pressed

¼   teaspoon salt
¼   teaspoon black pepper
3   tablespoons sliced almonds

1. Preheat oven to 475°.
2. Cut broccoli into 3-inch-long spears; cut thick stems in half lengthwise. Place broccoli in a single layer on a jelly-roll pan coated with cooking spray.
3. Combine olive oil and garlic; drizzle broccoli with oil mixture, and toss well. Sprinkle with salt and pepper. Bake at 475° for 14 minutes (do not stir).
4. While broccoli roasts, cook almonds, stirring constantly, in a small skillet over medium heat 2 minutes or until toasted. Sprinkle roasted broccoli with toasted almonds. Yield: 4 servings (serving size: about 1 cup).

CALORIES 97; FAT 6.1g (sat 0.7g, mono 3.9g, poly 1.1g); PROTEIN 5.2g; CARB 8.6g; FIBER 4.8g; CHOL 0mg; IRON 1.5mg; SODIUM 184mg; CALC 81mg

Honey—combined with fresh ginger, orange rind, and orange juice—is all that's needed to concoct this spicy-sweet glaze. Round out your meal with white rice.

The weight of the bricks helps the chicken cook evenly, leaving the breast moist and juicy, while the legs cook fully. Marinating the chicken tenderizes the meat and also adds a pleasant tangy flavor.

Chicken Under a Brick

Prep: 5 minutes • Cook: 40 minutes • Other: 8 hours

1 (3¼-pound) whole chicken
½ cup light mayonnaise
⅓ cup cider vinegar
¼ cup water

2 tablespoons sugar
1 tablespoon chopped fresh rosemary
Cooking spray

1. Remove backbone from chicken using kitchen shears. Combine mayonnaise and next 4 ingredients in a large heavy-duty zip-top plastic bag; add chicken. Seal and turn to coat. Marinate in refrigerator 8 hours, turning bag occasionally.
2. Remove chicken from marinade, and discard marinade. Heat a large cast-iron skillet over medium-high heat. Coat pan with cooking spray. Add chicken to pan. Place 2 bricks wrapped in heavy-duty foil over chicken, pressing down to flatten. Cook 20 minutes; turn chicken over. Reposition bricks. Cook an additional 20 minutes or until chicken is done. Remove skin from chicken, and cut into quarters. Carve chicken. Yield: 4 servings (serving size: about 4 ounces).

CALORIES 290; FAT 10.5g (sat 2.1g, mono 4.7g, poly 3.5g); PROTEIN 75g; CARB 4.7g; FIBER 0g; CHOL 253mg; IRON 4mg; SODIUM 397mg; CALC 44mg

serve with
Summer Succotash

Prep: 5 minutes • Cook: 10 minutes

2 center-cut bacon slices
1 cup frozen baby lima beans
2 ears corn
1 large garlic clove, minced

1 cup grape tomatoes, halved
¼ teaspoon salt
¼ teaspoon freshly ground black pepper
1 tablespoon chopped fresh basil

1. Cook bacon in a large nonstick skillet over medium-high heat until crisp. Remove bacon from pan, reserving drippings in pan; crumble bacon, and set aside.
2. While bacon cooks, thaw lima beans in a colander under warm water.
3. Cut kernels from ears of corn. Add corn and garlic to drippings. Sauté 4 minutes or until corn is golden. Stir in lima beans, tomato halves, salt, and pepper. Sauté 3 minutes or until thoroughly heated. Stir in bacon and basil just before serving. Yield: 4 servings (serving size: about ⅔ cup).

CALORIES 104; FAT 1.3g (sat 0.4g, mono 0.4g, poly 0.3g); PROTEIN 5.8g; CARB 19.2g; FIBER 4.5g; CHOL 3mg; IRON 1.2mg; SODIUM 210mg; CALC 23mg

Thanks to a deli rotisserie chicken, this dish lets you enjoy Thai cuisine with minimal effort. We packed this classic curry dish with colorful peppers and used light coconut milk to cut some of the fat. Serve it over fragrant jasmine rice to soak up the sauce.

Thai Green Curry Chicken

Prep: 5 minutes • Cook: 10 minutes

Cooking spray
1 medium onion, halved and vertically sliced
1 small zucchini, halved lengthwise and sliced
1 small red bell pepper, cut into thin strips
2 teaspoons green curry paste
2 cups thinly sliced roasted chicken breast

1 cup fat-free, less-sodium chicken broth
⅔ cup light coconut milk
3 tablespoons fresh cilantro leaves
Lime wedges (optional)
Cilantro sprigs (optional)

1. Heat a large nonstick skillet over medium-high heat. Coat pan with cooking spray. Add onion, and sauté 5 minutes. Add zucchini and bell pepper, and sauté 3 minutes; stir in curry paste. Add chicken, broth, and coconut milk to pan; bring to a boil. Reduce heat, and simmer 3 minutes. Spoon evenly into 4 bowls; sprinkle evenly with cilantro. Serve with lime wedges, and garnish with cilantro sprigs, if desired. Yield: 4 servings (serving size: 1 cup chicken mixture).

CALORIES 159; FAT 4.7g (sat 2.6g; mono 0.9g; poly 0.6g); PROTEIN 23.9g; CARB 4.9g; FIBER 0.8g; CHOL 63mg; IRON 1.1mg; SODIUM 224mg; CALC 22mg

serve with
Cucumber, Pineapple, and Mint Salad

Prep: 5 minutes

1 medium cucumber, coarsely chopped
1 cup coarsely chopped pineapple
2 green onions, thinly sliced

3 tablespoons chopped fresh mint
1 tablespoon seasoned rice vinegar
1 tablespoon fish sauce

1. Combine all ingredients in a medium bowl; toss well. Chill until ready to serve. Yield: 4 servings (serving size: ¾ cup).

CALORIES 37; FAT 0.1g (sat 0g; mono 0g; poly 0g); PROTEIN 1.4g; CARB 8.5g; FIBER 1.1g; CHOL 0mg; IRON 0.6mg; SODIUM 424mg; CALC 30mg

For variation and added crunch, toast the pita wedges while you're preparing the chicken and bean mixture. For crispy wedges, split the pita rounds in half, coat the cut sides with butter-flavored cooking spray, and stack the split rounds. Cut the rounds into wedges, and place the wedges on a large baking sheet. Bake the pita wedges at 350° for 10 minutes or until golden and crisp.

Roasted Chicken and White Beans with Greek Dressing

Prep: 8 minutes

2½ cups shredded skinless, boneless rotisserie chicken
1 (15.5-ounce) can cannellini beans, rinsed and drained
1 cup chopped red onion
Greek Dressing
2 (7-inch) whole wheat pitas, each cut into 8 wedges

1. Combine first 3 ingredients in a large bowl. Drizzle Greek Dressing over chicken mixture, and toss well. Serve with pita wedges. Yield: 4 servings (serving size: 1¼ cups chicken mixture and 4 pita wedges).

CALORIES 400; FAT 14g (sat 5g, mono 5.9g, poly 2.5g); PROTEIN 36.3g; CARB 31.5g; FIBER 5.6g; CHOL 93mg; IRON 3.1mg; SODIUM 550mg; CALC 159mg

Greek Dressing

Prep: 3 minutes

1½ tablespoons red wine vinegar
1½ tablespoons olive oil
½ teaspoon dry mustard
2 tablespoons minced fresh rosemary
¾ cup (3 ounces) crumbled feta cheese
½ teaspoon freshly ground black pepper
2 garlic cloves, minced

1. Combine all ingredients in a small bowl. Yield: 4 servings (serving size: 2 tablespoons).

CALORIES 108; FAT 9.8g (sat 3.9g, mono 4.7g, poly 0.7g); PROTEIN 3.3g; CARB 1.8g; FIBER 0.3g; CHOL 19mg; IRON 0.3mg; SODIUM 238mg; CALC 113mg

Cooking meat loaf in single-serving portions cuts the cooking time in half and keeps the ground turkey moist. Be sure to gently shape the turkey mixture into loaves—overworking the mixture will make them tough. For a hearty meal, serve with green beans and mashed potatoes.

Sage Turkey Meat Loaves with Onion and Cider Gravy

Prep: 10 minutes • Cook: 25 minutes

1½ pounds ground turkey
1 cup shredded peeled apple (about 1 medium)
½ cup dry breadcrumbs
2 tablespoons minced fresh sage
½ teaspoon salt
½ teaspoon black pepper
Cooking spray
Onion and Cider Gravy

1. Preheat oven to 425°.
2. Combine first 6 ingredients in a large bowl. Divide turkey mixture into 6 equal portions, shaping each into an oval-shaped loaf. Place loaves on a broiler pan coated with cooking spray. Bake at 425° for 25 minutes or until a thermometer inserted in center registers 165°.
3. While meat loaves bake, prepare Onion and Cider Gravy. Serve meat loaves with gravy. Yield: 6 servings (serving size: 1 meat loaf and about ¼ cup gravy).

CALORIES 283; FAT 11.9g (sat 3.9g, mono 4g, poly 3.4g); PROTEIN 22.5g; CARB 21g; FIBER 1.2g; CHOL 95mg; IRON 1.6mg; SODIUM 567mg; CALC 33mg

Onion and Cider Gravy

Prep: 3 minutes • Cook: 34 minutes

1 tablespoon butter
1 large Vidalia or other sweet onion, vertically sliced
1 cup apple cider
1 cup fat-free, less-sodium chicken broth
1 tablespoon cornstarch
1 tablespoon water
¼ teaspoon salt

1. Melt butter in a large nonstick skillet over medium-high heat; add onion. Cook 10 minutes or until golden brown, stirring frequently.
2. While onion cooks, bring cider and broth to a boil in a medium saucepan; boil 23 minutes or until reduced to 1 cup. Combine cornstarch, water, and salt; add to reduced cider mixture, stirring constantly with a whisk. Cook over medium heat 1 minute or until slightly thickened. Stir in onion. Yield: 4 servings (serving size: about ¼ cup).

CALORIES 64; FAT 1.9g (sat 1.2g, mono 0.5g, poly 0.1g); PROTEIN 0.8g; CARB 11.2g; FIBER 0.5g; CHOL 5mg; IRON 0.2mg; SODIUM 190mg; CALC 12mg

Don't reserve turkey and cranberries just for the holidays. This meal uses dried cranberries, which you can find year-round. Serve with a buttered baked sweet potato.

Seared Turkey Cutlets with Cranberry–Caramelized Onion Salsa

Prep: 2 minutes • Cook: 12 minutes

2 teaspoons olive oil
8 ounces turkey cutlets (about 4 cutlets)
3/8 teaspoon salt, divided
1/4 teaspoon freshly ground black pepper, divided
1 cup prechopped onion

1/4 cup water
3 tablespoons sweetened dried cranberries, chopped
2 tablespoons white balsamic vinegar
Chopped fresh parsley (optional)

1. Heat oil in a large nonstick skillet over medium-high heat. Sprinkle turkey with 1/8 teaspoon salt and 1/8 teaspoon pepper. Add turkey to pan; cook 2 minutes on each side or until done. Divide turkey between 2 plates; keep warm.
2. Add onion to pan. Cook 3 minutes, stirring frequently; add remaining 1/4 teaspoon salt and remaining 1/8 teaspoon pepper. Cook 5 minutes or until onion is tender and golden, stirring frequently. Stir in water, cranberries, and vinegar; cook 2 minutes or until cranberries are tender. Remove from heat; stir in parsley, if desired. Yield: 2 servings (serving size: 2 turkey cutlets and about 1/2 cup salsa.)

CALORIES 249; FAT 7.4g (sat 1.4g, mono 4.2g, poly 1.6g); PROTEIN 23.8g; CARB 22g; FIBER 2.1g; CHOL 63mg; IRON 1mg; SODIUM 494mg; CALC 32mg

serve with
Roasted Brussels Sprouts à l'Orange

Prep: 3 minutes • Cook: 14 minutes

2½ cups trimmed Brussels sprouts (about 8 ounces), halved lengthwise
2 teaspoons olive oil
1/4 teaspoon salt

1/8 teaspoon black pepper
1/2 teaspoon grated orange rind
2 tablespoons fresh orange juice

1. Preheat oven to 425°.
2. Place Brussels sprouts in a large bowl. Add oil, salt, and pepper; toss to coat. Place Brussels sprouts in a single layer on a foil-lined baking sheet. Roast at 425° for 7 minutes. Turn Brussels sprouts over, using a wide spatula. Bake an additional 7 minutes or until tender and browned.
3. Place Brussels sprouts in a bowl. Combine orange rind and juice in a small bowl. Drizzle juice mixture over Brussels sprouts; toss well. Yield: 2 servings (serving size: 1⅓ cups).

CALORIES 96; FAT 4.9g (sat 0.7g, mono 3.3g, poly 0.7g); PROTEIN 4g; CARB 12g; FIBER 4.4g; CHOL 0mg; IRON 1.7mg; SODIUM 319mg; CALC 51mg

Look for fresh pizza dough in your supermarket's bakery, or purchase it from your local pizza parlor.

Two-Tomato Turkey Sausage Pizza

Prep: 10 minutes • Cook: 18 minutes

1 pound pizza dough
Cooking spray
2 (4-ounce) links turkey Italian sausage
1 tablespoon oil from sun-dried tomatoes
4 oil-packed sun-dried tomatoes, drained

6 (0.67-ounce) slices reduced-fat Provolone cheese (such as Sargento)
2 cups grape tomatoes, halved
Crushed red pepper (optional)

1. Preheat oven to 450°.
2. While oven preheats, shape pizza dough into a 15½ x 10½–inch rectangle on a work surface; transfer to a large baking sheet coated with cooking spray. Place in oven on bottom rack while oven continues to preheat, and bake 10 minutes.
3. While crust prebakes, cook sausage in a skillet over medium-high heat until browned, stirring to crumble.
4. Remove crust from oven; rub with sun-dried tomato oil, and sprinkle with sun-dried tomatoes. Top with cheese, sausage, and grape tomato halves. Bake at 450° on bottom rack for 8 minutes or until crust is golden and cheese melts. Cut pizza into 6 rectangles, and sprinkle with crushed red pepper before serving, if desired. Yield: 6 servings (serving size: 1 piece).

CALORIES 312; FAT 12.5g (sat 3.5g, mono 4.9g, poly 3.5g); PROTEIN 17.7g; CARB 36.9g; FIBER 2.3g; CHOL 42mg; IRON 2.6mg; SODIUM 761mg; CALC 183mg

serve with
Lemony Romaine Wedges with Cucumber

Prep: 4 minutes

3 tablespoons fresh lemon juice
3 tablespoons olive oil
¼ teaspoon salt

¼ teaspoon black pepper
3 heads romaine lettuce, halved lengthwise
2 cups thinly sliced pickling cucumber (about 2)

1. Combine first 4 ingredients in a small bowl, stirring with a whisk. Place a lettuce wedge on each of 6 plates; sprinkle with cucumber slices and drizzle with dressing. Yield: 6 servings (serving size: ½ romaine heart, about ⅓ cup cucumber slices, and 1 tablespoon dressing).

CALORIES 80; FAT 7g (sat 1g, mono 4.9g, poly 0.8g); PROTEIN 1.2g; CARB 4.1g; FIBER 1.8g; CHOL 0mg; IRON 0.8mg; SODIUM 103mg; CALC 30mg

desserts

Brownie Bites
Flourless Chocolate Cakes
Vanilla Sponge Cakes with Fresh Berry Filling
Peach-Pineapple Crumble
Chocolate-Raisin Bread Pudding
Chocolate and Caramel Bread Pudding
Lemon Pudding Cake
White Chocolate–Cherry Rice Pudding
Triple-Chocolate Pudding
White Chocolate Panna Cotta
Glazed Apples in Caramel Sauce
Marsala-Poached Figs
White Chocolate–Hazelnut Tarts
Blueberry-Lemon-White Chocolate Tarts
Raspberry–Cream Cheese Tarts
Dulce de Leche Tartlets
Berry-Lime-Angel Food Mini Trifles
Hazelnut–Sugar Cookie S'mores
Strawberry-Kiwi Freeze
Cherry-Merlot Granita
Raspberry and Coconut Parfaits with Coconut-Walnut Crunch
Banana-Caramel Sundaes
Mexican Hot Fudge Sundae
Coffee Ice-Cream Sundae with Dark Chocolate–Sea Salt Almond Bark
Chocolate-Toffee Ice-Cream Pie

Cocoa nibs, which are broken bits of husked cocoa beans, add delicate chocolate flavor and delicious nutty crunch to baked goods. You can find cocoa nibs at upscale supermarkets and gourmet cookware stores. When you make this recipe, don't be alarmed that the batter is very wet—the end result will be moist, tender minicakes.

Brownie Bites

Prep: 5 minutes • Cook: 8 minutes

½ cup self-rising flour
⅔ cup sugar
3 tablespoons unsweetened cocoa
4 large egg whites
2 tablespoons canola oil
3 tablespoons chocolate liqueur (optional)

⅓ cup cocoa nibs
Cooking spray
Roasted salted almonds (such as Blue Diamond), coarsely chopped (optional)
Powdered sugar (optional)

1. Preheat oven to 400°.
2. Lightly spoon flour into a dry measuring cup; level with a knife. Combine flour, sugar, and cocoa in a medium bowl, stirring with a whisk.
3. Whisk egg whites until foamy in a separate bowl. Add oil and liqueur, if desired, stirring with a whisk. Add egg white mixture to flour mixture, stirring just until moistened. Fold in cocoa nibs. Spoon batter evenly into 24 miniature muffin cups coated with cooking spray. Sprinkle batter evenly with almonds, if desired.
4. Bake at 400° for 8 minutes. Remove from pans; cool on wire racks. Sprinkle with powdered sugar, if desired. Yield: 24 servings (serving size: 1 brownie bite).

CALORIES 61; FAT 2.4g (sat 0.8g, mono 0.9g, poly 0.4g); PROTEIN 1.2g; CARB 8.8g; FIBER 0.3g; CHOL 0mg; IRON 0.4mg; SODIUM 43mg; CALC 15mg

With rich chocolate flavor and a warm gooey filling, these hot-from-the-oven minicakes are the perfect indulgence at the end of a busy day. Many supermarkets stock ground pecans in the nuts section; if you can't find them already ground, chop pecan halves or pieces, and grind them in a food processor, minichopper, or spice grinder.

Flourless Chocolate Cakes

Prep: 10 minutes • Cook: 10 minutes • Other: 10 minutes

1 large egg
¼ cup sugar
2 teaspoons unsweetened cocoa
1½ tablespoons chopped pecans, ground
1 tablespoon warm water

1 ounce bittersweet chocolate, melted and cooled slightly
Cooking spray
Powdered sugar (optional)
Strawberries (optional)

1. Preheat oven to 425°.
2. Separate egg, placing egg white and egg yolk in separate medium bowls. Add sugar and cocoa to egg yolk, stirring with a whisk. Add pecans, water, and chocolate, stirring with a whisk.
3. Beat egg white with a mixer at high speed until stiff peaks form. Gently fold half of egg white into egg yolk mixture; fold in remaining egg white. Spoon batter evenly into 4 (4-ounce) ramekins coated with cooking spray.
4. Bake at 425° for 10 minutes or until almost set. Transfer to a wire rack; cool 10 minutes. Garnish with powdered sugar and strawberries, if desired. Yield: 4 servings (serving size: 1 ramekin).

CALORIES 124; FAT 6.2g (sat 2.1g, mono 1.9g, poly 1.8g); PROTEIN 2.5g; CARB 17.3g; FIBER 1.1g; CHOL 45mg; IRON 0.6mg; SODIUM 18mg; CALC 10mg

choice ingredient

Cocoa powder is made from ground roasted cacao seeds that have had most of the fat removed. When you are using less real chocolate in light baking, incorporate some cocoa powder to deepen the chocolate flavor without adding a lot of extra fat.

If you don't have a Texas-size or other jumbo muffin tin, spoon the batter into 8 regular-size muffin cups coated with cooking spray; bake for 15 minutes, and serve two small sponge cakes per serving. Adding water to unfilled muffin cups distributes the heat evenly in the pan during baking and prevents burning.

Vanilla Sponge Cakes with Fresh Berry Filling

Prep: 5 minutes

1½ cups blueberries
1½ cups sliced strawberries
2 tablespoons sugar

Vanilla Sponge Cakes, halved horizontally
½ cup frozen reduced-calorie whipped topping, thawed

1. Combine berries and sugar in a medium bowl, stirring until juice forms.
2. Place bottom half of a sponge cake on each of 4 individual serving plates. Spoon ¾ cup berry mixture over cake bottoms. Top berry mixture with 2 tablespoons whipped topping and top half of sponge cake. Serve immediately. Yield: 4 servings (serving size: 1 fruit-filled cake).

CALORIES 325; FAT 3.6g (sat 1.7g, mono 1g, poly 0.5g); PROTEIN 7.4g; CARB 70.5g; FIBER 3.4g; CHOL 55mg; IRON 2.3mg; SODIUM 288mg; CALC 222mg

Vanilla Sponge Cakes

Prep: 5 minutes • Cook: 20 minutes • Other: 6 minutes

Butter-flavored cooking spray
1 cup all-purpose flour
2 teaspoons baking powder

½ cup turbinado sugar
1 large egg
1 (6-ounce) container low-fat vanilla yogurt

1. Preheat oven to 375°.
2. Coat 4 cups of a Texas-size muffin tin with cooking spray. Lightly spoon flour into a dry measuring cup; level with a knife. Combine flour, baking powder, and turbinado sugar in a medium bowl. Combine egg and yogurt in a small bowl; add yogurt mixture to flour mixture, stirring just until moistened. Spoon batter into prepared muffin cups; add water to unfilled cups to a depth of 1 inch. Coat batter with cooking spray.
3. Bake at 375° for 20 minutes or until cakes spring back when lightly touched. Cool cakes 1 minute in pan; remove cakes from pan, and cool 5 minutes on a wire rack. Yield: 4 servings (serving size: 1 cake).

CALORIES 262; FAT 2g (sat 0.7g, mono 0.7g, poly 0.3g); PROTEIN 6.9g; CARB 54.6g; FIBER 0.9g; CHOL 47mg; IRON 2mg; SODIUM 228mg; CALC 254mg

No one will ever guess that the key ingredient to the buttery topping of this fresh, fruit-filled dessert is a pineapple cake mix. Select a cored pineapple with a generous amount of juice in the container to use in the batter.

Peach-Pineapple Crumble

Prep: 9 minutes • Cook: 38 minutes

 1 cored fresh pineapple
 3 cups sliced peeled peaches (3 large)
Cooking spray
 ¼ cup butter, melted

 1½ cups pineapple supreme cake mix (such as Duncan Hines Moist Deluxe)
 2 cups vanilla low-fat frozen yogurt
 ¼ cup chopped pecans, toasted (optional)

1. Preheat oven to 350°.

2. Drain pineapple, reserving 3 tablespoons juice. Chop pineapple to measure 3 cups.

3. Combine chopped pineapple, reserved juice, and peach slices in an 11 x 7–inch baking dish coated with cooking spray. Stir butter into cake mix until smooth. Spread batter over fruit; coat with cooking spray.

4. Bake at 350° for 38 minutes or until golden and bubbly. Serve warm with frozen yogurt. Sprinkle each serving with 1 tablespoon pecans, if desired. Yield: 8 servings (serving size: ⅛ of crumble and ¼ cup frozen yogurt).

CALORIES 333; FAT 10.6g (sat 5.5g, mono 2g, poly 0.3g); PROTEIN 5.1g; CARB 58.4g; FIBER 1.8g; CHOL 18mg; IRON 0.4mg; SODIUM 83mg; CALC 90mg

This easy recipe uses cinnamon-swirl bread and dark chocolate–covered raisins as its base, which keeps the ingredient list short. Serve this luscious dessert in teacups for an elegant presentation.

Chocolate-Raisin Bread Pudding
Prep: 5 minutes • Cook: 55 minutes • Other: 10 minutes

4 large eggs
1 cup sugar
2 cups 1% low-fat milk
5 cups (½-inch) cubed raisin cinnamon swirl bread (such as Pepperidge Farm)

1 cup dark chocolate-covered raisins (such as Raisinets)
Cooking spray

1. Preheat oven to 350°.
2. Combine eggs and sugar in a large bowl, stirring with a whisk. Stir in milk. Add bread, stirring to saturate. Stir in raisins. Spoon mixture into an 8-inch square baking pan coated with cooking spray. Let stand, uncovered, 10 minutes.
3. Bake at 350° for 55 minutes or until set. Serve warm. Yield: 8 servings (serving size: ⅛ of pudding).

CALORIES 349; FAT 8.5g (sat 3.5g, mono 2.1g, poly 1.4g); PROTEIN 8.7g; CARB 63.3g; FIBER 2.3g; CHOL 95mg; IRON 1.7mg; SODIUM 187mg; CALC 88mg

We updated classic bread pudding by baking the bread in a chocolate-pudding mixture topped with chocolate-covered caramel candies. While the dessert bakes, the center becomes moist and the candies melt, creating a sweet chocolate-caramel sauce. For added goodness, top the warm pudding with ice cream, and drizzle it with caramel sauce before serving.

Chocolate and Caramel Bread Pudding

Prep: 8 minutes • Cook: 38 minutes

2½ cups 1% low-fat milk
1 (1.4-ounce) package sugar-free chocolate cook-and-serve pudding mix
7 cups (½-inch) cubed Italian bread
Cooking spray

2 (1.7-ounce) packages chocolate-covered caramel candies (such as Rolo), chopped
Vanilla fat-free ice cream (optional)
¼ cup fat-free caramel sundae syrup (such as Smucker's)

1. Preheat oven to 350°.
2. Combine milk and pudding mix in a medium bowl, stirring well with a whisk. Stir in bread until coated. Pour bread mixture into an 8-inch square pan coated with cooking spray; sprinkle with chopped candy.
3. Bake at 350° for 38 minutes. Spoon pudding evenly into each of 6 individual serving bowls; top each serving with ice cream, if desired, and drizzle evenly with syrup. Yield: 6 servings (serving size: ⅙ of pudding and 2 teaspoons caramel syrup).

CALORIES 357; FAT 6.8g (sat 3.6g, mono 1.2g, poly 1g); PROTEIN 10.3g; CARB 62.7g; FIBER 1.9g; CHOL 6mg; IRON 2.1mg; SODIUM 540mg; CALC 229mg

shortcut kitchen tip

To quickly chop the chocolate-covered caramel candies, place the candies close to each other on a cutting board. Then use a sharp, heavy chef's knife, and rock the knife back and forth, pressing the thickest part of the blade down on the candies.

Prepare this recipe in the summertime when you're craving a dessert that's not too heavy. Lemon rind and juice provide tartness, which is balanced by the sweetness of the fresh berries. This dessert is not quite a pudding and not quite a cake—it's something in between. A puddinglike layer forms under the tender cake topping as it bakes. It tastes best when served warm.

Lemon Pudding Cake

Prep: 3 minutes • Cook: 28 minutes • Other: 5 minutes

- 1 (9-ounce) package yellow cake mix (such as Jiffy)
- ½ cup fat-free milk
- ¼ cup reduced-fat sour cream
- 1 lemon

- Cooking spray
- ⅔ cup boiling water
- 2 cups mixed berries
- Frozen fat-free whipped topping, thawed (optional)

1. Preheat oven to 350°.

2. Combine first 3 ingredients in a medium bowl. Grate rind, and squeeze juice from lemon to measure 1 teaspoon and 2 tablespoons, respectively. Stir rind and juice into batter just until blended. Spoon batter into an 8-inch square baking dish coated with cooking spray. Pour boiling water over batter (do not stir).

3. Bake at 350° for 28 minutes. Remove from oven; let stand 5 minutes. Spoon cake into 8 individual serving bowls; top with berries and whipped topping, if desired. Serve warm. Yield: 8 servings (serving size: ⅛ of cake and ¼ cup berries).

CALORIES 168; FAT 3.4g (sat 1g, mono 0.9g, poly 0.9g); PROTEIN 2.4g; CARB 33.2g; FIBER 0.9g; CHOL 3mg; IRON 0.8mg; SODIUM 229mg; CALC 18mg

When you're looking for a quick dessert, turn to this superfast pudding that's spiced with ground cinnamon and flecked with cherries. This shortcut method of using an instant pudding mix delivers the characteristic creamy texture of rice pudding without the long cooking time.

White Chocolate–Cherry Rice Pudding

Prep: 4 minutes • Cook: 7 minutes

3½ cups 1% low-fat milk, divided
⅓ cup dried cherries
2 tablespoons light brown sugar
¼ teaspoon ground cinnamon
1 tablespoon butter
⅛ teaspoon salt
1 cup instant rice
1 (1-ounce) package sugar-free white chocolate instant pudding mix
Cinnamon sticks (optional)

1. Bring 1½ cups milk, dried cherries, and next 4 ingredients to a boil in a medium saucepan over medium heat, stirring occasionally. Stir in rice; cover, and reduce heat to low. Simmer 5 minutes, stirring occasionally.
2. While rice mixture cooks, prepare pudding mix according to package directions using remaining 2 cups milk. Stir prepared pudding into rice mixture. Serve warm. Garnish with cinnamon sticks, if desired. Yield: 8 servings (serving size: ½ cup).

CALORIES 156; FAT 2.6g (sat 1.6g, mono 0.7g, poly 0.1g); PROTEIN 5g; CARB 27.9g; FIBER 0.7g; CHOL 8mg; IRON 0.9mg; SODIUM 141mg; CALC 142mg

Modest in appearance yet boasting an intense flavor and a made-from-scratch taste, this simple, satisfying chocolate pudding is the quintessential weeknight dessert. Place plastic wrap on the surface of the hot pudding to prevent a skin from forming during chilling.

Triple-Chocolate Pudding

Prep: 5 minutes • Cook: 19 minutes • Other: 5 minutes

1 (5-ounce) package chocolate cook-and-serve pudding mix
1 large egg yolk
4 cups 1% low-fat chocolate milk
1 ounce semisweet chocolate, chopped

1 teaspoon vanilla extract
Frozen reduced-calorie whipped topping, thawed (optional)
Semisweet chocolate shavings (optional)

1. Combine first 3 ingredients in a medium saucepan. Bring to a boil over medium heat, stirring constantly with a whisk. Boil 2 minutes, stirring constantly. Remove from heat. Add chopped chocolate and vanilla, stirring with a whisk until chocolate melts. Cool 5 minutes.

2. Spoon ½ cup pudding into each of 8 individual serving bowls. Serve warm, or cover surface of pudding with plastic wrap, and chill thoroughly. Top each serving with whipped topping, if desired; sprinkle with chocolate shavings, if desired. Yield: 8 servings (serving size: 1 pudding).

CALORIES 169; FAT 2.8g (sat 1.6g, mono 0.2g, poly 0.1g); PROTEIN 5.2g; CARB 31.3g; FIBER 0.7g; CHOL 31mg; IRON 0.7mg; SODIUM 187mg; CALC 151mg

Panna cotta is an Italian dessert made from heavy cream that is usually served with fresh berries, caramel topping, or chocolate sauce. We substituted fat-free half-and-half and fat-free sweetened condensed milk for the heavy cream and added a little white chocolate for flavor. Since this impressive dessert needs to chill at least 8 hours before serving, plan to make it ahead, and store it in the refrigerator until ready to serve.

White Chocolate Panna Cotta

Prep: 4 minutes • Cook: 3 minutes • Other: 8 hours

1 envelope unflavored gelatin
2 cups fat-free half-and-half, divided
3 ounces white chocolate, chopped
1 cup fat-free sweetened condensed milk

½ teaspoon vanilla extract
Raspberries (optional)
Mint sprigs (optional)

1. Sprinkle gelatin over 1 cup half-and-half in a small saucepan; let stand 1 to 2 minutes. Cook, stirring constantly, over medium heat 3 minutes or until gelatin dissolves; remove from heat. Add chocolate, stirring until chocolate melts.
2. Gradually stir in remaining 1 cup half-and-half, condensed milk, and vanilla. Pour ½ cup custard into each of 6 stemmed glasses or 6-ounce custard cups. Cover and chill 8 hours or until ready to serve. Serve with fresh berries and garnish with mint, if desired. Yield: 6 servings (serving size: 1 panna cotta).

CALORIES 281; FAT 4.6g (sat 2.8g, mono 1g, poly 0.5g); PROTEIN 5.8g; CARB 48.4g; FIBER 0g; CHOL 9mg; IRON 0.1mg; SODIUM 148mg; CALC 216mg

choice ingredient

Pure vanilla has one of the most complex tastes, and there's no mistaking its unique flavor and aroma. Don't be tempted to use imitation vanilla—it is made from chemicals and lacks the depth of flavor of the real thing.

This no-fuss treat comes together in minutes. The sauce, made of butter, apple juice, and a homemade caramel sauce, reduces while the apples bake, creating a velvety glaze. Make extra Caramel Sauce, and store it in the refrigerator to serve over pound cake or ice cream later in the week.

Glazed Apples in Caramel Sauce
Prep: 6 minutes • Cook: 45 minutes

4 Granny Smith apples, peeled and cored
⅔ cup no-sugar-added apple juice

2 tablespoons butter, melted
Caramel Sauce

1. Preheat oven to 375°.
2. Cut each apple horizontally into 5 slices. Reassemble each apple, and place in an 11 x 7–inch baking dish. Combine apple juice and melted butter; pour over apples. Bake, uncovered, at 375° for 45 minutes or until apples are tender, basting with juices every 15 minutes.
3. Place an apple stack on each of 4 individual serving plates. Pour ¼ cup Caramel Sauce into center of each stack, allowing sauce to flow over sides. Serve immediately. Yield: 4 servings (serving size: 1 apple and ¼ cup caramel sauce).

CALORIES 247; FAT 8.7g (sat 5.4g, mono 2.2g, poly 0.8g); PROTEIN 2.5g; CARB 41.9g; FIBER 1.7g; CHOL 22mg; IRON 0.2mg; SODIUM 102mg; CALC 98mg

Caramel Sauce
Prep: 1 minute • Cook: 18 minutes

1 cup sugar
⅓ cup water
1 tablespoon butter

½ cup fat-free evaporated milk
½ teaspoon vanilla extract

1. Combine sugar and water in a large skillet. Cook over medium heat 15 minutes or until golden (do not stir). Brush crystals from sides of pan with a wet pastry brush, if necessary.
2. Remove pan from heat; let stand 1 minute. Carefully add butter, stirring until butter melts. Gradually add milk, stirring constantly. (Caramel will harden and stick to spoon.) Cook, stirring constantly, over medium heat 2 minutes or until caramel melts and mixture is smooth and slightly thickened. Remove from heat; stir in vanilla. Yield: 4 servings (serving size: ¼ cup).

CALORIES 116; FAT 2.8g (sat 1.8g, mono 0.7g, poly 0.1g); PROTEIN 2g; CARB 20.7g; FIBER 0g; CHOL 8mg; IRON 0mg; SODIUM 60mg; CALC 81mg

This stylish dessert requires little preparation, and you can easily halve or double the recipe to serve fewer or more diners. Give the figs a gentle squeeze to check for their ripeness; they should be quite soft. Serve the figs with toasted pecan halves and small wedges of Gruyère or fontina cheese.

Marsala-Poached Figs

Prep: 3 minutes • Cook: 10 minutes

½ cup marsala
1 (3-inch) cinnamon stick
3 black peppercorns

1 tablespoon honey
6 fresh Black Mission figs (about 8.5 ounces), halved

1. Combine first 4 ingredients in a medium saucepan. Bring to a boil; cook 7 minutes or until syrupy. Add figs; cook 1 minute or until thoroughly heated. Yield: 6 servings (serving size: 2 fig halves and about 2 teaspoons sauce).

CALORIES 72; FAT 0g (sat 0g, mono 0g, poly 0g); PROTEIN 0.4g; CARB 13.3g; FIBER 1.2g; CHOL 0mg; IRON 0.2mg; SODIUM 2mg; CALC 15mg

choice ingredient

Fresh figs need very little adornment and cooking, thanks to their subtle, sweet flavor and dense texture. For a quick, pleasurable ending to a meal, serve figs raw, or gently simmer them in a sauce for just a few minutes. Figs are available twice a year, with the first crop available from June through July, and the second crop coming in early September and lasting through mid-October.

These creamy, nutty tarts received our Test Kitchens' highest rating. They're easy and fast for every day, but because this dessert needs time to chill, it's also a terrific make-ahead option.

White Chocolate–Hazelnut Tarts

Prep: 11 minutes • Cook: 12 minutes • Other: 30 minutes

½ (15-ounce) package refrigerated pie dough (such as Pillsbury)
1 (1-ounce) package sugar-free white chocolate instant pudding mix
1½ cups fat-free milk
¼ cup chocolate-hazelnut spread (such as Nutella)
¼ cup chopped hazelnuts, toasted
Chocolate shavings (optional)

1. Preheat oven to 450°.
2. Roll pie dough into a 14-inch circle. Cut 4 (5-inch) circles from dough; press each circle into a 4-inch tart pan with removable bottom. Pierce bottom and sides of dough; bake at 450° for 12 minutes or until golden.
3. While crusts bake, combine pudding mix and milk, stirring with a whisk for 2 minutes.
4. Spread 1 tablespoon hazelnut spread over bottom of each warm crust. Spoon pudding mixture evenly over hazelnut spread in each crust. Chill in refrigerator 30 minutes or until ready to serve.
5. Sprinkle tarts evenly with hazelnuts and chocolate shavings, if desired. Yield: 8 servings (serving size: ½ tart and ½ tablespoon hazelnuts).

CALORIES 200; FAT 10.8g (sat 2.8g, mono 5.1g, poly 2.8g); PROTEIN 3.1g; CARB 22.2g; FIBER 0.8g; CHOL 3.5mg; IRON 1mg; SODIUM 268mg; CALC 70mg

Try dipping the remaining candied peel in melted dark or white chocolate, and save the simmering liquid for flavoring teas, cocktails, or tossing with fresh fruit.

Blueberry-Lemon-White Chocolate Tarts

Prep: 5 minutes • Cook: 8 minutes • Other: 30 minutes

4 (3-inch) graham cracker tart shells
4 ounces ⅓-less-fat cream cheese, softened
¼ cup lemon curd
1½ ounces white chocolate, chopped and melted (such as Ghirardelli)
¼ cup wild blueberry preserves (such as Bonne Maman)
¼ cup Candied Lemon Peel (optional)

1. Preheat oven to 350°.
2. Place graham cracker shells on a baking sheet. Bake at 350° for 8 minutes or until toasted.
3. Combine cream cheese and lemon curd in a medium bowl; beat with a mixer at medium speed until creamy. Stir in melted chocolate. Spoon cream cheese mixture evenly into tart shells. Cover and chill 30 minutes. Top each serving with 1 tablespoon blueberry preserves and 1 tablespoon Candied Lemon Peel, if desired. Yield: 4 servings (serving size: 1 tart).

CALORIES 363; FAT 16.5g (sat 7.6g, mono 5g, poly 3.1g); PROTEIN 4.7g; CARB 50.3g; FIBER 3g; CHOL 36.7mg; IRON 0.4mg; SODIUM 301mg; CALC 41mg

Candied Lemon Peel

Prep: 5 minutes • Cook: 5 minutes • Other: 2 hours

2 large lemons
1½ cups sugar, divided
1 cup water

1. Carefully remove rind from lemons using a vegetable peeler, making sure to avoid white pithy part of the rind. Cut rind into 1 x ⅛–inch-thick strips.
2. Combine 1 cup sugar and 1 cup water in a medium microwave-safe bowl. Microwave at HIGH 2 minutes; stir in lemon rind. Microwave at HIGH 3 minutes, stirring every minute.
3. Spread remaining ½ cup sugar on a parchment-lined baking sheet. Using a fork, remove lemon peel from sugar syrup; add to sugar on baking sheet, and toss well. Spread rind in a single layer on baking sheet; let stand at room temperature until dry. Remove peel from sugar, and store in an airtight container. Discard remaining sugar. Yield: 16 servings (serving size: 1 tablespoon).

CALORIES 27; FAT 0g (sat 0g, mono 0g, poly 0g); PROTEIN 0.2g; CARB 7.7g; FIBER 0.6g; CHOL 0mg; IRON 0.1mg; SODIUM 0mg; CALC 8mg

Mascarpone, Italy's version of cream cheese, is a sweet, delicate triple-blended cheese made from cow's milk that is often used in both sweet and savory dishes. Here, we used only a small amount and stretched it with cream cheese to get the richness of the mascarpone with reduced calories and fat. Store the remaining mascarpone in the refrigerator for up to 1 month.

Raspberry–Cream Cheese Tarts

Prep: 8 minutes • Other: 3 hours

1 (8-ounce) package fat-free cream cheese, softened
2 tablespoons mascarpone cheese, softened
⅓ cup sugar
1 teaspoon vanilla
6 mini graham cracker pie crusts
⅓ cup seedless raspberry jam
1½ cups fresh raspberries

1. Combine first 4 ingredients in a large bowl. Beat with a mixer at high speed 1 to 2 minutes or until smooth. Spoon cheese mixture evenly into crusts.
2. Place jam in a medium bowl; stir with a whisk until smooth. Add raspberries, stirring until coated; spoon evenly over cheese filling in each tart. Serve immediately, or refrigerate 3 hours or until thoroughly chilled. Yield: 6 servings (serving size: 1 tart).

CALORIES 305; FAT 11.1g (sat 4g, mono 4.3g, poly 2.1g); PROTEIN 7.5g; CARB 44.6g; FIBER 3g; CHOL 15mg; IRON 0.6mg; SODIUM 361mg; CALC 91mg

Looking for a quick dessert that's ideal for a weeknight potluck or party? These petite tarts are the answer. With just the right amount of crunch from the candy bar pieces to complement the rich, smooth dulce de leche filling, they'll disappear fast!

Dulce de Leche Tartlets

Prep: 5 minutes • Cook: 5 minutes • Other: 2 minutes

1 (1.9-ounce) package mini phyllo shells (such as Athenos)
⅓ cup canned dulce de leche
1 cup reduced-calorie frozen whipped topping, thawed

1 (1.4-ounce) English toffee candy bar, finely chopped (such as Heath or Skor)

1. Preheat oven to 350°.
2. Arrange phyllo shells on a baking sheet. Bake phyllo shells at 350° for 5 minutes or until crisp. Cool slightly.
3. Spoon about 1 teaspoon dulce de leche into each shell, and top each serving with about 1 tablespoon whipped topping. Sprinkle tartlets evenly with chopped candy. Yield: 15 servings (serving size: 1 tartlet).

CALORIES 180; FAT 7.7g (sat 2.8g, mono 2.2g, poly 0.6g); PROTEIN 1.3g; CARB 23.4g; FIBER 0.1g; CHOL 14mg; IRON 0.5mg; SODIUM 83mg; CALC 64mg

choice ingredient

Dulce de leche, a sweet Spanish sauce, is made by cooking milk and sugar until it reduces to a thick, amber-colored syrup. Preparing home-made dulce de leche can take up to 3 hours; for quick weeknight cooking, we recommend purchasing a can at your supermarket or a Latin market. Look for dulce de leche alongside the canned milks. Since it is similar in flavor and texture to caramel, you can substitute caramel sauce.

In a traditional trifle, liqueur moistens cake that's layered with custard and fruit. In our lighter, parfaitlike version, we used the sweet juice from mashed blackberries and blueberries to soak into the cake and lime zest to flavor the whipped topping. Fresh strawberries and raspberries will also work well in this recipe.

Berry-Lime-Angel Food Mini Trifles

Prep: 10 minutes

1 tablespoon grated lime rind
2 cups reduced-calorie frozen whipped topping, thawed
1½ tablespoons fresh lime juice

1¼ cups blackberries, divided
1¼ cups blueberries, divided
2 cups (½-inch) cubed angel food cake

1. Fold lime rind into whipped topping; set aside.
2. Place lime juice and 1 cup each blackberries and blueberries in an 8-inch square glass dish. Mash berry mixture using the back of a spoon.
3. Layer half of cake cubes evenly in each of 4 dessert glasses. Top evenly with half of berry mixture and half of reserved topping mixture. Repeat layers with remaining half of cake cubes, berry mixture, and topping mixture. Top each trifle with 1 tablespoon each remaining blackberries and blueberries. Yield: 4 servings (serving size: 1 mini trifle).

CALORIES 192; FAT 4.6g (sat 4.1g, mono 0g, poly 0.3g); PROTEIN 2.5g; CARB 38.1g; FIBER 4g; CHOL 0mg; IRON 0.6mg; SODIUM 187mg; CALC 53mg

shortcut kitchen tip

Mashing the berries releases their juice, which adds flavor and moisture to the cake. To easily mash the berries, place them in an 8-inch square glass dish or other container with a wide, flat bottom, and use the back of a spoon.

In this takeoff of the campfire classic, we replaced the customary graham crackers with sugar cookies. We slathered them with chocolate-hazelnut spread, sprinkled them with dried apricots and hazelnuts, and, of course, sandwiched them with marshmallows.

Hazelnut–Sugar Cookie S'mores

Prep: 10 minutes • Cook: 2 minutes 20 seconds

2 tablespoons chocolate-hazelnut spread (such as Nutella)
8 rectangular sugar cookies (such as Pepperidge Farm Bordeaux)
2 tablespoons finely chopped dried apricots
16 miniature marshmallows
4 teaspoons chopped hazelnuts, toasted

1. Spread ½ tablespoon chocolate-hazelnut spread on each of 4 cookies; sprinkle each with ½ tablespoon apricots and 4 marshmallows. Place on a microwave-safe plate; microwave at HIGH 20 seconds or until marshmallows puff. Sprinkle evenly with hazelnuts, and top with remaining cookies. Yield: 4 servings (serving size: 1 s'more).

CALORIES 150; FAT 6.7g (sat 2.2g, mono 2.1g, poly 2.2g); PROTEIN 2.3g; CARB 20.8g; FIBER 1.3g; CHOL 5mg; IRON 0.7mg; SODIUM 54mg; CALC 15mg

Use ripe, juicy strawberries and kiwi to achieve the best flavor for this light, refreshing dessert.

Strawberry-Kiwi Freeze

Prep: 10 minutes • Cook: 1 minute • Other: 9 hours

1 cup sugar
1 cup water
2 teaspoons fresh lime juice

4 cups strawberries
1½ cups cubed peeled kiwifruit (about 4 kiwifruit)

1. Combine sugar and water in a medium saucepan. Bring to a boil over high heat; cook 1 minute. Remove from heat; cool 1 hour. Stir in lime juice; set syrup aside.
2. Place strawberries in a food processor; process until smooth. Stir in half of syrup. Pour strawberry mixture into an 8-inch square glass dish. Rinse processor bowl; wipe dry. Add kiwifruit; process until smooth. Stir in remaining syrup.
3. Use a measuring cup to drizzle kiwi mixture in a swirl pattern over the strawberry mixture. Cover and freeze 8 hours. Yield: 8 servings (serving size: about ½ cup).

CALORIES 148; FAT 0.5g (sat 0g, mono 0.1g, poly 0.2g); PROTEIN 1g; CARB 37.3g; FIBER 2.8g; CHOL 0mg; IRON 0.4mg; SODIUM 2mg; CALC 27mg

shortcut kitchen tip

To easily create a swirl pattern, pour the red strawberry mixture into an 8-inch square glass dish. Then scoop the green kiwi mixture into a measuring cup, and slowly drizzle it in a swirl pattern over the strawberry mixture.

This frozen dessert doesn't require an ice-cream maker—just freeze the mixture in a pan, and scrape it with a fork. For a nonalcoholic version, use 1 cup black cherry juice (such as Knudsen) in place of the merlot.

Cherry-Merlot Granita
Prep: 5 minutes • Cook: 3 minutes • Other: 8 hours

1 cup water
¼ cup sugar
1 cup ice cubes

1 large navel orange
1 cup frozen pitted dark sweet cherries
1 cup merlot

1. Combine water and sugar in a small saucepan. Bring to a boil; reduce heat, and simmer 3 minutes. Remove from heat; stir in ice cubes.

2. While sugar mixture comes to a boil, grate rind, and squeeze juice from orange to measure 1 tablespoon and ½ cup, respectively.

3. Place cherries and sugar mixture in a blender; process 1 minute or until puréed, stopping as necessary to scrape sides. Stir in rind, juice, and merlot; pour into an 8-inch square pan. Cover and freeze 8 hours or until firm.

4. Remove mixture from freezer; scrape entire mixture with a fork until fluffy. Yield: 8 servings (serving size: about ½ cup).

CALORIES 70; FAT 0.3g (sat 0.1g, mono 0.1g, poly 0.1g); PROTEIN 0.3g; CARB 11.9g; FIBER 0.5g; CHOL 0mg; IRON 0.2mg; SODIUM 1mg; CALC 8mg

Chambord—a ruby-red liqueur made with black raspberries, honey, and herbs—heightens the fruity flavor of this dessert, making it worth the splurge. Make the Coconut-Walnut Crunch ahead, and after it cools, store it in an airtight container for up to a week. The sauce is also delicious spooned over yogurt and vanilla ice cream.

Raspberry and Coconut Parfaits with Coconut-Walnut Crunch

Prep: 15 minutes

1 cup raspberry sorbet
Coconut-Walnut Crunch
1 cup coconut sorbet

½ cup fresh raspberries
2 tablespoons Chambord (raspberry-flavored liqueur)

1. Layer ¼ cup raspberry sorbet, 1 tablespoon Coconut-Walnut Crunch, and ¼ cup coconut sorbet in each of 4 (8-ounce) tall glasses. Top each with 1 additional tablespoon crunch.
2. Combine raspberries and Chambord in a small bowl. Top parfaits evenly with raspberry mixture. Serve immediately. Yield: 4 servings (serving size: 1 parfait).

CALORIES 310; FAT 12.7g (sat 5.4g, mono 2.8g, poly 3.5g); PROTEIN 3.8g; CARB 43.4g; FIBER 2.8g; CHOL 0mg; IRON 1mg; SODIUM 15mg; CALC 22mg

Coconut-Walnut Crunch

Prep: 2 minutes • Cook: 8 minutes

¼ cup regular oats
2 tablespoons chopped walnuts
2 tablespoons flaked sweetened coconut

⅛ teaspoon ground nutmeg
1½ teaspoons canola oil

1. Preheat oven to 350°.
2. Combine all ingredients in a small bowl, stirring until oats are moistened. Spread mixture on a jelly-roll pan. Bake at 350° for 8 minutes or until lightly browned. Cool in pan on a wire rack. Yield: 4 servings (serving size: 2 tablespoons).

CALORIES 74; FAT 5.4g (sat 1.2g, mono 1.5g, poly 2.2g); PROTEIN 1.9g; CARB 5.3g; FIBER 0.9g; CHOL 0mg; IRON 0.4mg; SODIUM 8mg; CALC 5.5mg

Candy-coated almonds give this superfast, simple ice-cream sundae a little something extra special. For variety, try substituting your favorite sugared or candied nut for the almonds.

Banana-Caramel Sundaes

Prep: 8 minutes

2 large bananas
1⅓ cups vanilla low-fat ice cream
¼ cup fat-free caramel topping (such as Smucker's)

⅓ cup chopped cinnamon-coated almonds

1. Cut each banana in half crosswise and then in half lengthwise to make 8 quarters. Place 2 banana quarters in each of 4 stemmed glasses or 4 individual serving bowls. Top each serving with ⅓ cup ice cream and 1 tablespoon caramel topping; sprinkle each serving with about 1 tablespoon almonds. Yield: 4 servings (serving size: 1 sundae).

CALORIES 320; FAT 5g (sat 1.7g, mono 2.5g, poly 0.8g); PROTEIN 3.8g; CARB 64.6g; FIBER 2.6g; CHOL 12mg; IRON 0.5mg; SODIUM 155mg; CALC 90mg

choice ingredient

Cinnamon-coated almonds are great to use for embellishing recipes that only need a few ingredients. Try them on desserts like ice-cream sundaes or as part of sweet-and-savory recipes such as salads. Look for the almonds either with the other nuts in your supermarket or near the produce section.

Instead of using Mexican chocolate for the fudge, we developed the same flavor using more common ingredients. Here, ground cinnamon lends a subtle hint of spice, while coffee adds richness to the semisweet chocolate. To ensure a smooth sauce, stir the cornstarch-milk mixture until all lumps have dissolved before cooking it.

Mexican Hot Fudge Sundae

Prep: 6 minutes • Cook: 2 minutes

1 teaspoon cornstarch
½ cup evaporated fat-free milk
⅓ cup strong brewed coffee
¾ cup semisweet chocolate chips
2 tablespoons powdered sugar

½ teaspoon ground cinnamon
½ teaspoon vanilla extract
4 cups vanilla light ice cream
¼ cup pine nuts, toasted

1. Place cornstarch in a small saucepan. Gradually add milk, stirring with a whisk until blended. Stir in coffee. Cook over medium-high heat 1 minute or until mixture just begins to simmer. Remove from heat; stir in chocolate chips. Cook, stirring constantly, over medium-high heat until mixture comes to a boil; cook 1 minute until mixture is smooth and slightly thickened. Remove from heat; stir in powdered sugar, cinnamon, and vanilla extract.
2. Spoon ½ cup ice cream into each of 8 dessert bowls. Top each serving with 2½ tablespoons sauce and ½ tablespoon pine nuts. Yield: 8 servings (serving size: 1 sundae).

CALORIES 290; FAT 12.5g (sat 5.9g, mono 3.9g, poly 2g); PROTEIN 7.2g; CARB 40.2g; FIBER 1.5g; CHOL 27mg; IRON 1mg; SODIUM 94mg; CALC 214mg

choice ingredient

Cornstarch is ideal for making quick sauces because it thickens liquids much faster than flour. Be sure to remove the sauce from the heat after it has thickened; if it cooks too long, the cornstarch will lose its thickening power, causing the sauce to separate and become thin.

Savor the best of both salty and sweet in this surprising combination of sea salt and chocolate bark. When paired with coffee ice cream, this must-try recipe is utterly delightful.

Coffee Ice-Cream Sundae with Dark Chocolate–Sea Salt Almond Bark

Prep: 11 minutes • Other: 20 minutes

½ cup bittersweet chocolate chips (such as Ghirardelli)
¼ cup whole natural almonds, chopped and toasted
½ teaspoon coarse sea salt
3 cups coffee light ice cream (such as Edy's)
6 tablespoons refrigerated canned fat-free whipped topping (such as Reddi-wip)

1. Place chocolate chips in a microwave-safe 1-cup glass measure. Microwave at HIGH 1½ minutes or until chocolate melts, stirring after 1 minute. Add almonds, stirring just until combined. Spread mixture evenly on a jelly-roll pan lined with wax paper; sprinkle evenly with sea salt. Freeze 20 minutes. Break into pieces.
2. Spoon ½ cup ice cream into each of 6 individual serving bowls; top each serving with whipped topping and broken bark pieces. Yield: 6 servings (serving size: ½ cup ice cream, 1 tablespoon whipped topping, and about ¾ ounce chocolate bark).

CALORIES 322; FAT 14.2g (sat 7.6g, mono 2.9g, poly 2.7g); PROTEIN 7g; CARB 43g; FIBER 0.8g; CHOL 2mg; IRON 0.5mg; SODIUM 281mg; CALC 19mg

You'll love the added crunch that toffee bits give this frozen pie. To quickly soften the ice cream, place it in a microwave-safe bowl, and microwave at HIGH 10 to 15 seconds.

Chocolate-Toffee Ice-Cream Pie

Prep: 8 minutes • Other: 8 hours

4 cups chocolate low-fat ice cream (such as Edy's), softened and divided
1 (6-ounce) reduced-fat graham cracker crust
¼ cup fat-free chocolate syrup (such as Smucker's), divided
¼ cup milk chocolate toffee bits, divided
2 cups fat-free frozen whipped topping, thawed

1. Spread 2 cups ice cream in bottom of crust; drizzle with 2 tablespoons chocolate syrup, and sprinkle with 2 tablespoons toffee bits. Spread remaining ice cream over toffee bits. Freeze 8 hours or until firm.
2. Top pie with whipped topping, and drizzle with remaining 2 tablespoons syrup; sprinkle with remaining 2 tablespoons toffee bits. Yield: 8 servings (serving size: 1 wedge).

CALORIES 268; FAT 7.8g (sat 2.5g, mono 2.5g, poly 2.2g); PROTEIN 3.8g; CARB 46g; FIBER 0.3g; CHOL 8mg; IRON 0.7mg; SODIUM 175mg; CALC 80mg

suppertime
shortcuts

When you don't have much time, use some favorite shortcuts from *Cooking Light* to simplify your meal preparations.

1. Keep your pantry, fridge, and freezer well stocked.

2. Save prep and cook time by using convenient potato products, such as refrigerated or frozen wedges, quarters, hash browns, and mashed potatoes. If you're using fresh potatoes, leave the skin on to save prep time and to preserve nutrients and fiber.

3. Forgo coring, peeling, and slicing fresh fruit yourself. Look in the produce section for presliced apple; seeded or unseeded melon chunks; cored pineapple; and bottles of sliced fresh citrus sections, mango, and papaya.

4. Keep bottled whole peeled garlic cloves on hand to add flavor to meats or side dishes.

5. Gather and prepare all of your ingredients before you start cooking.

6. Simplify side dishes by using couscous, quick-cooking grits, precooked microwaveable rice, and fresh pasta (it cooks more quickly than prepackaged dry).

7. For quick-cooking chicken, use cutlets instead of breasts. Or use one of the many precooked chicken products now available: rotisserie chicken, packaged preshredded or grilled chicken, or chopped frozen chicken. Also consider cooking a large amount of chicken to cut and freeze for later use.

8. Buy peeled and deveined shrimp. Ask someone in your seafood department to cook your shrimp while you finish your grocery shopping.

9. Use baby spinach instead of regular fresh spinach so you won't have to trim stems or chop.

10. Eliminate chopping and slicing veggies by using packaged prechopped vegetables from the produce section of your supermarket, such as broccoli florets, shredded cabbage angel hair slaw, carrots, celery, mixed stir-fry vegetables, and onion.

Nutritional Analysis

How to Use It and Why

Glance at the end of any *Cooking Light* recipe, and you'll see how committed we are to helping you make the best of today's light cooking. With chefs, registered dietitians, home economists, and a computer system that analyzes every ingredient we use, *Cooking Light* gives you authoritative dietary detail like no other magazine. We go to such lengths so you can see how our recipes fit into your healthful eating plan. If you're trying to lose weight, the calorie and fat figures will probably help most. But if you're keeping a close eye on the sodium, cholesterol, and saturated fat in your diet, we provide those numbers, too. And because many women don't get enough iron or calcium, we can also help there, as well. Finally, there's a fiber analysis for those of us who don't get enough roughage.

Here's a helpful guide to put our nutritional analysis numbers into perspective. Remember, one size doesn't fit all, so take your lifestyle, age, and circumstances into consideration when determining your nutrition needs. For example, pregnant or breast-feeding women need more protein, calories, and calcium. And men older than 50 need 1,200mg of calcium daily, 200mg more than the amount recommended for younger men.

In Our Nutritional Analysis, We Use These Abbreviations

sat	saturated fat	**CHOL**	cholesterol
mono	monounsaturated fat	**CALC**	calcium
poly	polyunsaturated fat	**g**	gram
CARB	carbohydrates	**mg**	milligram

Daily Nutrition Guide

	Women Ages 25 to 50	Women over 50	Men over 24
Calories	2,000	2,000 or less	2,700
Protein	50g	50g or less	63g
Fat	65g or less	65g or less	88g or less
Saturated Fat	20g or less	20g or less	27g or less
Carbohydrates	304g	304g	410g
Fiber	25g to 35g	25g to 35g	25g to 35g
Cholesterol	300mg or less	300mg or less	300mg or less
Iron	18mg	8mg	8mg
Sodium	2,300mg or less	1,500mg or less	2,300mg or less
Calcium	1,000mg	1,200mg	1,000mg

The nutritional values used in our calculations either come from The Food Processor, Version 8.9 (ESHA Research), or are provided by food manufacturers.

Metric Equivalents

The information in the following charts is provided to help cooks outside the United States successfully use the recipes in this book. All equivalents are approximate.

Cooking/Oven Temperatures

	Fahrenheit	Celsius	Gas Mark
Freeze Water	32° F	0° C	
Room Temperature	68° F	20° C	
Boil Water	212° F	100° C	
Bake	325° F	160° C	3
	350° F	180° C	4
	375° F	190° C	5
	400° F	200° C	6
	425° F	220° C	7
	450° F	230° C	8
Broil			Grill

Liquid Ingredients by Volume

¼ tsp			=	1 ml
½ tsp			=	2 ml
1 tsp			=	5 ml
3 tsp = 1 tbl		= ½ fl oz	=	15 ml
2 tbls = ⅛ cup		= 1 fl oz	=	30 ml
4 tbls = ¼ cup		= 2 fl oz	=	60 ml
5⅓ tbls = ⅓ cup		= 3 fl oz	=	80 ml
8 tbls = ½ cup		= 4 fl oz	=	120 ml
10⅔ tbls = ⅔ cup		= 5 fl oz	=	160 ml
12 tbls = ¾ cup		= 6 fl oz	=	180 ml
16 tbls = 1 cup		= 8 fl oz	=	240 ml
1 pt = 2 cups		= 16 fl oz	=	480 ml
1 qt = 4 cups		= 32 fl oz	=	960 ml
		33 fl oz	= 1000 ml	= 1l

Dry Ingredients by Weight

(To convert ounces to grams, multiply the number of ounces by 30.)

1 oz	=	¹⁄₁₆ lb	=	30 g
4 oz	=	¼ lb	=	120 g
8 oz	=	½ lb	=	240 g
12 oz	=	¾ lb	=	360 g
16 oz	=	1 lb	=	480 g

Length

(To convert inches to centimeters, multiply the number of inches by 2.5.)

1 in	=		2.5 cm
6 in	=	½ ft	= 15 cm
12 in	=	1 ft	= 30 cm
36 in	=	3 ft = 1yd	= 90 cm
40 in	=		100 cm = 1m

Equivalents for Different Types of Ingredients

Standard Cup	Fine Powder (ex. flour)	Grain (ex. rice)	Granular (ex. sugar)	Liquid Solids (ex. butter)	Liquid (ex. milk)
1	140 g	150 g	190 g	200 g	240 ml
¾	105 g	113 g	143 g	150 g	180 ml
⅔	93 g	100 g	125 g	133 g	160 ml
½	70 g	75 g	95 g	100 g	120 ml
⅓	47 g	50 g	63 g	67 g	80 ml
¼	35 g	38 g	48 g	50 g	60 ml
⅛	18 g	19 g	24 g	25 g	30 ml

index